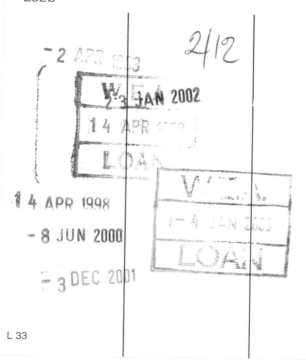

THE EMPEROR JULIAN

ROBERT
BROWNING

THE
EMPEROR
JULIAN

WEIDENFELD AND NICOLSON   LONDON

Weidenfeld and Nicolson
11 St John's Hill London SW11

ISBN 0 297 77029 2

Printed and bound in Great Britain by
Morrison & Gibb Ltd, London and Edinburgh

For Ruth

Contents

Preface   *xi*

1   The Age of Constantine and Julian   1
2   Childhood and Youth   31
3   Manhood and Freedom   48
4   The Chance of Power   67
5   Julian in Gaul   79
6   From Rebel to Emperor   105
7   Constantinople   123
8   Antioch   144
9   Julian and the Christians   159
10 Persian War and Death   187
11 Epilogue   219

Note on Sources   *236*
Suggestions for Further Reading   *238*
Julian's Family Tree   *241*
Table of Dates   *242*
Maps   *245*
Index   *249*

Illustrations

Between pages 116 and 117

1 Miniature chalcedony bust of Julian (*Hermitage Museum, Leningrad*)
2 Ninth-century manuscript showing Julian sacrificing (*Bibliothèque Nationale, Paris*)
3 Ivory pyxis with relief of Christ in the dress of a classical teacher (*Staatliche Museen, Berlin*)
4 Reliefs on a fourth-century sarcophagus showing Biblical scenes executed in the classical manner (*Grotte Vaticane, Rome,* Photo: *Mansell Collection*)
5 An idealized portrait of Julian (*The Louvre, Paris*)
6 Silver bowl depicting Persian king hunting wild boar (*Freer Gallery of Art, Washington*)
7 Bust of Constantine (*Museo dei Conservatori, Rome*)
8 Cameo of the head of Constantius II (*British Museum, London*)
9 Gold medallion showing Julian beardless in military uniform (*British Museum, London*)
10 Coin portrait of Julian bearded and wearing diadem (*British Museum, London*)
11 The Porta Nigra, Trier (Photo: *Landesmuseum, Trier*)
12 A view of Antioch (Photo: *Committee for the Excavation of Antioch, Princeton University*)

Maps

1 Gaul in the fourth century 245
2 The Roman Empire in the fourth century 246–7
3 Asia Minor and Syria in the fourth century 248

Preface

Julian has tantalized the speculative historian and the imaginative artist for sixteen centuries. The Middle Ages, for which he was the incarnation of evil, could not overlook the grandeur of his character and his achievements. To the men of the Renaissance he spoke with a voice which they recognized as their own. In the Age of Enlightenment he stood for reason, battling heroically but in vain against the prevailing superstition. The nineteenth century often saw in him a tragic outsider, a man of genius born out of his time. In our own age several tendencies are discernible. Some have put Julian on the psychoanalyst's couch and sought in the traumas of his youth the explanation of his striking personality and behaviour. Others have represented him as a muddle-headed enthusiast of little real importance. Others again have seen in him a man of unusual ability in whom, because of his position, all the sharpest contradictions of his age and class were embodied.

My own sympathies incline to the last view. So far from being an outsider, Julian seems to me to be very much a man of his time, sharing alike its superstition and its rationalism, its pragmatism and its concern for dogma. If in the end most of his efforts proved either fruitless or unnecessary, this does not mean that Julian was unimportant. Had he been so, he would have been as forgotten as are most of his predecessors and followers. If I occasionally speculate on Julian's state of mind, it is with the humility of the historian who is cautious of *passe-partout* explanations of the diversity of human behaviour. I have tried to depict Julian as a man of his age grappling with the problems of his age, and doing so with a knowledge which, though both wide and deep, owed more to tradition than to experience. His failures were not those of the dreamer or the fool. He misjudged situations. In particular, he was wrong about the urban upper classes of the east. Yet, as Joseph Bidez observed, although he made mistakes, they were understandable mistakes. That he was an outstanding personality even his enemies admitted; whatever might be thought of his religious views, he was a brilliant writer and one of the great generals of his age. And he was a tragic figure, a man of infinite promise, cut off before his prime. An American student once compared him with President John F. Kennedy. The comparison will not bear close analysis. But the feeling behind it suggests why Julian became the subject of legend within a few years of his death.

I am glad to express my gratitude to Dumbarton Oaks Center for Byzantine Studies, where my appointment as Visiting Scholar enabled me to do much of the preliminary work and some of the writing of this book; to Andrew Wheatcroft and Benjamin Buchan, who helped to turn a manuscript into a book; to Olivia Browne, who assisted with the illustrations; and to Susan Archer, who typed it all, and retyped much of it.

ROBERT BROWNING

1 The Age of Constantine and Julian

THE FOURTH CENTURY of our era saw the early stages of a vast and complex transformation of European society that was not completed until the end of the sixth century. Historians have traditionally thought of this transformation in terms of decadence from an earlier perfection – 'The Decline and Fall of the Roman Empire'. This scheme of thought, inherited from the men of the Renaissance, has led to majestic syntheses, from Gibbon to Seeck and Rostovtzeff, and provides the stereotyped categories through which most of us view the end of the ancient world and the beginning of the Middle Ages. We are all prisoners of our predecessors' ideas.

The present generation has taken a new look at the great transformation. Historians from Piganiol and Mazzarino to A. H. M. Jones and Peter Brown have tried to look again and more closely at what happened during those crucial centuries, without deciding in advance what they expect to find. They have not looked for a simple, unilinear development, a single 'explanation'. Rather they have recognized the complexity and the internal contradictions of human affairs. These historians do not form a school. Indeed their disagreements are many and fundamental. But they have in common an awareness of the new insights into the workings of human communities furnished by the social sciences. They have been influenced by the currents of thought associated with Max Weber and Karl Marx, without nailing the colours of either to their mast-head.

If the present account of the main changes in Mediterranean society in the fourth century sometimes presents a confused and contradictory picture, this is because an attempt has been made to take into account the work of recent historians. Not only are they dissatisfied with the old answers. They often ask new questions. And none of their answers is simple.

For Edward Gibbon the age of the Antonines was a golden age, which he depicts with judicious eloquence in the second chapter of *The Decline and Fall*. That its perfection was secretly flawed he knew: 'It was scarcely possible that the eyes of contemporaries should discover in the public felicity the latent causes of decay and corruption. This long peace, and the uniform government of the Romans, introduced a slow and secret poison into the vitals of the empire.' Modern scholars have often argued that the flaws were less latent than they appeared to Gibbon. Be that as it may, all are in agreement that the third century, and particularly its second and third quarters, saw the Roman empire shaken by a deep, prolonged and violent crisis. The armies whose duty it was to defend the frontiers marched to Rome to set their rival candidates upon the throne. No emperor ruled for long, and sometimes three or four rival claimants fought one another for supreme power. Barbarian peoples from the north raided deep into the Mediterranean world, burning and plundering as they went. Even Athens was captured and sacked by a force of Goths from north of the Danube. In the south the pastoralists of the desert threatened the settled life of the African provinces. A renascent Persia threatened Roman power in the east. The silver and bronze coinage with which ordinary citizens transacted their daily business was subject to an inflation and debasement that soon reduced it to less than a millionth of its former value. The delicate balance between the orders of society was upset. The old landmarks and the old certainties of life were swept away. Men were driven to self-help, often of a savage and violent kind. It was a grim and brutal age. An army largely recruited from outside the Mediterranean area fought for the spoils of Mediterranean civilization. Cities were destroyed, and with them a whole pattern of life based on the existence of a class of rentier landowners animated at least in part by civic pride. The division of responsibility between the central government and the cities, upon which the Roman empire had rested, ceased to work. Desperate and often unworkable expedients were tried, the outcome of which was to put an ever-increasing load of responsibility upon an imperial government that was weak, disorganized and subject to repeated usurpation. Faced with an unpredictable and frightening world men turned to new gods, who promised more direct and personal salvation than the old city deities or the Olympic pantheon. Or they resorted to sorcery and magic, seeking to constrain rather than to cajole the capricious and mysterious powers upon whom their fate seemed to depend. Superstition offered more comfort than reason.

Yet we must not exaggerate the chaos and discontinuity of the third century. There were important differences between region and region. On the whole the Greek east preserved the bonds of society better than the Latin west, which had had Roman civilization forced upon it. Though many rich families were reduced to penury, there was no wholesale replacement of the old governing classes. Their wealth was principally in land, not in money or movable goods. And land was an essential factor of production. In the west some of the old senatorial families survived, and sometimes, by adroit and timely trimming of their sails, even increased the extent of their estates. Others adopted and absorbed the new provincial or barbarian war-lords who rose to brief power. In the east there were probably fewer territorial magnates. But in many regions the city ruling classes survived, though they were unable or unwilling to practise the munificence of their forebears. It was primarily from this class of urban landowners that the intellectual leaders of the empire were recruited. And on the whole the intellectuals had an easy time in the harsh third century. Their economic base was not seriously undermined. And though they had to learn to keep their heads down at times, they still found prestige and patronage. Plotinus calmly lectured on the philosophy of Plato – and inadvertently transformed it into something else – to senatorial audiences in the troubled Rome of Gallienus. So there was no abrupt break in the intellectual tradition of antiquity. Doctrines, values and ways of looking at things were transmitted from the age of the Antonines to that of Constantine. Yet at the end of the dark age they were often subtly different from what they had been before it began. There had been changes of emphasis, changes in the meaning of words and concepts, changes in the goals men set themselves when they took up the weight of an intellectual tradition already a thousand years old. Things could never again become as they had been.

Men in positions of power did what they could to impose order on a disintegrating society, if only from self-interest. The measures they took were determined by the resources at their command and by their own personal view of what was wrong with society, as well as by their intelligence and their strength of character. Aurelian attached great importance to shared religious practices and beliefs. And in his reign the worship of the Divine Sun, *Sol Invictus,* became the official cult of the Roman State. Other deities were either to be identified with the Divine Sun, such as

Apollo, or in one way or another brought into line as manifestations or aspects of the new, universal, unique deity. The new religion owed something to Iranian ideas, and much to the traditional religions of the Fertile Crescent. It was symptomatic of a new openness among the rulers of the Roman world towards intellectual and spiritual influences from the east. Like most 'official' religions, however, the cult of *Sol Invictus* hardly answered the anxieties and aspirations of the common man, and never gained the passionate acceptance of the masses. Yet it was able to accommodate without difficulty the cult of Mithras, which was widespread in the army, and thus cannot be dismissed as an intellectual construction, imposed from above.

Diocletian (AD 284–305) took a broader view of the ills of society and of the remedies that they called for. He sought to check the galloping inflation and its social consequences by a policy of price-fixing. An imperial decree set out what was henceforth to be the price of every conceivable commodity or service, and established severe penalties for those who bought or sold above the fixed price. Copies of the decree, in Latin or in Greek, have turned up from every corner of the empire. Needless to say it was ineffectual. The rationing or control of distribution that must accompany price-fixing, even as a short-time policy, was beyond the capacity of the governmental apparatus. And even had it been technically possible, it was socially impossible in a society in which differences of status – and sometimes of class – were marked by sharp differences in standard of living and style of life. In any case there is no reason to suppose that the inflation of the third century was caused by rising costs of production.

Diocletian was more successful in tackling problems of political power. He institutionalized and at the same time brought under control the power of the war-lords by separating military and civil functions, and rigidly excluding senators from the former. Civil and military careers were to be quite distinct, and to be open to quite different classes of citizen. This policy, together with the strengthening of the central apparatus of the State, served to bring the armies under control, at any rate for the time. The central organs of the State were made more effective, and more capable of coping with the new burdens laid upon them, by a series of measures. New offices, unknown to the republic and the principate, were created, to deal with financial, judicial and military affairs throughout the empire. They were completely distinct from the old Roman annual magistracies, which became empty, though prestigious, honours. For the first time the Roman empire had something corresponding roughly to departments of state under ministers. Provincial administration was made more effective by the reduction in size of the larger provinces, and by the grouping of provinces into large regions, each controlled – as far as civilian affairs went – by a kind of super governor or regional commissioner.

To provide a more stable revenue for the State the old taxation system was abandoned. Formerly the land-tax – the basic tax in any agrarian society – varied in its rate and in its manner of collection from province to province. In some places it was fixed, in others variable, collected here in money, there in kind. Land in Italy itself was exempt from taxation. Diocletian caused the whole of the empire, Italy included, to be surveyed and divided into notional units called *iuga*. The *iugum* was essentially the area of land cultivated by one man and his family. Its area would vary from region to region, depending on climate, fertility, nature of crop and so on. But the tax payable on one *iugum* and on the man who cultivated it – one *caput* – was in principle the same wherever the *iugum* and its *caput* were situated. The general rate could however be varied from year to year in accordance with projected needs.

The *iugum* and the *caput* were the two sides of the same coin: land without a tiller, or a man without land, were alike unproductive and untaxable. Hence to make the system work the man had to be kept on his land. The earliest surviving legislation ordering runaway tenants to be dragged back in chains to the farms that they had abandoned dates from some years after Diocletian's abdication and death. But the custom certainly began to establish itself under the Tetrarchy as the logical implication of the new system of taxation.

The system of constraint was not limited to farmers. The inflation had destroyed or weakened normal economic incentives. The uncertainties of life made it often tempting to abandon an ancestral way of life, or simply to run away from intolerable difficulties. The State met every such threat by forbidding men to change their occupations. More and more categories of citizens were tied to their professions, which became hereditary. If there was a shortage of bakers, then bakers were forbidden to change their jobs, and a baker's son not only had to be a baker, but had to marry a baker's daughter. If city councillors sought to escape the obligations of office, then they too were forbidden to move, and membership of the council became hereditary. If difficulties arose in the transport of corn from Egypt to Rome, then shipowners were tied to their trade, and obliged to make one voyage per year under government charter between Alexandria and the port of Rome. The system, which is largely revealed to us by fourth-century legislation, originated under Diocletian. It betokens a new attitude of the governors to the governed, a new relationship between State and citizen, the product of crisis and of the breakdown of traditional structures.

Yet although almost every citizen from the highest to the lowest was supposed to be tied to his job, the narrative sources for the fourth century reveal a very different picture. It was a period of accelerated social mobility. Governments warn, threaten, rant; but no one appears to take much notice. In the copious narrative literature of the fourth century, pagan and Christian, scarcely a single individual seems to be prevented from doing what he wants because he is legally tied to his job, though of course there were many other constraints on men's freedom. It is a strange contrast. The legislator and the ordinary citizen seem to inhabit not so much different worlds as parallel universes. The lesson should not be lost on historians of the later Roman empire. Its rulers were making what was largely a vain attempt to stem the tide of history, to freeze a rapidly changing society into rigid immobility, as much for administrative convenience as for any other motive.

To return to the topic of taxation. The new land-tax could not, in conditions of hyper-inflation, be collected in silver or bronze coin. And the average farmer did not have occasion to acquire many gold coins. So it had to be collected in kind, thus giving the State a hedge against inflation. To deal with this a network of granaries, storage depots, transport units and collection points was set up, all manned by civil servants under one of the great officers of State, usually the Praetorian Prefect. As conditions became more lastingly stable under Constantine and his sons, it sometimes became convenient for the State – and occasionally for the taxpayer too – for the land-tax to be collected in money from farmers who sold their crops on the market, and for the government to buy the commodities it needed by compulsory purchase. This substitution of taxes in money for taxes in kind – *adaeratio* – becomes frequent and important in the fourth century. As the government determined both the rate of commutation and the rate of compulsory purchase, it could and often did manipulate these to its own advantage. But its freedom of manoeuvre was limited. It was useless to squeeze the primary producers to starvation or to drive the goods that it needed off the market.

Side by side with the basic land-tax were other taxes, paid in uninflated gold coin or bullion, and payable by urban artisans, senatorial landlords and others who escaped the land-tax. These taxes provided the State with the gold necessary to pay – or bribe – its largely barbarian army. Ideally this gold found its way back into the productive system as soldiers bought manufactured goods or foodstuffs. In fact a good deal of it was hoarded or exported.

To secure more effective decision-making Diocletian took a colleague as Augustus, Maximian, like himself a soldier from the northern frontier provinces. Each of the two emperors appointed a junior colleague, or Caesar, who was to act as his deputy, and eventually as his successor, thus preventing bloody struggles for power. The two Augusti and the two Caesars were to move about the empire as the military situation required, always available where they were most needed. The capital of the empire was no longer to be the Eternal City, but the camp – *Castra*. This collegiate exercise of sovereignty was in no sense a division of the empire, such as took place after the death of Theodosius in 395. The junior Augustus and the two Caesars were representatives and delegates of the supreme Augustus, without any policy-making initiative of their own. And the regions that they ruled were not fixed, but determined by the needs of the moment. It was a formula for unity, not for division; for centralization, not for devolution.

To reinforce the concept of unity the senior emperors adopted their junior colleagues. This was an admission of the strength of the dynastic idea. Loyalty – and above all the loyalty of the army –was given to a man, and might readily be transferred to his son if he seemed to be of his father's mettle. It was not freely given to a committee. It was not surprising that the Tetrarchy, as the system of four emperors was termed, broke down soon after Diocletian, worn out and sick, stepped down from his throne to cultivate his cabbages by the Dalmatian shore.

Marcus Aurelius in the second century sought to be approachable, to underline his humanity, to live like his fellow-citizens, or at any rate the richer among them. 'Take care not to be dyed in purple,' he warns himself. What men looked for in the great crisis was not a fellow-citizen, but a saviour. Only superhuman power could save the world. So Diocletian and his colleagues and successors had to be larger than life, remote from their fellows, surrounded by an aura of power. Their life-style became hieratic and ritualized. No longer could they be approached as near equals. They lived in vast palaces, rarely seen by their subjects. When they did appear, they were raised high above the heads of the crowd, surrounded by guards in glittering armour, preceded by trumpeters. Clad in purple from head to foot, resplendent in jewels, the emperor did not deign to notice the applause of his loyal subjects. Immobile, gazing into space, trying to look twice his size, he posed as a superman. His every movement was surrounded by protocol and ceremony. He was addressed in terms more appropriate to a god than to a man. All that pertained to him, his palace, his decrees, his treasury, his correspondence, the hem of his garment, was called sacred. Men fell on their faces in adoration before him, even if they only heard his voice issuing from behind a curtain. We can form some idea of the image of himself that a fourth-century emperor tried to project from the huge head of Constantine now in the Museo dei Conservatori in Rome. The statue to which it originally belonged, and which stood in the apse of the great basilica that he built overlooking the Roman Forum, was more than forty feet high. The face, with its great beak of a nose and its firm mouth, is cold and impassive. The greatly enlarged eyes stare out into space, high above the heads of ordinary mortals. It is the face of a man raised above everyday human concerns, used to contemplating higher things. And above all it is a face of power. The emperor is no *primus inter pares*, he is *dominus et deus*.

The reality, of course, was somewhat different. Yet it is difficult to understand how a man so raised above and cut off from his fellows ever seriously discussed affairs of state with his principal officers, or indeed how he ever had an ordinary conversation. Those very features of his situation that made him appear to the ordinary man as a saviour and protector prevented the fourth-century emperor from having that day-to-day familiarity with the problems of the empire and their possible solutions that Augustus or Trajan acquired from constant intercourse with their fellow citizens.

The superhuman emperor's power rested in the last resort upon his command of the army. The Roman army of the Principate had been recruited by a combination of voluntary service and conscription from Roman citizens and non-citizens within the empire and in large measure from the Mediterranean world. And it was commanded by amateurs in the course of their political career. The army of Diocletian and his successor had to maintain more men under arms than Trajan or Marcus Aurelius. Exact figures are lacking. But the strength of the Roman army in the fourth century was in the neighbourhood of 400,000. Modern industrial societies can mobilize a much larger proportion of their population. While 400,000 out of perhaps 25 million may not appear a high proportion, for ancient society with its low productivity the extra burden imposed by the increase in the size of the army was considerable.

The army of the principate had been almost entirely stationed in the frontier provinces, and often on the frontier itself. There was no strategic reserve. Reinforcements could be brought to a threatened frontier only by withdrawing units from other frontiers. And they took a long time to move. Diocletian established a distinction between the static units on the frontiers, whose only task was defence, and the mobile field army that could reinforce and counter-attack. His successors maintained and further institutionalized the distinction. The result was an army consisting of two fundamentally different kinds of unit, the *limitanei* and the *comitatenses*. The *limitanei*, who manned the frontier fortresses, were largely an infantry force, less well equipped and trained than the field army, and largely maintained by the produce of the frontier lands that they and their families tilled. The *comitatenses*, largely mounted units, were maintained out of the land-tax, and were better equipped, trained and paid than the frontier forces. The distinction however was never absolute. Units were transferred from one force to the other. And at the middle of the fourth century there were still many units that do not seem clearly to have belonged to either category. As with so many reforms in the ancient world, the old lived on side by side with the new.

By the beginning of the fourth century there had been Christian communities in the Roman empire for 250 years. The earliest communities had been established in cities like Corinth, Thessalonica, Antioch, Alexandria, and Rome itself. At first they may have awaited the speedy second coming of Christ. Soon they began to come to terms with the world and with the Roman State. Their members were mostly humble people – urban artisans and shopkeepers for the most part, both free men and slaves. And in general they offered a low profile. Christianity was merely one among a number of oriental religions offering personal salvation, which drew their membership from men who had little concern with the sophisticated intellectual tradition of the Greco-Roman world. But the Christians differed from most other groups of dissidents in the quality of their organization. The bishops who headed the little communities were in constant correspondence with one another, and met in formal and less formal synods and councils. A Christian going from one city to another found himself at once accepted by the local community. Their organization gave to the Christians a sense of solidarity and a unity of doctrine and practice that most other religious groups lacked.

The early Christians were not a pressure group. Their communal life was marked by inwardness and the pursuit of spiritual goals. They did not seek to influence the Roman State or the authorities of their own cities. The existence of the Roman empire was a fact of life in this world that had to be taken into account. But the Christians were neither for it nor against. They mingled freely with their pagan fellow-citizens, worked with them, traded with them, held office with them when the situation required it. They avoided taking part in pagan sacrifices when they could, shunned the gladiatorial fights of the amphitheatre because of their cruelty and the mimes and ballets of the theatre because of their moral obliquity and their pagan content. But a Christian could hold a provincial priesthood without provoking the condemnation of his fellow Christians, since such an office was essentially civic rather than religious.

As time went on the communities grew. Some were attracted to Christianity by the gentle life-style of the Christians, others by the desire to belong to a self-conscious group with an inner life of its own, others by the promise of salvation in the hereafter. But the communities remained firmly rooted in urban society. The vast mass of peasantry was scarcely touched. And the growth was most marked in the eastern, Greek-speaking areas of the empire, and to a lesser extent in north Africa and Italy itself. There were few Christians in the rest of the Latin-speaking west, and they were mainly persons of eastern origin, not fully absorbed into the communities in which they lived. Men and women of the upper classes began to appear among the Christian communities, though they were still predominantly lower class. It is this social expansion upwards that explains the efforts of Christian leaders like Clement of Alexandria (died *c.* 215) and Origen (185–253/4) to fit the Greek philosophical tradition to Christian revelation and to provide an intellectual framework for Christian doctrine that could satisfy men who knew and respected the classical heritage of thought.

Like any inward-turned communities the Christians tended to split into factions on points of doctrine or practice. But the organization of the bishops was strong enough and efficient enough to preserve unity. Most of the dissident groups withered away once the driving force of their founders was removed. Others persisted for centuries as tiny conventicles of self-styled true believers, arrogantly sure of the purity of their doctrine, but without influence on the mass of the Christian population.

Busy with their own internal affairs and concentrating on matters of no interest to those outside the faith, the Christians were generally accepted by their fellow-Romans with amused tolerance, when they were noticed at all. But their way of life was sufficiently distinct from that of the pagans round them to make them suitable scapegoats when things went wrong. Ugly rumours sometimes circulated that they went in for incest and cannibalism. Here and there communal tension led the Roman authorities to intervene. There were trials and condemnations. Men and women were put to death, sometimes in circumstances of particular cruelty. Those who thus bore witness to their faith – martyrs they were called in Greek – were particularly revered by their fellow-Christians. The circumstances and manner of their condemnation and death were recorded – or made up – and circulated among other Christian communities. To many pagans their conduct was merely obtuse persistence in error, and typical of the pigheaded stupidity of their co-religionists. To others their steadfastness in the face of death was evidence of the sincerity and seriousness of their convictions. In a sense the blood of the martyrs was the seed of the Church.

There has been much discussion of the precise nature of the charge upon which the Christian martyrs were condemned. Was it the technical charge of belonging to an association that did not fulfil the rather strict requirements of Roman law? Or was it a charge of political disaffection, because they would not offer a pinch of incense on the altar of Rome and Augustus? Or was being a Christian a criminal activity in itself, and the challenge to offer the incense merely a means of proving that the accused was a Christian? And if so why was Christianity alone – or almost alone – among the many religions in the empire – regarded as illicit? It may be that these questions are scarcely worth asking. Roman criminal law had not the refinement and sophistication of Roman civil law, largely because it mainly concerned the lower classes. And at moments of acute communal tension other factors than strict interpretation of the law doubtless carried weight with provincial governors. Yet so far as the evidence points in any one direction, it appears to indicate that Christians were condemned because they were Christians, and not because they were guilty of treason or illicit association. The concept of an illicit religion was familiar enough to the Romans. As early as 186 BC the Senate had declared illegal the orgiastic cult of Bacchus and prescribed severe penalties for those who continued to take part in its observances. Christianity was probably proscribed either by a similar enactment or by the interpretation of existing law. The grounds would not be theological but social. Religions were proscribed because they were socially disruptive and threatened to disturb the peace, not because they were erroneous. Doctrine had nothing to do with the matter. Practice was what counted.

Be that as it may, up to the middle of the third century persecution was the exception, and was always local, never general. Most Christian communities lived their life undisturbed for generations. There was no 'Christian problem' in the Roman empire.

The great crisis of the third century affected the Christians in two ways. First of all the uncertainty and fear in which men lived drove them more and more to seek supernatural aid, protection and comfort. The Christian communities were particularly well adapted to provide just this. It is clear that the growth of Christianity, both geographically and socially, was accelerated in the generations of crisis. It would be foolish to attempt to quantify. But in some areas Christians became a substantial and important minority, if not actually a majority. And they began to include more men of substance who played a leading role in their communities. The leaders of the Church, the bishops, tended to be drawn more from this new class than from their humbler co-religionists. These new Christian leaders were men of education, who knew their way about in the quarters where power was exercised, and who could make their views heard. Yet we must not exaggerate the change. Over the empire as a whole the Christians were still a small minority. They were still concentrated mainly in the east. And they were still confined to the cities, and absent from the countryside. Their preoccupations were still mainly with their inner life, their attitude one of passive neutrality towards the Roman State, which always represented a potential threat.

The other new development was that the rulers of that State themselves sought aid and protection from the higher powers. Where old institutions and old customs had clearly not guaranteed the security of society men in power turned to new religious beliefs and practices. It was a world in which all, from the highest to the lowest, saw the direct intervention of the supernatural everywhere, and sought to engage it in their own interests. Just as an individual's fortunes depended on his entertaining the right beliefs and performing the right actions in his relations with the unseen powers, so the fate of the empire depended on the beliefs and actions of its citizens and above all of its rulers. For an emperor it was of cardinal importance to know what powers controlled the universe and to do what they wanted him to do. And he had a duty to see that his subjects also did nothing displeasing to the capricious higher powers. This is the attitude that underlies Aurelian's attempt to subsume all other religions under the cult of *Sol Invictus* and to make it the official religion of the Roman State. Such it remained in theory – though interpretations of it might differ – until after the death of Diocletian. In this new religious climate the Christians were an awkward exception. They would not let themselves be taken under the syncretistic umbrella of *Sol Invictus*, but insisted on proclaiming that their god and their god alone ruled the universe. And they were by now too numerous and influential to be passed over. Their continuing refusal to recognize the one God and his many manifestations, in whose protection the empire lay could only be an affront to that god. They could bring untold harm upon their fellow-citizens by perversely persisting in their particularism. It was the duty of the emperor as the ruler of the State under God to put a stop to their harmful activities. The authorities of the State could no longer turn a blind eye to the Christians, intervening only when local conditions seemed to threaten communal discord. It was their duty to take the initiative and pursue the Christians with the utmost vigour of the law.

Such perhaps was the theory. In practice most Christian communities continued to flourish and to grow unmolested most of the time. But there were two waves of persecution that differed from earlier persecutions in being general instead of local, and in being set on foot by the initiative of the central government. The first of these was under Decius, a Pannonian senator who found himself proclaimed emperor against his will in 249, and who died fighting the Goths in 251. Decius was a defender of Roman traditions, the neglect of which he saw as the chief cause of the disorders of the times. He required all citizens to perform a symbolical act of sacrifice. Many Christians refused and paid for their refusal with their lives. Decius evidently desired to break up what he thought was a dangerous empire-wide dissident movement, whose activities were harmful to the empire as a whole. By prosecuting and condemning in particular the clergy, who were more likely to stand up and be counted than the ordinary layman, he hoped to strike at the organization of the church, and so cause the movement to collapse. The same policy was continued, though with less rigour, by Decius' successor Valerian.

The second wave of persecution came under Diocletian and his successors, after half a century of peaceful growth of the Christian Church. It lasted from 303 to 312, and was triggered off by a response of the oracle of Apollo at Delphi. The god declared that if he was silent or no longer gave the accurate predictions he had given in the past, it was the Christians who were to blame. They were casting a kind of spell on the whole world. The god's response was evidently prearranged. The idea behind it however was one shared by most Christians and pagans of the time. All alike believed in witchcraft and in the manipulation of demonic powers. The persecution was severe and long lasting, though its rigour varied from region to region. Many were put to death. Many more were branded or mutilated or sent to forced labour in the mines. The Christians were by now too numerous and influential to be eliminated in this way. Diocletian's own wife and daughter were at any rate sympathetic to Christianity, and one of his senior ministers became a martyr. The Christians were no longer a semi-clandestine group. There was little general hostility to them among their fellow-citizens. Few can now have believed the stories of incest and cannibalism. The Church emerged from the Great Persecution probably stronger than before.

However a kind of time bomb had been left behind, in the form of hostility between those who had compromised under pressure, perhaps handing over the Church books to the authorities or putting the ritual pinch of incense on an altar, and those who had stood firm and often suffered for it. The two groups often set up rival bishops and clergy in the same city and spent more energy in denouncing one another than in converting the pagans. There had been divisions within the Church before, but they had been largely on matters of doctrine. For the first time the Christian communities were rent by a dispute on church organization. And there was more at stake than before. The Church had become wealthy, and owned not only its ecclesiastical buildings but estates of all kinds that produced considerable revenues. It was not just a community of the faithful, preoccupied with its own inner life. It was becoming a major economic organization. The acrimony of the dispute varied from region to region. In some areas where the split was deepest, such as Africa, religious radicalism became a vehicle for social and economic discontent. Landless peasants roved the countryside in bands, denouncing the church of the collaborators and setting fire to the barns of the rich.

The Tetrarchy did not long survive its founder Diocletian. When he abdicated in 305 he obliged his colleague Maximian to resign with him, and a regular hand-over of power took place according to the rules of the new constitution. The two Caesars, Constantius and Galerius, became Augusti, and two new Caesars were chosen, Severus in the west and Maximinus Daia in the east. Constantius died at York in July 306, and the troops immediately proclaimed as emperor his young son Constantine. Galerius, 2000 miles away in Nicomedia, had no choice but to accept the *fait accompli* and recognize the legitimacy of Constantine. He insisted, however, that he should take his place as junior Caesar, while the other

surviving members of the second Tetrarchy were each promoted one grade
higher. But the damage had been done. What soldiers in Britain had
achieved soldiers elsewhere aspired to achieve. Maxentius, the son of
Diocletian's colleague Maximian, felt that he had been passed over, and
induced the garrison and people of Rome to proclaim him emperor in
October 206. Maximian, who had never wanted to retire, soon joined his
son. There were now six rival emperors. Maximian and Maxentius defeated
the armies of Galerius and Severus and gained control of Italy, Africa and
Spain. They then came to terms with Constantine, who controlled Gaul
and Britain. The alliance was cemented by the marriage of Constantine to
Fausta, daughter of Maximian and sister of Maxentius. Dismayed at the
disarray of the empire, Galerius summoned Diocletian from his retirement
at Salona to set matters right. A conference was arranged at Carnuntum
on the Danube in November 308. Maximian, whom no one really wanted,
went into retirement for the second and last time. Severus, who had been
taken prisoner by Maxentius, had been forced to commit suicide in
captivity. A third Tetrarchy was patched up with Galerius and Licinius
as Augusti, while Constantine and Maximinus Daia were to be Caesars.
It was never more than a paper construction. Maxentius, whom it ignored,
remained in effective control of Italy and Africa, while his father
Maximian, ostensibly in retirement, stirred up revolts against Constantine
in Gaul until he met his death in 310. In their turn Constantine and
Maximinus Daia insisted on equality of status with Galerius and Licinius.
When Galerius died in May 311 Diocletian's orderly system, designed to
smooth over succession to power and to avoid civil war, was already in
ruins.

Constantine at Trier, Licinius at Sardica (Sofia), and Maximinus Daia at
Nicomedia behaved like independent rulers, though formally recognizing
one another's legitimacy. Maxentius ruled in Rome, unrecognized by his
colleagues. The system of delegation of power designed by Diocletian to
preserve the unity of the empire seemed more likely to lead to its
fragmentation. We do not know what the other three emperors thought
of the political problem. Constantine, it is abundantly clear, realized
from the start that effective unity meant rule by one man, with all
decisions emanating from a single source. The panegyric delivered before
him at Trier by the rhetorician Nazarius says nothing of his link with the
founders of the Tetrarchy – one of whom had just died as a rebel in
Constantine's own territory. Instead the orator harks back to the memory
of his father Constantius and to his alleged descent – by a faked pedigree –

from the third-century emperor Claudius Gothicus. Constantine was marked out from birth for imperial power, he declares.

Constantine lost no time in making trial of his destiny. In 311 he seized Spain without a battle, and in 312 in a lightning campaign defeated and killed Maxentius at the Milvian Bridge outside Rome and so became sole ruler of the western half of the empire. Licinius, who feared that Maximinus Daia might follow Constantine's example, hastily recognized Constantine's new position. Once again a marriage, this time between Licinius and Constantine's sister Constantia, cemented the alliance. Meanwhile Maximinus Daia, feeling himself threatened by the new power group, attacked Licinius' army in Thrace, and a new civil war seemed inevitable. Only Maximinus' death in 313 from natural causes prevented it.

The peace between Constantine and Licinius was an uneasy one. Each realized that he could survive only if the other were removed, yet for a time neither wished to strike the first blow. In 316 open hostilities began, though it would be hard to say which party was the aggressor. They were brought to a close by negotiation only after Constantine had ousted Licinius from Pannonia and Thrace and gained control of the whole of the European part of the empire. Once again a Tetrarchy was established, with two Augusti and two Caesars. But this time the Caesars were the real sons of the Augusti. Constantine nominated his two sons Crispus and Constantine II, Licinius his son Licinianus. The two latter Caesars were babies, and Crispus was only fourteen. They were the heirs presumptive of their fathers, but not their colleagues.

The new peace was as transient as the old. From 320 relations between the rulers of east and west became tense, and in 324, in a short war terminated by a decisive battle at Chrysopolis, on the Asiatic shore of the Bosphorus, Constantine overthrew Licinius and his infant son. Both died in captivity shortly afterwards.

The Roman empire was united under a single ruler for the first time for forty years. And so it remained until Constantine's death in 337. Crispus, his eldest son, was executed on his father's orders in 326, and his step-mother Fausta a few months later. The real motive for Constantine's untypical severity remains unknown, though politics rather than adultery seem to have provided the background. The young Constantine II was joined as Caesar in 324 by his brother Constantius, in 333 by his brother Constans, and in 335 by his cousin Dalmatius, a son of Constantine's half-brother Flavius Dalmatius. But these princes were in no sense colleagues of Constantine in power. At best they acted as his lieutenants in particular matters. Their main role was as potential successors. Constantine was firmly committed to dynastic succession, as opposed to the system of selection and adoption on which the Tetrarchy had rested.

To summarize Constantine's achievements in power would need a book as long again as the present volume. And our subject is Julian, not Constantine. Yet a brief sketch of his character and of the principal modifications he made in the system of government and the organization of society is essential for the understanding of what follows.

Born at Naissus (Nish) about 280, Constantine had spent much of his youth as a hostage at Galerius' court for his father's good behaviour. His mother Helena, an ex-barmaid whom Constantius had married – if indeed they were ever formally married – early in his military career, had had to be put aside when Diocletian nominated Constantius as Caesar. Her successor as Constantius' wife was Maximian's daughter Theodora. So the young Constantine had little direct contact with either of his parents, and little by way of formal education. His background was the camp and the imperial headquarters, not the city. Yet he was anything but an ignoramus. He respected education in others, and sought to make up for its deficiency in himself. In later life he even attained a certain mastery of the turgid and involved Latin that passed at the time for good style. His own spontaneous utterances, however, were far more pregnant and incisive than the convoluted exercises in rhetoric in which he evidently took great pride. For Constantine was a man of impulse and of action. Quick to seize the essentials of a practical problem, he was bored by theoretical considerations. His taste in literature and art was simple and superficial, as was his approach to moral and religious problems. His personal and family life was straight-laced and prudish. If his impulsive character and the exigencies of politics led him to have his son and his second wife put to death, not even his enemies could charge him with sexual irregularity. In a way he was typical of the upper class of the northern provinces, combining a plain, no-nonsense attitude with a somewhat ambivalent envy of the sophisticated culture of the Mediterranean world. What made him untypical was his untiring energy, his ability to gain and retain the loyalty of men who were his intellectual superiors, and his judgement and skill in battle. Any general can win one battle, but it takes an outstanding commander to win all his battles. At the same time he was, like most of his contemporaries, a deeply religious man. He shared their belief in constant supernatural intervention, and their desire for protection and salvation, and he was ready to see manifestations of higher powers everywhere. The breadth and scope of his political ambition made him especially eager to establish a personal relationship with these powers. He needed a hot-line to god.

Ancient official portraiture was no more realistic than are the representations of heads of state on coins and postage stamps today. Yet the pictures of Constantine have sufficient in common to give us an idea of his appearance. The great head in the Museo dei Conservatori at Rome is no doubt idealized. But it is recognizably the same man as appears in the early coin portraits. He must have been an imposing and magnetic figure. In later life he put on weight, and there are hints in the coin portraits of a double chin. And he grew his hair longer. But he never gives the impression of a man who took things easily. He understood and enjoyed power.

His long reign was in a sense a continuation of the Tetrarchy. There was the same strengthening of the central government, which intervened more and more in what had traditionally been left to local initiative. The army continued to grow, and the division between frontier garrisons and mobile field army was more systematically carried out. The numbers and powers of government officials increased. The attempt to freeze society by preventing social mobility continued and received further development. The new taxation system was improved by the addition of new impositions on classes of citizens who had hitherto escaped untaxed. And the strongly authoritarian style of government inaugurated by Diocletian was maintained.

But in more important ways Constantine broke new ground. And it is with a brief survey of these that the present chapter will conclude. His economic policy was far more successful than that of Diocletian. Instead of trying to freeze prices by administrative action he increased the amount of gold coin in circulation and succeeded in establishing a stable relation between gold coin and the baser metals. A single monetary system thus replaced the double system of the Tetrarchy. And there is evidence that gold coins really circulated once again and were used in everyday commercial transactions. The stabilization of the monetary system carried out by Constantine was a pre-condition of the economic growth that seems to have taken place in the later fourth century. The secret of his victory over inflation escapes us. He must have had far more gold bullion under his control than had any of his predecessors, since the resources of the empire were once again unified. His new gold *solidus*, struck at seventy-two to the pound, was issued in vast numbers, and became the model for Byzantine gold coinage for the next eight centuries. But the decisive factor must have been the new political confidence engendered by his unbroken series of victories and his reunification of the empire.

Diocletian's power had rested firmly on the army. And the men whom he put in key positions were almost exclusively soldiers from the Rhine and Danube provinces. The old ruling class, and in particular the Roman Senate, was systematically excluded from power. Constantine depended no less on his army. But he saw that a broader basis of support was essential if he was not to be faced with the disaffection of a class whose wealth, power and prestige were still vast. So, cautiously at first, but with more freedom later, he began appointing to high positions men of families long excluded from office, or of senatorial families who had never held high office before. The strict separation of civil and military careers was maintained. And military command was still mainly exercised by new men from the frontier provinces. But a beginning was made in the fusion of the two groups. And men of power and influence in their cities and their provinces were drawn into the power structure of the central government. In part this concession to the senators was the price paid for the new tax that Constantine imposed on them. But it was more than that. Constantine was a man of a conservative cast of mind. And he was certainly hoping in part to re-establish the state of affairs before the great crisis of the third century, however difficult it might be in fact to square this aim with the rest of his policy. A final motive was probably the desire to win the support of an influential group in western Roman society who had been alienated by his new religious policy.

Constantine had been brought up in the official religion of the late Roman State, the worship of *Sol Invictus,* and as a man of his time he was in tune with the supernatural, and convinced that his own destiny and that of the empire over which he ruled depended on the establishment of a correct relation with the unseen powers of the universe. He was familiar, as an outsider might be, with Christianity. Probably some members of his family were already Christians. His mother Helena became a devout Christian later. She may have had links with the Christian Church since her childhood. The matter is uncertain, as our sources are all heavily impregnated with hindsight. He certainly numbered Christians among his courtiers and friends from his earliest days in power. The Diocletianic persecution had never been carried out by his father Constantius in the regions that he governed. Constantine, like many men of his time, sought religious experiences, and not unnaturally found them. While he was still in Gaul he had a vision of Apollo, who was in the theology of the time an aspect or manifestation of the supreme sun god.

On his forced march towards Rome in 312 he had a dream, in which Christ appeared to him and told him that if he put a Christian monogram – the Greek letters Chi and Rho – on the shields of his soldiers, he would win victory over Magnentius. Constantine hastily had the sign painted on the shields of at least some of his soldiers. And on 28 October 312 he defeated Magnentius' forces at the Milvian Bridge, killed their leader, and at one stroke became master of half the empire. Another story, less well attested and almost certainly a later invention, is that on the eve of the battle he and his army saw a cross in the sky surrounded by the words 'in this sign conquer' in Greek. Whatever the truth of the matter may be, Constantine had sought the support of the god of the Christians in his decisive struggle and he had not been disappointed. His attitude to religion was a pragmatic one. If it worked, it was true. What he took to be a Christian observance had worked, so the Christian god was powerful and able to protect him. The Christian Church was therefore deserving of his favour. Indeed it was both his duty and his interest to protect it.

When he met Licinius at Milan in February 313 the two emperors issued joint instructions to officials on the treatment of Christians in the areas under their jurisdiction, the so-called Edict of Milan. This document sets aside the discriminatory legislation in force since 303, and orders not only complete toleration for Christian beliefs and observances but the restoration of all property confiscated from the Church during the Great Persecution. Its theology is – no doubt deliberately – woolly and vague: generic terms like 'divinity', 'supreme divinity', 'whatever there may be of divine and celestial' abound, and there are no specifically Christian terms. It was a text designed to be interpreted in different ways by different readers. The argumentation it uses is exactly that used by the persecutors – that the troubles of the empire were due to neglect of correct worship. Only Constantine now interpreted correct worship in a way favourable to the Christians. It is noteworthy that of the coins issued in his name in 313 some show the emperor with the chariot of the sun on his shield, and with the profile of the sun-god – *Sol Invictus* – behind him, while in others he has Romulus and Remus and the she-wolf on his shield and a tiny Chi-Rho monogram on his helmet.

Historians have sometimes described the events of 312–13 as the conversion of Constantine. 'Conversion' is a word of many meanings, and Constantine certainly changed his attitude, and that of the Roman State, towards the Christians at this time. But his true conversion was a long process, ending only with death-bed baptism, a process in which Constantine not only deepened his understanding of the new religion and his commitment to it, but allowed himself to be taken over by the Christian Church that gradually dominated his court, provided his most intimate advisers, taught his sons, and made him the judge of its disputes and its principal propagandist. It was a conversion not merely of Constantine himself but of the Roman State. Only the barest outline of these complex changes can be presented here.

For the Christian Church the sudden end of persecution and the new favour that they enjoyed was a welcome relief. But the new situation brought many problems. The Christians, except for a few sectarian conventicles, had long accepted the existence of the Roman State as a fact of life and played in it whatever part their station required. They were used to its neutrality, and prepared to bear its hostility. It was like the weather, unpredictable, omnipresent and without deep significance. No Christian thinker in his wildest dreams had imagined a Roman State that consistently favoured the Christians, still less a Christian emperor, as Constantine became. Many old attitudes had to be changed, many new questions answered. The heads of the Christian community were its bishops. But what if the emperor, who was the head of the State, was also a member of that community? How were the respective spheres of emperor and bishop to be demarcated? And what of the Roman empire itself, which pagans had treated as a special creation of providence and Christians as a fortuitous political organization? Was the concept of a Christian empire possible, and what were its implication? When there were differences within the Christian community, as there were in many regions after the persecutions, what would be the attitude of the State when faced with rival groups, each claiming to be the only true Christians? And how ought the Christian communities to greet imperial intervention in such a dispute?

The Christians gradually worked out a theological justification for the existence of a Christian emperor and a Christian empire. Its successive stages can be traced in the writings of Eusebius of Caesarea, Church historian and one of Constantine's principal religious advisers. It culminated in the picture of Constantine painted in the speech that he delivered in 336, in celebration of the emperor's thirty years of rule:

E.J.—2

The divine Logos, which is above, throughout and within everything, visible and invisible at once, is the lord of the universe. It is from and through the Logos that the emperor, the beloved of God, receives and wears the image of supreme kingship, and so guides and steers, in imitation of his Lord, all the affairs of this world. . . . Constantine, like the light of the sun . . . illuminates those farthest from him with his rays . . . and harnessing the four Caesars like spirited coursers beneath the single yoke of his royal quadriga, he moulds them to harmony with the reins of reason and unity, guiding his team like a charioteer, controlling it from above and ranging over the whole surface of the earth illuminated by the sun, and at the same time present in the midst of all men and watching over their affairs. . . . God is the model of royal power and it is He who has determined a single authority for all mankind. . . . Just as there is only one God, and not two or three or more, since polytheism is really atheism, so there is only one emperor. . . . He has received the image of the heavenly monarchy, and his eyes lifted on high he governs the affairs of this world in accordance with the ideas of his archetype, fortified by the imitation of the sovereignty of the heavenly King [Eusebius, *Speech on Constantine's 30th Anniversary* 3.4–5, 5.1–4].

The echoes of the worship of *Sol Invictus* in this curious panegyric were no doubt even clearer to the ancient hearer or reader than they are today.

The Christian emperor, then, was not merely a member of the Church among others: he was the special vehicle of providence, more fully in the image of god than his fellow-Christians, and hence obedience to him was part of the duty of a Christian citizen. Or at any rate obedience in all worldly matters. The demarcation between the office of bishop and that of Christian emperor was still left vague. Constantine took to calling himself 'bishop of those outside the church', thereby implying that he had a quasi-episcopal function and a special responsibility for the spiritual welfare of those citizens who had not yet embraced Christianity. He also called himself, or was called by his flatterers 'the equal of the apostles' and 'thirteenth apostle'. This title too implied ultimately superiority to the church hierarchy, whose authority depended on the apostolic succession of its members. But the implications of these and other titles given to Constantine were never rigorously worked out. The emperor himself was a practical man and no theologian. And the leaders of the Christian

Church were largely carried away by a wave of euphoria and by the ever-increasing responsibilities laid upon their shoulders by a church rapidly growing in members and in wealth.

Some Church leaders did not share in this euphoria. From the earliest days after the Edict of Milan the authorities were forced to decide between rival claimants to represent the Christian Church. If there were two Christian groups hostile to one another, as there were in many cities and provinces as a result of the Great Persecution, the question arose to which of them confiscated Christian property was to be restored, to which exemption from taxation was to be accorded, to which the ever more numerous privileges of the Christian Church were to be granted. As early as 316 Constantine decided in favour of Bishop Caecilian of Carthage, whose legitimacy was challenged by the rigorist Donatists. And like any other Roman magistrate he executed his own decision. From 316 to 320 there was systematic persecution of the Donatist counter-church in Africa by the imperial authorities. When Constantine defeated Licinius and gained control of the eastern provinces, he found the Christian communities sharply divided by a dispute on the nature of Christ – was he, and by implication the Holy Spirit also, inferior to and created by God the Father, or were they of the same substance? This deep theological difference, which led to the establishment of rival bishops and rival churches in many cities, was itself a long-term result of the adoption by Christian thinkers of the concepts and methods of classical Greek philosophy in the generation of Clement of Alexandria and Origen.

The matter could not be left to sort itself out. Not only were there the usual problems of who was to receive the by-now considerable privileges due to the Christian Church. Constantine himself had progressed in his understanding of and commitment to Christianity since 312. It was clear to him that he had a special duty to ensure that God was worshipped in the way most pleasing to Him, and to bring those in error to recognition of the truth. He carried out this duty by calling, on his own initiative, a council of the whole Church throughout the empire, and by presiding at most of the sessions of the 381 bishops who attended. The council pronounced in favour of equality of Father and Son. The opposing party, called Arian after one of its leading members Arius, a priest of Alexandria, was excluded from all the benefits and privileges of the Christian Church and from the administration of Church property, and its leading members were subjected to persecution, arrest and deportation by the State authorities. Religious communities, however, thrive on persecution up to a point.

The Arians refused to be corrected, and responded to persecution with polemic and denunciation of their rivals, and attempts to win support in high places. The time was to come when they in their turn would have the upper hand and enjoy the active support of the civil authorities. When Constantine let himself be drawn into arbitrating in ecclesiastical disputes he began a stage in the relationship of State and Church that was marked by cruelty, hypocrisy and bigotry on both sides and which offered a most unedifying spectacle to the still very large and influential pagan elements in Roman society.

In the meantime the freedom of pagan religious observance was limited by a series of State interventions as Constantine's commitment to Christianity deepened and as Christians held more and more of the key positions in his court. In 318 sacrifices and magical practices in private houses were forbidden. The measure was directed as much against sorcery, in which Christian and pagan alike firmly believed, as directly against traditional ceremonies. But the bracketing together of pagan religion and sorcery was ominous. Temples in many cities of the empire were demolished or despoiled because of something offensive in the cult centred in them. But otherwise there was little direct interference with public pagan practice. In 320 Sunday was declared a public holiday, to be observed by all. A public proclamation after the victory over Licinius affirms the freedom of pagan worship, and at the same time makes contemptuous observations regarding pagan belief and practice. There could be no doubt in any one's mind which way things were moving.

At the same time Constantine showered benefits upon the Christian Church. From 313 tax exemptions and direct gifts were granted to the various local churches. In 318 litigants were permitted to bring their case for trial before the local bishop, whose verdict was to be as valid as that of a regular court. Slaves could be manumitted by declaration in a church before a bishop or priest. Christian churches had hitherto been modest and inconspicuous buildings, where they were not merely private houses converted to religious use. Constantine began a tradition of vast monumental churches, modelled on civil public buildings and supported by imperial munificence. One such great basilica was built by the Lateran palace at Rome, which had belonged to Constantine's wife Fausta and was now put at the disposal of the bishop of Rome. Across the Tiber another great basilica rose on the Vatican hill, the traditional site of the burial of Peter and Paul. On the road to Ostia, outside the walls, a basilica in honour of St Paul was built; though much modified in the course of the centuries, its immense hangar-like interior exemplifies the austere grandeur that in Constantine's eyes befitted a church. In Palestine great churches were built in Jerusalem and Bethlehem. In other provincial cities similar building programmes were carried out. They were financed by the transfer to the Church of vast imperial landed estates, often accumulated over centuries, the income from which made possible the construction and maintenance of these costly edifices. The churches also received gifts of movable wealth. Constantine gave more than a ton of gold and nearly ten tons of silver to the churches of Rome alone. From being a poor organization the Christian Church became a great property-owner. As such it began to take over the role of the city and its landowner class in providing the elements of social security. Hospitals, orphanages, charities for widows and the aged grew up under church control and funded by church estates.

Christianity had already begun to make headway among the upper classes of the cities and the empire long before Constantine. But the support he gave to the Church increased the tempo of Christian penetration of the ruling class. Some converts were moved by the manifest success of Christianity, others were sincere believers who had lain low because of the social discrimination against Christianity, still others hedged their bets by keeping a foot in both camps, like the bishop whom Julian met in Troad who also publicly worshipped Apollo. Between devout and enlightened Christians on the one hand and pagans emotionally or intellectually committed to their cult on the other, there was a vast grey area in which moved the doubters, the *arrivistes*, the men who were not really interested in religion.

Constantine in general gave preference to Christians over pagans in making public appointments, and his court in particular was strongly Christian. His children were given a strict and even bigoted Christian education. But there was no ban on paganism in public life. Side by side with Christian consuls, prefects of the city of Rome, and praetorian prefects, Constantine appointed pagans to the same offices. And he made no abrupt break with the pagan traditions of the Roman State. The Vestal Virgins still watched their ever-burning fire in the heart of the Forum. The Senate still began its proceedings with a formal sacrifice on the altar of Victory in the Senate House. The emperor himself still retained the ancient priestly office of Pontifex Maximus. Constantine fought against paganism by transferring its economic assets to the Christians, and by social discrimination in their favour, not by political repression. That was to come later, and to be begun by his sons.

The last, and not the least important, of Constantine's innovations was his establishment of a new capital at Constantinople. It is important not to let our understanding of this event be warped by hindsight. We know that Constantinople remained the capital of the east Roman or Byzantine empire for eleven centuries. This knowledge was concealed from Constantine and his contemporaries. Rome had long ceased to be the effective centre of government of the empire. In the turbulent third century the capital was where the emperor was. And the emperor was usually with his army in one of the frontier zones, not half-way down the peninsula of Italy. With the emperor moved his court and the high officers of state. Rome became a backwater, its Senate lost the power and influence it had maintained in the early empire, and the rich senatorial families were more and more reduced to a life of antiquarian make-believe and *dolce far niente*. The Tetrarchs institutionalized the new administrative system. None of them set foot in Rome for more than a brief visit. Their courts and centres of government were strung along the new life-line of the empire that stretched from the lower Rhine to the Arabian desert. Trier, Milan, Sirmium (Sremska Mitrovica), Sardica (Sofia), Nicomedia, Antioch were the new centres of power, where the mobile headquarers of emperors settled for months or years. In establishing his own administrative headquarters at a point along this line Constantine was doing only what his predecessors had done for three generations, and what the military and political situation called for.

The new city, on the site of the ancient Megarian colony of Byzantium, was built to celebrate Constantine's victory over Licinius on 18 September 324, which made him master of the Roman world. At first he hesitated where to found his city. Sardica, Ilium, Chalcedon, perhaps Thessalonica, were all considered. Finally the emperor's choice fell on Byzantium. Its situation at the crossing of the sea route between the Mediterranean and Black Seas and the land routes between Europe and Asia, together with its magnificent deep water harbour, turned the scales. And Constantine may well have been moved by the breath-taking beauty of its situation. The outline of the walls of the new city were traced on the ground by Constantine in the first half of November 324. Before the year was out coins were issuing from its mint, and the first imperial decrees dated from Constantinople belong to 325. By 330 the new city, whose palaces and squares and colonnades engulfed the old town of Byzantium, was completed on the ground. On 11 May 330 it was formally dedicated by Constantine, and this date was celebrated through the centuries as the 'birthday' of Constantinople.

Thus far Constantine had done nothing that was not in the tradition of imperial behaviour. The Hellenistic kings had founded cities – either on the site of earlier settlements or *de novo* – in celebration of their victories, and called them after their own names. Augustus founded Nicopolis ('the city of victory') at the entrance to the Gulf of Ambracia to commemorate his victory there over the fleet of Antioch. Since then the Roman empire had become studded with imperial foundations or refoundations – Claudiopolis, Traianopolis, Hadrianopolis – the list is endless. Constantine was merely acting out his role in founding Constantinople. What is important is to discover when and how the city began to be something more than an ordinary imperial foundation. To do this the historian has to cut his way through the tangle of legend that has overgrown the original contemporary sources. There is no room here for the details of this complex exercise in historical criticism, which has most recently and admirably been performed by Gilbert Dagron in *Naissance d'une capitale: Constantinople et ses institutions de 330 à 451* (Paris 1974). An over-simplified summary of results must suffice.

From the start Constantinople was expressly a Christian city. It lacked the temples and altars and cult sites that were often the most conspicuous landmarks in an ancient city. In their place it had a series of churches, some on a new and monumental scale, built or sponsored by the emperor himself. This did not prevent the actual foundation ceremonies – both those of 324 and those of 330 – being largely pagan in inspiration and form. There was no Christian tradition for the foundation of a city. And the old ceremonies still moved men's hearts and minds. So Constantine set up a statue of Apollo with a radiate crown on a column in the main square, walked through the streets carrying a globe surmounted by a statue of victory (the symbol of his imperial Roman power) and buried beneath a triumphal column the archaic statue of Pallas Athene, the Palladium, on which the fortune of Rome was said to depend. All this was accompanied by psalmody and prayers to the god of the Christians. The religious ambivalence of the age could not be better illustrated.

The mention of the Palladium reminds us that Constantinople was from the beginning a kind of second Rome. Even while the city was still being built its bishop was addressed as 'bishop of the new Rome', and a court poet wrote of it as *altera Roma*. Constantine induced a certain number of senatorial families to establish themselves in the new city. Like Rome it was divided into fourteen regions, and with a little imagination seven hills were found within its walls. Constantine's intention is clear enough – to establish a new Christian city named after himself that would have the standing and authority of Rome and be a second national capital as well as the real administrative centre. The realization of this intention, however, required a long series of measures, most of which were carried out by Constantine's successors, and which culminated in the declaration in the twenty-eighth canon of the church council of Chalcedon that Constantinople was the equal of Rome. It was only slowly that the territory of the city was withdrawn from the provincial administration and made subject to a prefect of the city appointed by the emperor like that of Rome. It was only slowly, and mainly in the reign of Constantius II, that the city council of the new city became transformed into a second Senate, whose responsibility was imperial and no longer local, whose members were recruited from the highest-ranking officers of State, and which stood as the representative of a senatorial order, to which a man might belong either by birth or by promotion. It was only slowly that from a medium-sized provincial city Constantinople became a megalopolis, a gigantic urban community that could not be fed from its own hinterland but needed wheat from Egypt, cattle from Thrace and pigs from Asia Minor to feed its ever more numerous citizens. This whole development, which took more than two generations to complete, and of which the most important stages belong to the reign of Constantius rather than to that of his father, is compressed into a moment of time by historians of the following century, when they speak of Constantine founding a new capital city in the image of Rome. It was a development that could have been stopped at any time. The fruit could always be left to wither on the branch. Constantine spent little of the seven years that remained to him after 330 in his new city. The accession of a new king of Persia drew his attention to the eastern frontier. Death found him, on 22 May 337, at Nicomedia. Of the three sons who succeeded him, Constantine II was at Trier when his father died, and Constantius II at Antioch. The youngest, Constans, was only seventeen and it is not known where he was living. When the three met to settle their spheres of responsibility it was not at Constantinople but at Viminacium (Kostolac near Belgrade). Constantius, in whose domain the new city fell, and who in any case soon became sole ruler, spent his twenty-four years of power on the move between the Persian frontier and the Rhine at the head of his army. He passed through Constantinople many times, but never stayed for long. Julian, the first emperor to be born in Constantinople, passed only a few months of his short reign in the new capital. All of them made their contribution to its growth and development, but for none of them was it his first care. The fact that within less than a century Constantine's foundation had become a real permanent capital, a super-city, juridically, politically, economically and demographically different from the other cities of the empire, is evidence of the unerring intuition that the practical-minded Constantine showed for the needs of the time.

As it grew from 330 on, the new city upset the old political and social balance of the empire in a variety of ways. It was a Latin city in the middle of the Greek east. Not that all, or even most, of its inhabitants spoke Latin as their mother-tongue, though many did. But it was a centre of imperial power, not of local administration. And Latin was the language of imperial power. The emperor legislated in Latin, the army was commanded in Latin, the high officers of State and senior civil servants carried on their business in Latin. Men from the ruling class of the Greek cities had played a part on the larger stage of the empire before. The historian Cassius Dio was a case in point, thrice consul and holder of a series of high offices. But such cases were exceptional. In general the world of the Greek cities was culturally and politically self-contained. Its leaders left the business of running the empire to Latin-speaking westerners, whom they despised more often than not, while they got on with managing the affairs of their own cities and provinces. Now imperial power was on their own doorstep. A career that was empire-oriented rather than city-oriented became a possibility for many – not only for the richest and most influential, who might aspire to governorships and prefectships, but also for thousands of humble men who found jobs in the swelling bureaucracy of the capital, and for intellectuals like the rhetorician and philosopher Themistius, who abandoned the lecture rooms and theatres of the old cultural centres to become the adviser and friend of six emperors in succession. All this implied a re-evaluation by these men of their traditional culture and way of life, and a sharp division between those who accepted, or even welcomed the new shape of things, and those who did not. The writings of Libanius (314–c.393) are full of complaints against young men of good family who neglect the culture of their fathers and go off to learn Latin, or Roman law, or – horror of horrors! – shorthand. The deep malaise of a long-established ruling class comes out clearly.

Then the economic effects of the growth of Constantinople were profound. We cannot quantify them today. But constant railing about the
way the new city sucked in produce from all over the eastern world is
evidence of the disturbance of old trade patterns. And it was not just a
matter of foodstuffs and consumer goods. The grandiose building programme drained the eastern provinces of architects and craftsmen, and
probably of unskilled labour too. The temples and public buildings of
every eastern province were ransacked by imperial agents in search of
statues and columns to adorn the new city, which was compared by its
enemies with a harlot. Many welcomed the economic opportunities offered
by the vast demand of the new capital. For others it spelt personal ruin.

It would be hard to exaggerate the degree of social mobility that the
foundation of Constantinople introduced into the rather traditional society
of the Greek east. Contemporary sources are full of stories of men who
rose from nothing to positions of unimagined power and wealth, and of
others who from being big fish in a small pool rapidly found themselves
very small weak fish in a new pool whose boundaries they could not
discern. It was an age of great unease and uncertainty in the eastern world.

In the west the establishment of the new capital had less immediate
effect. But even here there were direct economic effects, particularly the
switching of the Egyptian corn surplus from Rome to Constantinople.
And politically the old Roman senatorial class, fantastically wealthy and
prestigious though it was, found itself challenged by a new eastern senate
of upstarts who had made their way to the top through government
service. Its reaction was to withdraw more and more from meaningful
participation in imperial affairs.

Such were some of the main trends in the age preceding the birth of
Julian that shaped the world in which he grew up and reigned.

2   Childhood and Youth

WHILE CONSTANTINE'S ARCHITECTS were building his new capital on the Golden Horn, and adorning it with statues and works of art from every part of the Greek world, a son was born to his half-brother Julius Constantius in one of the newly built palaces that lined the Sea of Marmara. The boy was given the name Flavius Claudius Julianus.

Constantine was not the man to put members of his family in decision-making positions. This was partly a matter of temperament: he liked to keep power in his own hands, and sought subordinates rather than collaborators. But it was more than that: the heritage of division and hatred within the family left by his father Constantius Chlorus made it impossible for him to trust any of his immediate kin.

When Constantius Chlorus was selected by Diocletian to be his junior colleague in 293, he was forced to repudiate the ex-barmaid from Asia Minor Helena, with whom he was no doubt linked by the kind of morganatic marriage known to the Roman lawyers as *concubinatus,* and to take as his wife the daughter of Diocletian's colleague Maximian. Her name was Flavia Maxima Theodora. By her he had two sons, Dalmatius and Julius Constantius. Meanwhile Helena brooded over the insult that had been offered her, and brought up her son Constantine to hate his half-brothers. When Constantine succeeded to imperial power on the death of his father in 306, one of his first acts was to summon his mother to court and establish her as the first lady of the empire.

Helena was a woman of strong character, combining passion with firmness of will. Her influence on her son was immense. Dalmatius and Julius Constantius were sent into a kind of house arrest in the provinces, surrounded by spies, and kept far from public office or military command.

For a time Julius Constantius lived in Toulouse, then a university town, where he probably attended the lectures of the leading rhetoricians and philosophers. Years later Helena relented something of her hatred for the children of her rival. By now she had the style and dignity of Augusta, and her name appeared on the coins along with that of her son. About the middle-twenties of the fourth century Julius Constantius was permitted to settle in Italy, where he had a great country house in Tuscany. In the meantime he had married Galla, daughter of a wealthy Italian family that for generations had held high office; two of her brothers became consuls, in 347 and 358. There were three children of the marriage, two sons and a daughter. For some reason that is no longer clear to us, he soon fell under suspicion again, and was expelled from Italy and forced to move from city to city, always under the watchful eye of Constantine's agents. For a time he found refuge in Corinth, and from there was allowed to go to Constantinople when Constantine established his new capital there. Helena had died the previous year, and Constantine now felt that he had nothing to fear from a half-brother who had passed an ineffectual and wasted life of *dolce far niente*. Julius Constantius was given high rank but no office.

Some time before coming to Constantinople, Julius Constantius' first wife Galla had died. He had soon remarried. His second wife was Basilina, the daughter of Julius Julianus, who had been praetorian prefect and virtual head of government under Licinius, Constantine's former colleague and rival. Constantine had praised his administration as a model to be followed by his own officials, and appointed him consul in 325. Basilina's mother was a wealthy woman in her own right, and owned great estates in Asia Minor. In May or June of 332 their only child, the future emperor Julian, was born. There is no indication that Constantine, who was in Constantinople at the time, took any notice of this addition to his family. Perhaps it was as well that he did not, for he was an impulsive man who did things he later regretted. Only six years earlier he had put to death his eldest son Crispus, the offspring of his first marriage, and a few months later he had his second wife Fausta, mother of three sons and two daughters, suffocated in her bath. The motivation of this family tragedy is unknown. Some alleged that Crispus had been falsely accused by Fausta of making sexual advances to her – the traditional Phaedra and Hippolytus motif. More probably Constantine's suspicion and fear had been aroused by Crispus' military successes – suspicion and fear on which Fausta played in order to advance the interests of her own sons. Be that as it may, Constantine was unlikely to be a mild benevelent uncle.

A few months after Julian's birth, his mother died. The baby was brought up, under his father's supervision, by nurses. The three older children of his father's first marriage, the youngest of whom, Gallus, was some six years older than Julian, formed part of the household. There must have been a large nursery. Maybe the young Julian, the baby of the family, was spoiled. What he lacked would be the security that comes from the close personal affection of a fond mother. There were too many eunuchs and slave women in the palace of Julius Constantius. The boy's maternal grandmother did what she could. He must often have gone to spend the summer in her villa on the southern shore of the Sea of Marmara, and perhaps visited some of her other Asian estates.

Slowly, Julian grew from a baby to a small boy, surrounded by luxury but rather short on affection. Let us not exaggerate, however. His lot was probably not all that different from that of other upper-class children whose mothers were alive. He may have been somewhat isolated when his elder half-brothers began to go to school – or rather to study under a tutor in the palace. As his sixth year came on, he too went to the schoolroom and learned to read and write, by methods that had not changed in a thousand years. One first learned the alphabet, letter by letter, then one combined letters to form syllables, first open syllables – BA BE BI BO BU – then closed syllables – BAB BAC BAD and so on. Only when one could read off any syllable at sight did one advance to words and short edifying maxims. It is astonishing how many boys – and girls – maintained their enthusiasm for literature after such a dreary introduction. The question arises in what language did he learn to read and write. Constantine's family were from a Latin-speaking area of the Balkans, and Constantine himself never learned to speak Greek well. Basilina's family, though they no doubt spoke Latin in their official capacities, were from Greek-speaking Asia Minor. The majority language of the new capital was Greek, though there were plenty of native Latin speakers to be found in its streets.

But we would be putting the question in a false perspective if we posed it in terms of native language. A man's mother-tongue in the late Roman empire might be Latin or Greek, or Syriac or Coptic or Armenian or one of a multitude of other languages that still survived. But Greek was the language in which the life of the cities of the eastern part of the empire was carried on, the language of scientific and technical communication, the language of culture. Latin was the language of the imperial government, of the army, the civil service, the higher courts of justice, and so on. Which language a man used depended on the role he was playing, not on

his mother-tongue. Julian certainly knew Latin, but Greek was the
language with which he was brought up to feel at home. He was not
being groomed to share imperial power, but to live a life of cultured leisure.

Suddenly everything was turned upside down. Constantine, who had been
in Constantinople for Easter on 3 April 337, set out for the eastern
frontier, to pursue the war against the Persians. His second son Constantius
had preceded him and was already at Antioch, taking charge of arrangements. Soon after he left the capital Constantine, who must have been
about sixty, was taken ill. Visits to baths and to shrines of martyrs proved
of no avail. After a week of high fever the emperor died on 22 May near
Nicomedia. Constantius had been summoned as soon as his father's illness
became serious, but arrived too late.

The old emperor, who did not really want a successor, had been slow
and indecisive to make arrangements for the succession. The army idolized
him, but hardly knew his three surviving sons, Constantine, Constantius
and Constans, who in any case distrusted each other. And there was
Constantine's brother to be taken into account – not the *fainéant* Julius
Constantius, but Dalmatius, who had held high office, and whose two sons
were already grown men. There was no shortage of candidates for power.
But Constantius was on the spot. He accompanied his father's body to
Constantinople, and organized his lying-in-state and burial in the Basilica
of the Holy Apostles. Julian's father must have been one of the guard of
honour, and have taken part in the solemn audiences before the bejewelled
catafalque on which the embalmed body of the emperor lay for weeks on
end. For no successor was proclaimed. Constantius issued laws in his
father's name for months after his death. Meanwhile he was negotiating
with his brothers and sounding out the feelings of the army officers. The
negotiations cannot have been easy. The eldest brother, Constantine, seems
to have anticipated events and issued proclamations in his own name as
early as June. For Julian's father it must have been a period of great
anxiety. At all costs he must not appear to seek power. And at the same
time he must not back the wrong candidate. By 9 September things had
been settled between the brothers, and on that day they were proclaimed
joint emperors, dividing the empire between them into three administrative zones. Minor appanages were found for Dalmatius and his sons, who
had to be content with the lower rank of Caesar.

But the devious Constantius was not content with the settlement.
Rumours were spread in the army at Constantinople that a will had been

found in the hand of the deceased emperor, concealed beneath his shroud, where it had been put by the bishop who attended at his deathbed. In the alleged will he accused his two half-brothers Dalmatius and Julius Constantius of having poisoned him, appointed his three sons co-emperors, and enjoined on them the duty of punishing his murderers. There can be no doubt that Constantius was behind these rumours. It was to him that the alleged will had been handed by Bishop Eusebius of Nicomedia. He may have intended merely to weaken the position of Dalmatius and his sons. If so, he displayed unusual naivety. The effect on the troops stationed in the capital was immediate. They rushed to the palaces of the late emperor's brothers, poured through the halls and gardens, seeking them out, and when they found them butchered them on the spot. Dalmatius and his two sons were put to death. Julian's father and his eldest son met the same fate. The second son, Gallus, was spared as he was ill and believed to be dying anyway. The soldiers took pity on Julian we are told, because he was only five years old. Some accounts say that he was grabbed by a priest and taken by a secret passage to the sanctuary of a nearby church.

Whether he saw his father and brother killed before his eyes we do not know. But the memory of that dreadful day never left Julian throughout his life. A mere child, he can have known nothing of the political tension following on Constantine's death. Suddenly, in all its brutality and irrationality, the problem of power was thrust before the mind of a child too immature to grasp what it was all about. Who was responsible he neither knew nor cared at first. But as he grew older it became clear to him that the man who could have stopped the murder but did not was his cousin the emperor Constantius.

Something had to be done about the boy. In the first days after the murder he was probably looked after by some of his father's household; perhaps his grandmother felt that her family connections were powerful enough to let her risk taking him in charge. Within a few weeks, however, Constantius made up his mind. Though his father's property was confiscated the child was to be allowed to live; but he was to be kept under constant surveillance well away from the capital. The place of exile chosen by the emperor for his cousin was Nicomedia (Izmit) about sixty miles from Constantinople at the end of a long arm of the Sea of Marmara. It had been an imperial residence under Diocletian, and had many palaces and villas suitable for so distinguished an exile. Its monuments and public buildings made it one of the loveliest cities of the east. There the six-year-old child was installed, with an appropriate establishment of nurses, servants and bodyguards. Constantine chose Eusebius, Bishop of Nicomedia, to be his guardian and it was he who chose his tutors, watched over his spiritual welfare, and sent his confidential reports to the emperor. He seems to have been a distant relation of Julian on his mother's side. But within a year Eusebius was translated to the bishopric of Constantinople and so his influence on his young ward was minimal. The boy prince's grandmother had estates not far from Nicomedia, in which she passed much of her time. A kindly and warm-hearted woman, she devoted much care and tenderness to the young orphan. In particular she gave him the run of a villa near the city, where Julian learned to know the countryside and developed an appreciation of nature that stayed with him all his life. It was probably during his years at Nicomedia that he learned to know his mother's brother, Julianus, who was one of his closest friends later in life.

What we can never know is how his grandmother or guardian explained to the traumatized child what had happened to his father and his eldest brother. Was there a conspiracy of silence, in which the matter was never mentioned? What kind of answer was given to the boy's inevitable questions? How did they assure him that his brother Gallus, who was being kept in similar forced residence 200 miles away at Ephesus, was not dead too? What did they say when he asked to return to the city in which he had been born and brought up? Whatever the answer to these questions may have been, their very existence suggests that, behind the surface of luxury and benevolence surrounding young Julian in Nicomedia, there was an ominous undertone, at best puzzling, at worst nightmarish. Yet Julian recalled his days at Nicomedia with pleasure and wept when, years later and in far-off Gaul, he heard of the earthquake that laid the city flat.

Perhaps his agreeable memories were mainly due to his tutor Mardonios. Mardonios was a Scythian, that is to say a native of the present-day Dobroudja, where the coastal cities were Greek, perhaps ethnically a Goth. He had been made a eunuch in childhood – doubtless he was a slave – and given a thorough literary education. He first appears as reader to Basilina. Probably he had been her teacher, and had been given his freedom by her father. He remained a member of Basilina's entourage after her marriage, but seems to have returned to his former masters after Basilina's death. It was no doubt through the influence of Julian's grandmother that he was appointed by Bishop Eusebius as private tutor to the boy, not long after his arrival in Nicomedia. He was a fresh link with Julian's mother, whom the boy could not remember, but whom he longed to know more about. As the adult with whom Julian was in closest daily contact during some of his formative years, he may have come in a strange way to replace his mother. At any rate the relations between master and pupil were warm and trusting. Julian afterwards referred to him as 'the tutor who brought me up', using the word normally applied to parents. Mardonios was a man of profound culture, with a feeling for Greek literature that he succeeded in transmitting to his young pupil together with a genuine appreciation of beauty, and firm, rather old-fashioned moral standards. The literature that they read was of course the literature of classical Greece, and above all the poets – Homer first and foremost, the tragedians, and Aristophanes. The Hellenic culture that men of the eastern empire defended and enjoyed in the fourth century was something they treasured from a long distant past. That men of their own day might write as well or better, that the life of their own times could provide as good examples of virtue and vice, of beauty and ugliness, never occurred to most of Julian's contemporaries. The men of the past had attained perfection. It remained only to appreciate it, and, so far as men could, to imitate it. Originality was excluded. Such a system of values could lead to a deadening, stifling education that cut off the springs of the human spirit at their source. However Mardonios seems to have been a good teacher and a simple upright man, who inspired the respect of his pupil and who could communicate to him his own genuine enthusiasm for the literature that they studied together. Julian, who had no school companions, seems to have read widely beyond the fairly narrow bounds of the traditional school curriculum of late antiquity. He could have been spoiled, in this day-long face to face confrontation with a teacher who stood so immeasurably lower than him in the social scale. But Mardonios made no concessions. Years later, as ruler of the world, Julian recalled his strict, schoolmasterly injunctions.

Often my tutor used to say to me when I was still a mere boy, 'Don't let all the boys of your age who rush off to the theatres lead you into the error of ever craving for these shows. Are you keen on horse-races? There is one in Homer, most cleverly described. Take the book and go through it. Do you hear them talking about the dancers of pantomime. Leave them alone. The lads dance a much more manly dance among the Phaeacians. For lyre-player you have Phemius, for singer Demodocus.'

Julian must have been a rather lonely boy – most princes are – ready to look on life in the distorting mirror of literature, a boy older than his years in some ways, in others a child without experience. If he lived a rather self-contained life of thought, it was not entirely a matter of temperament, for later on he displayed an eager and nervous sociability.

He was naturally brought up as a Christian. Both his father and his mother had been Christians, and Constantius and his brothers were almost fanatical adherents of the new faith. He would have been familiar with the Bible and the liturgy from an early age. But one must bear in mind that in the first half of the fourth century, education had not been Christianized. One learned to read the classical, pagan literature, not the gospels. The whole furniture of an educated man's mind was still Hellenic and pagan, and his Christian belief, if he was a Christian, came as something additional and external. The process of fusion between the two cultures had begun, but it had not gone very far. His tutor Mardonios must have been at least formally a Christian. But what he taught his pupil was Homer, not the Bible. And his firm moral position owed nothing at all to Christian revelation.

Julian was thoughtful, well-read, sensitive and serious. He no doubt reflected much on the Christian religion as he grew from babyhood to adolescence. But other and older traditions aroused a response in his heart too. He tells us himself how the power of the sun induced in him a kind of mystical experience of divinity (*Hymn to King Helios* 168.10ff). He was already a mystic, in search of a philosophy.

As Julian reached the age of ten or so, it would have been natural for him to proceed to a more advanced stage of education, in which he learned not merely to read literature, but to read it with understanding and appreciation. The teacher who provided this instruction was known as a 'grammaticus', and his task had been clearly set out centuries earlier: 'To read fluently, with attention to prosody, to explain the poetic figures, to understand readily the rare words and the allusions, to discover the etymology of words, to work out the regularities of language, and to criticize poetry, which is the highest task of the craft.' The pupil might also begin at the same time the study of rhetoric, the art of self expression in speech and writing.

What happened to Julian is not at all clear. There are indications that he may have been brought back to Constantinople about 342 to study under Nikokles the grammaticus, a man whom he later summoned to court when he was emperor, and who continued to defend his memory after his death. He may also have begun to study rhetoric under Hekebolios, a fashionable teacher, who was something of a Vicar of Bray. But these contacts may belong to a somewhat later period in his life. If he did return to Constantinople as a ten-year-old he must have enjoyed the sympathy of many of the citizens. Some hated Constantius, for a variety of reasons, including his theology. Others remembered how Julian had become an orphan. Others were captivated by his unassuming air as he walked through the streets of the city to Nikokles' school. Perhaps there were demonstrations of support for him. At any rate Constantius, whose natural state was to be torn between conflicting emotions, reversed his earlier decision and sent his young cousin back to Nicomedia, within a couple of years, perhaps accompanied by one of his teachers.

But he was not allowed to stay in Nicomedia for long. His official guardian, Bishop Eusebius, had died. Who replaced him we do not know. Whoever it was, he was in no position to protect the youth from the suspicion and indecision of Constantius. The division of the empire between the three brothers had not worked. The eldest, Constantine II, who was probably illegitimate, and to whom the westernmost provinces of the empire had fallen as his lot, was afraid that his brothers were preparing to eliminate him. He tried a pre-emptive strike, and was defeated and killed in battle at Aquileia in March 340. The result was to give the third brother Constans control of the whole empire from Britain to the western Balkans. Constans made no move against Constantius, but he gave support to Athanasius and the leaders of the Nicaean faction in the Church, whose hatred for the Arian emperor knew no bounds. Constantius was afraid, not so much of a direct military attack as of a *coup d'état* in the capital itself. If Julian and his brother were in one of the great urban centres, they could only too easily become involved in such an attempt. At the same time things were not going well on the Persian front, where the long years of peace had been broken in 341. It was probably in autumn of 344 that Constantius decided to put Julian and his brother under close surveillance – which amounted to house arrest. A messenger arrived in Nicomedia from the capital and told the youth to be ready to move. He had to leave behind him Mardonios, a bitter blow. His grandmother, too, was never to see him again. The sudden and unexpected separation from those closest to him was a fresh blow that Julian never forgot. Within a few days he was on his way along the dusty roads of Asia Minor in a convoy of mule carts of the imperial post.

His destination was an imperial estate known as Macellum, just north
of Mount Argaios, whose great peak, snowcapped for much of the year,
rises to more than 10,000 feet. On the other three sides spread the arid
lunar plateau of Cappadocia, whose surface was here and there interrupted
by fantastic outcrops of soft rock, like dead cities. They were indeed cities,
for Cappadocia, dry as it was, had quite a dense population, and those who
could carved themselves dwellings in the rock rather than building houses.
It was easier – one did not have to face problems of thrust – and these
cave dwellings were cooler in summer and warmer in winter than any
house could have been. It was not, however, to a cave that Julian was
brought, but to a sumptuous palace, a kind of imperial hunting lodge,
far from any inhabited locality. It had probably originally been built by
the kings of Cappadocia, before its annexation under Tiberius, 300 years
earlier. There he lived in the style that befitted his estate. Suitable teachers
had been sent with him to continue his education. All the luxuries that
wealth could provide were at his disposal. But his contacts with the
outside world were few and strictly controlled. And he was permitted no
companion of his own age.

As befitted his years, he was given a more thorough education in the
Christian religion than he had received before. A regular catechetic course
preceded baptism, which he received some time during his years in
Cappadocia. We do not know who was immediately responsible for his
religious education. But the man ultimately responsible was George,
Bishop of Caesarea, the nearby provincial capital. Julian had frequent
contact with George. For he tells us later that the Bishop had an excellent
library, containing not only Christian theology, but also works of the
pagan rhetoricians and philosophers, including many of the Neoplatonic
commentaries on the works of Plato and Aristotle. He lent Julian books
and allowed him to have copies made of those that interested him most.
For the first time the young prince learned to know directly the tradition
of Hellenic philosophy, which in the third and fourth centuries of our era
had undergone a renewal at the hands of men like Plotinus, Porphyry and
Iamblichus. Interpreting Plato in the light of the Neopythagorean philosophy of the second century, and probably also drawing upon Gnostic and
other oriental doctrines, these thinkers offered a view of the universe as
a hierarchically structured whole in which everything had its place, in
which the world of Value permeated the world of Reality, and in which
the material world of our sensual experience, though low in the cosmic
scale was yet connected by links of spirituality with that One, to which

all else was related as rays of lights are to the sun. At its best it was an impressive, and for some minds a satisfying, world-picture. At its worst it could be a tawdry rationalization of magic and popular superstition. In this philosophy the young Julian began to find an understanding of the deep emotion that as a child he had felt in contemplating the sun and its influence upon the world of life. The sun, said the Neoplatonists – or some of them, for there is no closed orthodoxy here – was a kind of reflection or analogy of the One that powers the universe as the sun powers the visible world. More and more deeply he read and thought his way into this new thought-world, at first with the wonder of a boy, soon with the passion of a young man.

Such thoughts did not necessarily imply a break with the Christianity in which he had been brought up. Christian and pagan alike thought in Neoplatonist terms, like fish swimming in the same water. Julian may have passed through a period of peculiarly devout Christianity, perhaps in part as a result of his growing familiarity with Neoplatonist philosophy. At any rate it is related by near-contemporary sources that he and his brother Gallus both dedicated churches in Caesarea. The one dedicated by Gallus, goes on the story (which in the form we have it belongs to the years after Julian's death), stood firm while that dedicated by Julian collapsed. It was possibly during his adolescent years at Macellum that Julian was ordained to the lowest religious order, that of reader. It was the duty of the reader to read or chant the lessons from the Old and New Testaments during the Eucharist. In antiquity this order was often conferred on very young men, and sometimes on children. It did not necessarily imply an intention to proceed to higher orders; many readers remained laymen. But it had become an essential stage towards the diaconate and the priesthood. It is a pity we know so little about when or how Julian was ordained. For though the readership implied no higher vocation, it could scarcely be conferred upon a man against his will, or even against his better judgement. When Julian was made reader he cannot yet have rejected Christianity, even if the interpretations that he gave to some parts of Christian revelation were his own.

If his eyes were opened to philosophy during the years of isolation at Macellum, they were also opened to other things. It was there that he came to understand what had really happened to his father, his eldest brother, his uncle and his cousins, and at whose door responsibility lay. He was now old enough to understand such matters, and in the absence of other informants he no doubt picked up his information from the

servants who surrounded him. If he attempted to discuss it with Bishop
George or his clergy, he is unlikely to have got very far. For Constantius
still wore the diadem as sole emperor. He was not the anointed of the
Lord, for the practice of coronation by the church had not yet begun. But
he clearly enjoyed the special favour of the Almighty. So along with the
bitter hatred of Constantius – who was at this time married to Julian's
half-sister, the daughter of the uncle he had had murdered – there was
sown in the young Julian's mind the conviction that some leading
Christians were less than honest.

During the journey to Macellum Julian probably looked forward to
being reunited with his elder brother Gallus, whom he had not seen for
some years. If so, he had a disappointment. For Gallus, now a young man
of eighteen or nineteen, shared neither Julian's intellectual interests nor
his sensitivity to beauty, and his character probably already showed the
streak of brutality that later became prominent. Thrown as they were on
each other's company, neither can have derived deep or lasting satisfaction
from it.

Julian spent about six years at Macellum, from 344 to 350. When he
went there he was a lad of eleven or twelve; when he left he was eighteen.
It is a period in a young man's life when many things happen. He reaches
puberty, he seeks to define his own identity, he gradually comes to terms
with a world that he is beginning to understand. Often, especially in a
society that sets a high importance on religion, he passes through a crisis
of faith or of metaphysics. Julian developed as others of his age. But we
can only piece together a very imperfect record of his development from
occasional hints in his later writings and from reports of doubtful reliability
made by others. The temptation to fit Julian into one or other of a number
of psychological stereotypes readily available today is strong. Yet we have
to bear in mind not only the inadequacy of the evidence, but also the
uncertainty whether the stereotypes themselves are relevant to a society
that was very different from ours. It is better to admit that we do not
know much that we would like to know about Julian. Some things,
however, can be stated with a degree of certainty. First Julian grew from
boy to man alone. It was not merely that he had no family, other than
Gallus, but he also had no companions of his own age with whom to form
the passionate and changing friendships of adolescence. 'No stranger came
near us', he writes later of this period in his life, 'none of our old friends
was allowed to visit us. We were cut off from any serious study and any
contact with free men; surrounded by a splendid entourage, we had no

companions but our own slaves: none of our friends of our own age came to see us, none was allowed to.' Mardonios, who was both a father and mother figure for him, was no longer there. No other adult enjoyed either the authority or the affection to guide the young prince as he grew up. Clergymen there were, no doubt, to instruct him in the Christian religion. But they seem to have performed their task in a perfunctory way, without any true commitment, and to have offered Julian no help in the moral and religious struggles through which he had to pass. Bishop George was an adventurer, who ended up by being lynched by his flock. He provided no model for an intensely serious young man. However, at least he had a library and would lend books from it. If Julian had to borrow his reading matter from a bishop in the nearest city, it must have been because he had few books of his own. Whether of set purpose or by oversight, Constantius had cut off his cousin from the intellectual communion that he had learned to value so much.

Then in addition to isolation, there was suspicion and even fear. 'We were like prisoners in a Persian fortress', he writes later. Puzzled though he may have been at first by his sudden departure from Nicomedia he soon realized that he and his brother were virtually under arrest. Their every movement was watched and reported to Constantius. Even the young slaves with whom they took exercise might note any careless word. Mysterious messengers came and went between Macellum and the capital. The atmosphere at best was eerie and disquieting. As Julian came to know the whole truth about the fate of his family, it became menacing. He can have been in no doubt that his cousin Constantius would murder him in a moment of panic as he had murdered his father and brother. In the absence of reliable information, rumour and speculation would have flourished. There must have been moments when Julian was in doubt whether he would survive until the next day. Whether these moments of intense emotion were worse than the long months of inescapable boredom only Julian himself could tell us, and he does not.

Such was the background against which Julian grew to physical, emotional and intellectual maturity. If he sought models, either to follow or to differ from, he had to seek them in literature, not in life. This only reinforced the backward-looking attitude instilled by Hellenic education, with its undervaluing of the contemporary world. If he sought answers to the problems that spring up in the mind of a young man – problems of conduct, problems about the nature of the universe – he got them from books, without the guidance of a sympathetic teacher or friend. The inexhaustible source of information – and misinformation – that a youth finds in his age-mates was blocked off for him. And the gap between what grown men and women preach and what they practise, which worries every young man from time to time, must have struck Julian with peculiar and personal sharpness and pathos.

He seems to have been a fairly fervent Christian in his early days at Macellum, when he took reader's orders and chanted the lesson in church. His knowledge of the Bible and of early Christian writings was detailed and precise. He can only have acquired this knowledge at Macellum. His later years were far too occupied with other matters. The Bible, as a Catholic writer observed, is a book full of traps for the faithful. Julian had a sharp eye for contradictions and inconsistencies, but he had no one in whom he had confidence to explain his difficulties to. He could only brood over them in silence, and in dissatisfaction at the superficial explanations furnished by his entourage. A naturally religious man, alert to the supernatural, he was incapable of a blind act of faith. Intellectual discontent with doctrine, moral discontent with the villainy and hypocrisy of many of the Christians who surrounded him, and perhaps above all with his bigoted and dangerous cousin and emperor, metaphysical discontent at a view of the world that often seemed to sweep the problem of evil under the carpet, all these undermined his earlier fervour. At the same time he was eagerly reading the works of the Neoplatonist philosophers, and finding in them a more acceptable explanation of his own simple mystic experiences and of the place of evil and pain in the universe. And it was an explanation that was couched in terms familiar to him from his earlier education with Mardonios, drawing its illustrations and its imagery from the classical literature which he knew and loved.

Julian passed through a religious crisis, or perhaps a series of crises, in the years at Macellum. We can only dimly discern the nature of the crisis, and approach it by a chain of uncertain inferences. Of its outcome, however, there is no doubt. He totally rejected Christianity and all its implications and institutions, and adopted the pagan monotheism of the Hellenizing intellectuals of the empire, who held out against the new faith, a monotheism in which there was room for the pantheon of the traditional gods and goddesses as allegories or manifestations or reflections of the true One. Writing in November 362 he says that he followed the way of error for twenty years, and that now with the help of the gods he has been following the true path for more than eleven years. This puts the date of his conversion in the last year of his exile at Macellum. It is unlikely to have happened suddenly. Julian was no Paul on the road to Damascus. It was rather the climax of months, or maybe years, of moral and intellectual struggle in the sinister solitude of his idyllic palace in the arid heart of Asia Minor.

Certain points may not be immediately clear to the present-day reader. First, Julian's acceptance of a Platonist idealism need not necessarily have led to a break with the Christianity in which he had been brought up. This philosophy was part of the intellectual climate of the times. Any Christian who sought an intellectual foundation for his faith – in Augustine's phrase *fides quaerens intellectum* – would turn to its concepts and its ways of thought. The great Cappadocian fathers, who were Julian's contemporaries, Basil, Gregory of Nyssa, Gregory of Nazianzus, were all in a sense Neoplatonists. Second, Julian's conversion did not involve accepting the tenets and practice of some other organized religion. Fourth-century paganism was vague in its outlines. The old cults of the Olympians and their Roman counterparts had long ceased to be practised except as an antiquarian exercise. Of the newer cults that had been superimposed upon the traditional religion, and all of which were monotheistic by implication, only three were still extensively practised – those of Isis, of Cybele, the *Magna Mater,* and of Mithras, the unconquerable sun, *Sol Invictus.* None of these had a body of doctrine that adherents were required to accept. None had a rigid organization. The public performance of these ceremonies was by now a serious criminal offence, and even private celebration of rites within the walls of a house could lead to denunciations and blackmail. Julian cannot at this stage in his life have had any direct acquaintance with the practice of pagan religion. He is much more likely to have met with magic. The boundary between magic and religion was particularly unclear at this time. Basically the magician seeks to compel higher powers – or the highest power – to do his will through the performance of occult ceremonies, while the worshipper seeks to do the will of the god and to draw as close to him as possible. But magic in late antiquity, as E. R. Dodds observes, makes much use of the debris of other people's religions. It is likely enough that among the slaves and attendants with whom his life was passed Julian had come across some who used half-understood pieces of pagan ritual, jumbled up with Christian and Jewish fragments, for the magical attainment of their trivial ends. Apart from this, his acquaintance with the surviving pagan cults was purely theoretical.

Visitors were few at Macellum. But one day the young Julian and his brother did receive an unexpected visitor. Constantius himself arrived to spend a few days at his hunting lodge and see his cousins. We do not know when he made this visit. Spring of 347 has been suggested; Constantius was at Ancyra (Ankara) in March of that year, and by early May had reached Hierapolis (not the better-known Phrygian city, now Pambukkale, but a crossing of the Euphrates at present-day Membidj), on his way to take command against the Persians in Mesopotamia. It would not be much of a detour to visit Cappadocia. But other dates are possible, such as summer 349, when Constantius was returning from Antioch to Constantinople, or September 350, when he travelled from Mesopotamia to Ancyra. In any case the disturbance of the calm at Macellum can be imagined. An emperor travelled with a vast personal entourage, accompanied by high officers of state, each with his suite, and a considerable body of troops. The palace would be fully occupied, and tents and bivouacs stretched as far as the eye could see. For Julian it would be a first confrontation with his father's murderer. No doubt they went on hunting parties together; Constantius was a keen sportsman, though Julian had no taste for such pastimes. There would be banquets where the tables groaned under the weight of game and the wine flowed like water; Julian had little taste for the pleasures of the table. Doubtless they attended church service together. There must even have been quiet conversations in the evening, when the reserved, guilt-ridden, suspicious and indecisive man on whose shoulders the burden of empire had fallen tried to establish contact with the withdrawn, intellectual son of the man he had had murdered. These overtures, from whichever side they came, were fore-doomed to break down in icy politeness and embarrassed silence. For all their striking differences of character the two men had one trait in common, a good opinion of themselves. It was hard for either to admit to himself that he might, in some small degree, have been wrong.

What part, if any, Constantius' visit played in Julian's break with Christianity we do not know. But it certainly marked a stage in his realization of the hypocrisy of mankind, including himself. His loathing of Constantius was probably equalled by his contempt for the role that he himself had had to play. All in all, the visit must have given Julian food for reflection for many a long day after the last of the emperor's cortège had vanished in the dust of the Asia Minor plateau.

Many young men in Julian's position might have sought distraction from the problems that faced them in a series of sexual experiments. Partners could easily enough have been found among the slaves and other humble members of the young prince's entourage. One point, however, on which Julian and his enemies were at one was the chastity of his life. This was partly a matter of upbringing. Constantine, only too well aware of the troubles arising from irregular unions in his own family, and doubtless driven on by a growing sense of guilt, insisted that in the education of his children the greatest emphasis be laid on the Christian conception of chastity. This may well have contributed to making them the neurotic creatures they appear to have been, though it did not prevent Constans, the youngest son, from developing a taste for young boys. No doubt the same lesson was instilled into the young Julian. Here it fell upon more fertile ground. Julian appears to have genuinely felt no need, at a conscious level, for any sexual relations. He describes himself as 'anaphroditos', probably meaning 'dead to sensual pleasure', and elsewhere makes it a principle of his conduct never to have sexual intercourse except in order to beget children. Unlike many unsensual men, however, he does not seem to have been censorious of the indulgences of others.

His reserve, the air of being withdrawn in an inner world that observers noticed in him, was only one side of his character, and one given emphasis by the isolation in which he passed his adolescent years. In other ways his was an outgoing character. He got on easily with his chosen associates in later life, and became the idol of the soldiers under his command. Perhaps 'command' is the important word here. Julian communicated well, but he liked to talk rather than to listen. He was at his best in situations in which he was firmly in control, though he fearlessly faced those in which he was not. The social distinctions of a hierarchical world interested him little, and he often offended the sensibilities even of his friends by the readiness with which he crossed social barriers. This whole aspect of his character must have been given an unnatural emphasis by the years at Macellum, when his only companions were persons separated from him by a social gulf so wide that in the outside world it could scarcely be crossed.

In 351 the years of exile suddenly ended. Julian, by now a bookish, thoughtful, sober young man, a little inclined to priggishness and more than a little pleased with himself, fundamentally and irrevocably opposed to the Christianization of upper-class society and of the Roman State that he saw going on around him, was recalled to the world as brusquely as he had been dismissed from it six years earlier.

3 Manhood and Freedom

AFTER THE DEATH of Constantine II at Aquileia in March 340, the Roman empire, while ideally remaining a single state, had been in fact divided between the brothers Constantius and Constans. Constans ruled the largely Latin-speaking west, Constantius the mainly Greek east. Thus it was Constantius who had to bear the brunt of the long war with the Persians that had broken out in the last days of his father's reign. It was a war of attrition, costly in men and in material resources. The aim of both sides was not to destroy the other – which would in any case have been beyond their powers – nor even to make large territorial gains. What each was trying to do was to establish and maintain an image, to convince the people of the Fertile Crescent that it was the supreme power in the region, and so to win their respect and allegiance. For right across the frontier of the two empires stretched a zone of a relatively unified culture. The native speech of the people was Aramaic. An eastern Aramaic dialect was the diplomatic language of the Sassanid Persian empire. A western dialect was rapidly developing as a literary tongue and vehicle of a rich Christian literature in the Roman city of Edessa and elsewhere. Over this basic Aramaic culture there had been superimposed in the west a Hellenic culture. Greek was the language of the upper classes. The cities transacted their affairs in Greek. Christian bishops corresponded with one another in Greek and preached in Greek in their cathedral churches. But the same bishops might well preach in Syriac (the name given to the wester Aramaic literary language) to the inhabitants of the surrounding countryside. Antioch, the second city of the eastern Roman empire was and always had been a Greek city, founded by Alexander's general Seleukos in the fourth century BC. Yet we know that the peasants who cultivated the land in its extensive territory mostly spoke Syriac, and that many of the Greek-speaking citizens understood Syriac, and might well speak it in the privacy of their homes. Men could and did move readily from one end to the other of this populous zone, which was the seat of an ancient civilization, without bothering too much about the frontier between the Roman and Persian empires. It was a centre of prosperity and advanced technology, important in the economy of both empires, and because of its wealth a much prized source of revenue. Hence the importance of impressing its inhabitants, on one's own side as well as on the other side of the frontier. Therein lay the key to the domination of the Middle East.

The Persian war dragged on. The Romans were more vulnerable to Persian attack than the Persians were to Roman, since they had more and larger cities within raiding distance of the frontier. In this way a long war was ultimately to the Persians' advantage. Constantius was anxious to bring the hostilities to a close by negotiation, but could hope to do so only after a major victory in the field.

In the western half of the empire the ineffectual and pleasure-loving Constans had become very unpopular with the army. Though there was no situation of war with a major foreign power, as there was in the east, the whole way of life of the western provinces depended on the maintenance of the Rhine and Upper-Danube frontier against the continuous pressure of the various German tribal confederations, themselves pushed from behind and eager both for booty and for land to settle on. Constans neglected the legions on which the security of the frontier depended, rejected the advice of his senior military commanders, and came to depend more and more upon favourites, often *arrivistes* of humble origin, who pandered to his pleasures. There was an underswell of discontent that needed only organization to turn it into open revolt. The organization was provided by Marcellinus, Constans' chief finance minister (*Comes rerum privatarum*). At a banquet given by him to celebrate the birthday of his son, at Augustodunum (Autun), on 18 January 350, while Constans was on a hunting trip nearby, all the leading military officers of Gaul were present. In the course of the banquet one of them, Magnentius, a man of imposing appearance, probably the son of a British father and a Frankish mother, and a pagan, put on the purple robe and was acclaimed by the assembled company as emperor. Within a few days Constans had been arrested and executed. A few months later two other counter-emperors were proclaimed, one in Rome and the other on the Danube frontier. But they did not succeed in establishing themselves. Indeed the Danubian candidate, an elderly general named Vetranio, was probably proclaimed at the instigation of Constantius' sister in order to prevent his troops going over to Magnentius. Within a short time he had made his peace with Constantius and was sent off to spend the evening of his days on an estate in Asia Minor.

Constantius, whose hands were full in the east, at first tried to negotiate with Magnentius, but soon became convinced that he would have to fight him. It was a daunting prospect. The distances were vast, the logistic problems almost insuperable, and the stakes immense. To complicate matters, the Christian Churches of east and west did not see eye to eye on doctrinal matters. The point at issue, to which reference has already been made (p. 23), was the position of the second person of the Trinity. Was the Son of the same nature as the Father, or was he in some way subordinate, however similar. The council of Nicaea, held by Constantine in 325 had decided that they were of the same nature, and this was the official doctrine of the Church. It was open to a number of philosophical as well as theological objections, and these were openly voiced by many churchmen in the sophisticated east. Athanasius, Bishop of Alexandria, a fiery and uncompromising Nicene, was expelled from his see and sent into exile. In time he contrived to escape to the west, where he was protected by Constans and later by Magnentius. From the safety of Rome he launched denunciations of his opponents and organized intrigues and conspiracies. The Arians of the east responded in kind. The mass of the eastern clergy sought a compromise position. But since they did not accept unquestioningly the creed of Nicaea, they were in the eyes of Athanasius and his friends Arians. Pamphlet followed pamphlet, counter-coup followed coup, and neither side scrupled to use the most violent methods against the other, including murder. For it was precisely the kind of dispute that can be used, even by those who do not understand what it is all about, to pay off old scores and to exteriorize their own dissatisfaction. It was an unedifying spectacle. And it was politically dangerous, as it created in east and west alike a sense of disaffection that could turn into collaboration with the enemy.

In this situation Constantius decided to appoint a junior colleague to take charge in the east while he fought Magnentius in the west. This kind of regional devolution of administrative decision while retaining the ultimate political power in the hands of the senior colleague had been tried several times in the preceding two generations. It was the obvious solution to the problem of administration in a society where communications are slow and in a state in which departmental organization is weak. The only thing wrong with it was that it did not work. Since Diocletian the colleagues in empire had always ended within a few years as opponents in civil war. Nevertheless Constantius had little choice, except of who was to be his colleague. An outsider would certainly become a rival for power. This much he had learnt from recent history. The only safe course was to appoint a member of his family. This was what his father Constantine had done, who had combined a strong sense of family with a murderous vindictiveness against any of his kinsmen whom he thought to be plotting against him. Constantius had diminished the scope of his choice by the massacre of his uncles and their offspring that he had allowed to take place in 337. He had two surviving sisters, both of whom were at the moment unmarried. His nearest male kinsmen were the brothers Gallus and Julian, sons of his paternal uncle. The fact that he was an accessory to the murder of their father may in a way have made them more acceptable candidates to Constantius. In promoting them, he could feel that he was atoning for his earlier crime. Gallus, who was by now twenty-five or twenty-six years of age, was chosen.

In the winter of 351 a messenger suddenly arrived at the princes' place of exile at Macellum, bidding Gallus to leave at once for Constantius' headquarters at Sirmium (Sremska Mitrovica near Belgrade). Despite the season, Gallus made haste, and on 15 March he was proclaimed Caesar at Sirmium and given the east as his sphere of operation. Both emperors swore solemn oaths of loyalty to one another before an assemblage of bishops and officers of State. To cement the new alliance Gallus was married to the elder of Constantius' sisters, Constantina. She was a good deal older than Gallus, and had been married sixteen years earlier to Hannibalianus, Constantine's nephew. Hannibalianus had been killed in 337 in the pogrom of his relations engineered by Constantius. Magnentius had offered to marry her as part of an agreement with Constantius, but the offer had been rejected by the emperor. Now at last, after thirteen years of widowhood she was again provided with a husband. She had a cruel nature – or perhaps she had been soured by her experience. At any rate a historian who had seen her, and whose judgement we can respect, even if we do not always agree with it, wrote of her as 'a Fury in human shape, continually inflaming her husband's rage, no less thirsty of human blood than he' (Ammianus Marcellinus 14.1.2).

This egregious pair of rulers, in whom the well-disposed may see the victims of circumstance rather than of original sin, set off for Antioch,

accompanied by an entourage befitting their state and by a group of senior
civil and military officers appointed by Constantius – some of whom, no
doubt, sent him secret reports. In the meantime Julian seems to have been
forgotten. However Gallus arranged to meet him at Nicomedia on his way
from Sirmium to Antioch in the late spring of 351. Julian succeeded in
obtaining, through the good offices of his brother and sister-in-law, permission to leave his place of exile and continue his studies. In addition he
was given the estate of his maternal grandmother, who had died in the
intervening time. He was nineteen or twenty years of age, a very rich man,
and for the first time in his life free to go where he liked, see whom he
liked, make what friends he liked – or more or less free.

A weak man might have found the stresses of freedom too much, and
turned to a meaningless round of pleasure-seeking. Julian's streak of
puritanism prevented that. He knew very well, too, that there were limits
to his freedom. He must keep away from concerns of State. The whole
sphere of imperial affairs – the army, the law, foreign policy, the financial
operations of the central government, anything that might give him
experience of power – was closed to him. He was to have no public career
such as Constantine had permitted to his half-brother Dalmatius. He was
to confine himself to life at the level of the cities, a life that was conducted
in Greek, not Latin. This was probably never spelled out in the frigidly
polite exchanges between Constantius and Julian, but it had no need to be.

Julian's greatest desire was to make up for the years of isolation at
Macellum and continue his education. He probably began once again to
attend the lectures of Hekebolios at Nicomedia. There was another
teacher of rhetoric at Nicomedia at this time, Libanius, whose reputation
was already spreading all over the Greek-speaking world. We possess many
of his speeches. They are marked by invariable good taste, archaism, a
kind of finicky refinement – no vulgar appeals to the emotions of his
hearers, no flowery décor, no poetry in prose. To modern ears his style is
flat and his meaning not always clear. To the men of his time he was the
embodiment of Attic purity. He embodied too the backward-looking,
inward-turning attitude with which many of the intellectuals of the Greek
cities greeted the invasion of their world by the sovereign power. For since
Constantine founded his new capital on the Bosphorus the central authority
of the empire was no longer distantly protective, leaving the cities of the
Greek east to run their own affairs, provided they paid their taxes. It was
on their doorstep, interfering more and more in day-to-day matters,
drawing into its service the richest men from the city councils and sending

their sons scurrying off to Rome or Berytus to fit themselves for a career in the civil service, instead of learning the subtle craft of imitating the models of the great Hellenic past. Julian longed to attend Libanius' lectures. But Libanius was an open pagan, contemptuous of the new imperial religion. At this stage of Julian's development this made him all the more attractive. Yet elementary prudence warned him that intimacy with Libanius might be misinterpreted by the bigoted and suspicious Constantius. Perhaps he was over-cautious. After six years of isolation it was hard to be sure what one could get away with. At any rate he avoided direct association with Libanius, but arranged to obtain copies of his lectures.

Julian was soon dissatisfied with the emptiness of the literary rhetoric of the time. He had a natural inclination towards directness and a distaste for mere verbal skill. And the questions over which he had brooded in his years of exile still burned within him. He had read much philosophy, and he had rejected the Christian view of the world. But philosophy is not something one reads, it is something one does. He needed to be trained in the practice of philosophy. And he longed to be initiated into the religious beliefs and rites of the pagan adherents of philosophy, beliefs and rites of which he had caught only fleeting glimpses through his reading. So he soon turned from the rhetoricians to the philosophers.

In the century or more that had elapsed since Plotinus (205–269/70), there had been developments in Neoplatonist thought. Plotinus had sought a direct, if momentary, union of the human spirit with the first principles of being by purely intellectual means. He was the type-specimen of the introvert mystic. Something of an intellectual snob, he despised everything that smacked of magic, or of popular religious practice. Well aware of Christianity, which though not yet a State religion was a far from negligible force in the society of his time, he refused to get involved with it. It was really beneath his notice. His leading pupil and successor was Porphyry (232/3-c. 305) a formidable philosopher, but a man of very different stamp from his master. He was, among other things, a textual scholar, interpreting the works of his predecessors, identifying their apparent contradictions, and explaining them away. He had a taste for what could be clearly set down in black and white. For Plotinus' occasion-ally vague hierarchy of orders of being, down which run the emanations of the One, and up which the soul struggles in its striving to reunite with the One, Porphyry substituted a complex structure in which every stage could be named and described, and a place found for every deity of the pagan pantheon. Lastly he saw the progress that Christianity was making among the upper classes and was determined to put a stop to it. Thoroughly familiar with the Bible and other early Christian texts, he was probably less familiar with the daily life and practice of Christian communities. Nevertheless, he was a well-informed and sincere opponent, with a sharp eye for contradictions and absurdities, and a firm philosophical standpoint of his own. His book *Against the Christians* no longer survives – for soon all book copyists had become Christians – and we can only partially reconstruct its arguments from later quotations and allusions, which were mainly hostile. It was by far the most systematic and radical critique of Christianity that the ancient world knew. Its application of historical criticism to the basic texts of Christianity was something not done so well again until the nineteenth century. In the end Porphyry left a philosophy that turned rather more on the interpretation of authoritative texts than that of Plotinus, and one in which belief was finding a place side by side with ratiocination. He writes:

> Four elements should be given emphasis in what concerns God: belief, truth, love and hope. One must believe because the only salvation lies in turning towards God, and having believed strive to one's utmost to learn the truth about him, and having learnt it love what one knows, and having loved it feed one's soul on good hopes throughout life.

For Porphyry the bonds between philosophy and religion were already beginning to break down.

Porphyry's pupil and successor was Iamblichus (*c.* 250–*c.* 325). Little of his writings survive and it has long been fashionable to sneer at him as a miracle-monger and demi-charlatan. Yet he was the father of the scholasticism of the Athenian school of the fifth and sixth centuries, as well as of the theosophy of many of his direct pupils. The truth seems to be that he was a highly respectable philosopher who, from character or conscious choice, tried to find room in his philosophy for much of the spiritualism and magic of popular superstition. Many of the phenomena with which he concerns himself would today be left to the psychologist to investigate. But there were no psychologists in the fourth century. Iamblichus sought to explain alleged instances of clairvoyance, of prophecy, of telekinesis, and so on from his own philosophical premises. If the whole of the universe flowed as an emanation from the first principle of being, then the humblest material objects contained within themselves a spark of the divine, a pale reflection of pure being that might enable them on occasion to transcend the laws of their limited nature. This proposition permitted a rational explanation of much that seemed inexplicable, and enabled the philosopher to accept every kind of religious or quasi-religious practice, from astrology to Zoroastrianism. It also opened the door wide to every kind of charlatanism and encouraged a kind of breathless expectation of the unexpected, which was a poor substitute for philosophical detachment. Philosophy had been taken over by religion, in a strange amalgam of rigid dialectic and enthusiastic ritualism. The philosopher's world was now populated with demons and spirits, who could be subjected to the human will. In this respect it was no different from the world of the Christian. The Fathers of the Church yield nothing to Iamblichus in demonology.

By the time Julian began to seek a guide in philosophy Iamblichus was dead. But some of his pupils were still alive. The chief among these was Aidesios. He was a Cappadocian, who had for years been living and teaching in Pergamum, in north-western Asia Minor. The author of serious studies on Aristotle, he was also a firm believer in oracles and divination, and in the approach to the gods – or to God – through occult rituals. At one time in obedience to an oracle he had left the city and bought a small farm in the depths of the country. This untypical 'dropping-out' probably reflected some kind of personal crisis. By now he was an old man, and in failing health. When Julian came to Pergamum, pressed lavish presents on him, and asked to become his pupil, Aidesios asked to be excused because of his age and his health. He may well have thought it imprudent, too, to take on a pupil whose activities were likely to be the subject of secret reports to Constantius, since some of his own religious practices belonged to that grey area between the permitted and the illicit. Instead he recommended Julian to address himself to one of his own pupils. 'If you are initiated into our mysteries', he went on, 'you will be ashamed to have been born a man and to have borne the human name. I wish Maximus were here, but he has been sent to Ephesus. I wish too that Priscus were here, but he has set sail for Greece. Of my closest friends only Eusebios and Chrysanthios are still here. Seek instruction from them.' This Julian did.

Eusebios taught a rather old-fashioned Neoplatonism. Only by intellectual effort could the soul mount towards its source. Spells and mystery cults were of no avail. He used to conclude all his lectures with a reminder that magical activities were mere illusions of the senses, tricks worked by charlatans with the aid of material devices. This repeated observation intrigued Julian, who sensed that there was more behind it than met the eye. One day he asked Chrysanthios about it. But Chrysanthios was giving nothing away. 'You would do better to ask Eusebios himself for an explanation,' he said. Later Julian plucked up the courage to go up to Eusebios after a lecture and ask him the meaning of his words. The philosopher answered him at length:

> Maximus is one of the older and more advanced students. His strength of character led him to despise logical demonstrations in these matters, and launch impetuously on a mad course. Not long ago he invited us to the temple of Hekate, and made us witnesses against him. We arrived there, and did reverence to the goddess. 'Sit down, my friends', said Maximus, 'and see what is going to happen, and how much superior I am to the run of you.' We sat down, and he burned a grain of incense and recited to himself some sort of hymn. So successful was his demonstration that the statue first began to smile and then seemed to laugh aloud. We were disturbed by what we had seen. 'Don't worry', said he, 'for you will soon see the torches which the goddess holds in her hands light up.' Hardly had he finished speaking when the torches burst into flame. At the moment we were in admiration of that theatrical miracleworker. But do not you marvel at any of these things – I do not – but be sure that the most important thing is to purify your soul by reason.

Julian did not follow his advice. 'Stick to your books,' he said, 'you have shown me the man I want.' And off he set for Ephesus to meet Maximus (Eunapius, *Lives of the Sophists* 7.2.5–12).

Maximus was a strange character, typical in a way of the age in which he lived. A native of Ephesus and a distant relation of Aidesios, under whom he studied. Negligible as a philosopher, he made a speciality of every kind of theurgy, divination and miracle-mongering. He seems to have been the kind of half-charlatan who deceived himself before he deceives others. His powerful personality and his imposing manner silenced criticisms. A writer who met him many years later, after he had been subjected to humiliation and torture because of his association with Julian, says his speech recalled that of Athena or Apollo in Homer.

> The very pupils of his eyes seemed endowed with wings . . . his beard was long and grey, his eyes revealed the impulses of his soul. Both to eye and ear his person had a kind of harmony. People who met him were

captivated through both senses, overborne by the rapid movement of his eyes and the swift course of his speech. Not even the most experienced ventured to contradict him in discussion. They yielded to him in silence, as if he were an oracle. So great was the charm that sat upon his lips [Eunapius, *Lives of the Sophists* 7.1.1–3].

If this was the impression that Maximus produced in broken old age, one can imagine how compelling was his personality in his prime, when Julian first met him.

He became a regular attendant at Maximus' lectures, and no doubt had private 'tutorials' with the great man, in which the Neoplatonist view of life as interpreted by Iamblichus was expounded. Much of what Julian had read in the library of Bishop George was now made clear. And new, exciting perspectives were opened of attaining communion with the One – or at any rate with one of its higher manifestations – by secret rites, unknown to the man in the street, strongly condemned by the ruling Christian view, and probably strictly illegal. Certainly dangerous for a kinsman of the emperor. The later Neoplatonists, or a section among them, had elaborated a kind of esoteric religion, revealed only to those whom they cared to initiate. The practice of it no doubt confirmed the feeling of solidarity among them, the sense of belonging to a group superior to the mass of mankind. Their Bible was a book called *Chaldaean Oracles*, written by a certain Julian, a Babylonian who had come to Rome in the early second century AD, together with the commentary which Iamblichus had composed upon it. Babylonians, real or spurious, enjoyed a reputation in the ancient world as astrologers and clairvoyants. Many of them made an uncertain living on the fringes of society as humble fortune-tellers. Julian the Babylonian, who came of a family of magicians, satisfied a real demand with his uncritical compilation of the degenerate debris of the ancient religions of his people, probably overlaid with influences from dualist, fire-worshipping Iran. Iamblichus provided pseudo-philosophical glosses upon this strange farrago, introduced into it many elements of traditional Greek religion, and imposed some kind of systematic structure on the whole.

Both the *Chaldaean Oracles* and Iamblichus' book on them survive only in casual quotations made by other writers. They smelt too much of brimstone for early medieval copyists. So we cannot reconstruct with any completeness the overgrown theology and theatrical ritual of the religion of the initiates. Their principal deity was Hekate, in Greek mythology a rather sinister goddess of the underworld. In the hands of the Babylonians and Iamblichus she had become fused with Cybele, the great Mother Goddess. Fire was her principal attribute – blazing torches in her hands, and hair that turned to flame. Her image was the material counterpart of a reality in a higher order of being. And the fire that accompanied her was the image of the divine fire, of which there was a spark in every human soul. Her worship involved the chanting of hymns and secret formulae, the lighting of torches and burning of incense, sudden blazes of light, obsessive music, theatrical effects – moving statues, doors opening of their own accord, and so on, and it normally took place in underground chambers. It sounds trivial, like something from a fairground. But so does almost any other religion, described from the outside. To those who had been taught the inner meaning of the rites, and brought to the right pitch of expectation, they may well have been profoundly moving and satisfying, discharging tension and creating a sense of well-being.

Julian longed to be initiated. Here at last was what he sought – a concrete, living embodiment of his conversion at Macellum. Now he could not merely believe in what he thought was the religion of his ancestors, he could live it. Maximus had none of the scruples that had held back Aidesios. As soon as he felt his pupil was prepared, he took him to the crypt, where the secret rites were enacted and their hidden meaning revealed to the new initiate. This initiation, with its words and music and incense and light filling the senses and charging the emotions, was a key experience in Julian's life. He now belonged to the elect, of whom more was demanded than of ordinary men, and to whose souls was promised a rebirth in the higher order of being. He had crossed a bridge that could never be recrossed.

Basically a religious man, as were so many in his age, having abandoned one religion it was almost inevitable that he should end up in another. But there was probably more to it. Starved of affection and isolated for so much of his youth, Julian had a need to be accepted and to belong to a group of some kind. In the Neoplatonist philosophers, with their interest in the Greek past, their intellectual rigour, their opposition to the course events were taking, their exteriorization of their deepest emotions in secret rites, he found just such a group. At last he was accepted as an equal by men whom he could respect. No doubt in the dangerous world in which they lived the initiates had secret signs by which they could recognize one another. Julian was now one of their number, sharing their secret knowledge, the consciousness of superiority, and their slight sense of danger. A little after his first initiation he was initiated once again, this time to the cult of Mithras, the Sun God. The place of initiation would again be underground. The Mithraic temple recently discovered in the city of London, or that at Aquincum, near Budapest, give an idea of what it was like. The new initiation was a natural sequence to the first, for in the eyes of these Neoplatonists all traditional religions were ways to the attainment of the Truth. And the cult of Mithras still had wide-spread adherence, despite the position of Christianity as the official religion of emperor and State.

Julian knew that he was surrounded by spies, and his participation in these forbidden rites must have been carried out with the greatest care and circumspection. Not that there was anything illegal in being a pagan. What was forbidden was public offering of sacrifice, in particular by night. For a close relation of the pathologically suspicious emperor to be caught in such activities would be doubly dangerous. None but his fellow-initiates and his closest personal servants can have known of them. Outwardly he was still a conforming Christian, attending church service on Sundays and feast days, possibly even reading the lesson from time to time, and observing all the prescriptions and taboos of Christianity. He was living a double life, a stimulating and exciting experience for a time, but one that in the long run dulls a man's ability to distinguish between illusion and reality.

For three years Julian continued his philosophical studies and his heady experiments in pagan theosophy and theurgy. Meanwhile his brother Gallus was in Antioch, with the rank and title of Caesar. Gallus' activities there are described in some detail by the historian Ammianus Marcellinus, a native of Antioch, who was there at the time. Thanks to Ammianus, Gallus has been seen by posterity as a kind of fiend in human shape, taking delight in cruelty for its own sake. Ammianus piles up suggestive epithets that imply disreputable motives and compares him with a lion that has tasted human flesh and so on. Recent studies have shown that Ammianus was less than just to Gallus, who had taken measures against the interests of the Antiochene upper class to which Ammianus belonged. Some have even suggested that Gallus enjoyed mass popular support and may even have been a social reformer. There seems to be no real evidence for this. And that Gallus was hot-tempered, easily provoked, and some-times very rash seems beyond doubt. The matter does not really turn on the character of individuals, but on fundamental questions of political power that rose again a few years later in the case of Julian. For this reason it is worth looking at the situation a little more closely.

Firstly Gallus was thrown in at the deep end, apparently without any training or experience of public affairs. And he was surrounded by officers of State appointed by and responsible to Constantius. He can scarcely have been expected to make independent political decisions at first. What he was expected to do was to be the personal representative of the emperor – not his delegate, exercising power on his behalf, but a kind of reflection of his charismatic person, to raise morale and ensure loyalty. Inevitably, communications being as poor as they were, he would have decisions thrust upon him, decisions that some senior civil servants would refuse to accept as being *ultra vires*. Gallus would then have to give way or to enforce an authority that in strict law he did not possess. Some of his alleged acts of wanton cruelty fall under this head. Secondly since the time of Diocletian a clear-cut separation of military and civil power had been established in the Roman empire. The two chains of command met only at the top, in the person of the emperor. Gallus' duties, in so far as they were more than ceremonial, were purely military. Contemporaries tell us that he was appointed to keep things under control on the eastern front while Constantius, with the bulk of the armed forces, marched against Magnentius. He did in fact succeed in doing just this – we hear of the suppression of revolts of the mountain peoples of the Taurus range and of the Jews, and of minor victories against the Persians, who never succeeded in pressing home an attack. Magnentius thought him important enough to try to have him assassinated. There was an inherent difficulty in his position, however, that his military successes only exacerbated. Though he exercised operational command of the armed forces, the provision of supplies – forage, rations, pay, equipment and so on, was in the hands of a civil official, the Praetorian Prefect, and his subordinates. Gallus had no authority over this department. Even a complaisant Praetorian Prefect might not be able to do all that a military commander would like him to do. An uncooperative Praetorian Prefect could frustrate his every move. This curious situation was not the result of perverseness or failure to think things through. It arose because an army had to be supplied out of the taxes – in money, kind and labour – paid by the local population. In ancient conditions there could be no effective concentration of all resources at the centre and redistribution of them to the points at which they were needed. So the provision of supplies for the army inevitably became the duty of the official responsible for the assessment and collection of revenue. When the emperor himself took the field, there was no problem. When a subordinate was in command, there had to be either detailed instructions from the top on conflicts of authority and jurisdiction, or an understanding growing out of long years of experience. Gallus had no experience. And the instructions he and the civil officials received from Constantius seem to have been unclear and equivocal. Constantius' natural suspicion and indication would have guaranteed this. We hear of a series of conflicts between Gallus and the civilian officials, not only on questions of military supply, but also on conditions among the civil population in the rear of the army. A typical case was before Gallus' departure for the eastern front during a Persian raid in force. He addressed a public meeting at Antioch. There were appeals from the crowd to save them from an expected famine. Gallus quite correctly, if unwisely, pointed to the governor of Syria, a subordinate of the Praetorian Prefect, who was standing beside him, and said that there would be no lack of food unless the governor wanted it so. This was taken to imply – perhaps rightly – that the governor was acting hand in glove with the wealthy citizens of Antioch who were hoarding corn at a moment when military needs were forcing the price up. The situation became more inflamed, and a few days later, as prices continued to rise, an angry crowd burnt down the house of one of the leading citizens and lynched the governor. Gallus returned from his journey to the front, ordered the rich hoarders to lower their selling price, and when they refused, condemned the leaders of the town council to death all together. This was probably illegal, and it was certainly an interference in civil affairs. It was also probably a bluff, and it seems to have worked. It was doubtless unwise, but Gallus had a war on his hands and could not wait. Actions like this alienated the high civil officials, and the wealthy citizens of the eastern provinces, who in any case came from the same social stratum as the officials. There was a mysterious plot against Gallus, the leaders of which were pursued and punished with the utmost severity. What reports reached Constantius in the distant west we do not know. But they were certainly tendentious and slanderous, since they came from the very people in whose sphere of authority – and enrichment, let us remember – Gallus was interfering. Constantius interpreted the interference with his officials as a challenge to his own authority. He had decisively defeated Magnentius at Mursa (the modern Sisak in Yugoslavia) in September 351, but only at the cost of terrible losses in men. Magnentius was still alive, and was not finally cornered and driven to suicide until August 353. During all this time, and even afterwards, until the last remnants of Magnentius' forces were rounded up and incorporated with his own army, Constantius was afraid of a revolt against him in the eastern provinces. There seem indeed to have been some senior military commanders who did consider rebellion. Gallus was not involved in their plot, which in the end never came to anything. But he would have been useful as a figure-head.

All these factors together played on Constantius' suspicious mind, until in 354 he decided that he must recall Gallus. In any case he was no longer necessary, now that Magnentius had been removed. The Praetorian Prefect Domitianus was sent from the imperial headquarters at Milan to Antioch with overt orders to persuade Gallus 'politely and frankly' to accompany him to Milan. Domitianus instead contacted Gallus' enemies, one of whom was his own son-in-law, and began collecting evidence of disaffection on the part of Gallus. He was probably acting according to secret orders. Finally he confronted Gallus with an ultimatum. 'Come with me to Italy or your supplies will be cut off.' Gallus had him arrested. Another officer pointed out to Gallus that he had no authority to remove any civil official, far less a Praetorian Prefect. Gallus appealed to his soldiers for protection, and they responded by tearing Domitianus and his colleagues to pieces. Constantius, hearing of all this, saw his worst suspicions confirmed, and it is probably at this point that he decided to destroy Gallus. Other officers were sent to invite him to come to Milan. In the end he went without a struggle, probably because he realized that he did not have any solid support, rather than from any high-minded resolve to spare the empire another civil war. In any case he seems to have thought that the matter could all be sorted out, misunderstandings cleared up and errors of judgement forgiven. On his way to Italy he stopped at Constantinople, where he presided at chariot races in the hippodrome. When he heard of this Constantius 'flared up beyond human measure'. He evidently interpreted Gallus' action as a usurpation of his own prerogative and an attempt to win the support of the people of the capital. It was almost certainly nothing of the kind.

The story need not be pursued in detail any longer. Gallus returned and was at once put under arrest at Pola. Constantius, torn between fear and guilt, hesitated at first what to do about him. Finally he gave the order for his execution, then changed his mind, but too late. In November 354 the Caesar was beheaded.

Julian had certainly been aware of his brother's difficulties. Though of such different temperaments, the two seem to have been on good enough terms. They met during Gallus' journey from Antioch to Italy. The news of Gallus' arrest and execution, though not wholly unexpected, must have been a dreadful blow to Julian, whose new life in Ephesus had seemed so assured. The whole sinister history of his family, and in particular the part Constantius had played in it, once again occupied the forefront of his mind. But worse was soon to come. Gallus' friends or supposed friends were arrested and put on trial one by one, while informers vied with one another in furnishing damning evidence against him. Julian's turn soon came. He was summoned to Milan. On his journey there he had a curious experience, which years later he recounted in a letter. The ship carrying him and his military escort put in at the little port of Alexandria Troas, opposite the island of Tenedos. Julian seized the opportunity to walk up to the site of Troy, a few miles away. It was a flourishing little town at that time. He was met by the local bishop, Pegasios, who courteously offered to show him the sights. First they went to the shrine of Hector, where to his amazement he found a fire still smouldering on the altar, and the statue of the hero still dripping with oil. 'What is this?', he said to the bishop, trying to sound his opinions, 'do the people of Ilion still offer sacrifice?' 'Is it strange', replied his guide, 'that they should show their respect for their distinguished fellow-citizen, just as we show ours for the martyrs?' Julian realized that this was no ordinary bishop. They went on to the temple of Athena of Troy, where again everything was in order, and where the bishop did not make the sign of the cross on his forehead or whistle between his teeth, as Christians did to ward off the evil spirits that still hung about pagan cult sites. The tomb of Achilles, too, which Julian had heard had been desecrated by the bishop, was intact. As the two men walked through the ancient city, discoursing on its antiquities, there grew upon each a conviction amounting to certainty that the other too was an initiate in the secret pagan cult. Nothing was openly said. But when Julian returned in the evening to his ship it was with a deep sense of relief. The gods whom he worshipped in his heart had brought him to a friend. He did not forget the courteous, civilized pagan bishop in future years.

When he reached Milan he was accused of having left Macellum without the emperor's permission, and of having had a meeting with his brother in Constantinople. He succeeded in showing that neither of these actions was taken in defiance of an imperial order. But this did not help him, for the real charge against him was of having participated in a plot to overthrow Constantius. He found an unexpected ally in Constantius' new wife,

Eusebia, a woman of wide culture and warm kindness. She made the most of her influence with her husband, who hoped at last to beget an heir by her, and had the emperor grant Julian an audience at which the two men were reconciled. He was not, however, allowed to return to his studies in Asia. A complicated affair of forged documents had led Constantius to believe, quite wrongly, that Silvanus, his commander-in-chief in Gaul, was plotting rebellion. So Julian was held under house arrest for some time at Comum, north of Milan. Again Eusebia intervened on his behalf, and he was finally allowed to return to his studies. But he was directed to pursue them, not in Asia Minor, but in Athens, where he would be far from any military garrison and unlikely to be contacted by disaffected generals. Nothing was more to his liking. The decision seemed to him to be an obvious instance of the gods protecting their own. Athens, the city of Plato and Aristotle, was by this time a quiet town in an out-of-the-way province, but renowned as a centre of learning and study. It had the prestige, and something of the atmosphere, of a university city – Oxford, or Göttingen, Leyden or Salamanca. To teach in Athens represented the crown of the career of a rhetorician or philosopher. Young men came from all over the Greek world and beyond to sit at the feet of the great teachers, and to profit by the network of correspondence and recommendation by which they furthered the careers of their pupils. To study in Athens had been Julian's dream, and suddenly it had come true.

We know a good deal about student life in Athens in the fourth century. The pupils of each teacher had a fierce loyalty to one another and to their master. There were fights between the different groups, in which heads were sometimes broken. Students were kidnapped by those of another group. Newcomers were met at the quayside by representatives of the various groups, who tried to press-gang them. There were bizarre initiation ceremonies, rags and processions of all kinds. Julian was older than the run of students, and he was the emperor's closest surviving relation. We may be sure that he was spared these manifestations of youthful boisterousness and received as an honoured guest in the city of Pallas Athene, when he arrived in the summer of 355.

The leading teachers of rhetoric at the time were Prohairesios of Armenia, a Christian, and Himerius of Prusa, a pagan. Julian does not seem to have attended their lectures with any regularity. The empty technicalities of rhetoric held little interest for him. And the tinselly style of Himerios' orations, which survive, was scarcely to his taste. What he was looking for was further instruction in Neoplatonist philosophy and further initiation into the half secret cult of the philosophers. He found both. Priscus, the pupil of Aidesios whose absence the old man had regretted when Julian first presented himself to him, was now teaching in Athens, and it was to him that Julian attached himself. They became close friends and explored together the arcane secrets of theurgy.

Julian spent some time visiting the ancient monuments of Athens, walking in the gardens of the Academy, where Plato had taught and where the school that he had founded eight centuries earlier was still in being, following the footsteps of Aristotle in the Peripatus. These summer and autumn months in Athens must have kindled in him a deeper feeling of the continuity of Hellenic intellectual life than he can ever have learnt at Pergamum or Ephesus. During his stay in Athens he became an initiate of the ancient mystery cult of Demeter in the temple at Eleusis. This pagan cult was tolerated because of its antiquity and its prestige. To many visitors to Athens in late antiquity it was no more than a tourist attraction. To Julian, as he looked on the symbolic objects in the sacred basket, took part in the sacred meal, heard the hierophant recite the ancient words that promised rebirth to the initiates, it was a profound allegory of the journey of man's soul towards communion with the One. He felt himself more than ever a man apart from his contemporaries, protected by the ancient gods, who were reflections or ministers of the Pure Being from which the universe eternally flowed and to which it eternally returned.

There were others in Athens at the time who saw things very differently. Gregory of Nazianzus, the future bishop of Constantinople, recognized by the church as a saint after his death, was one of Julian's fellow-students. It is unlikely that Julian knew him personally. They moved in different circles. But he knew Julian. Years later, after his death, and with the advantage of hindsight, he wrote a bitter attack upon Julian, in which he described him as he was in his student days. 'There seemed to me to be no evidence of sound character in his unsteady neck, his twitching and hunched shoulders, his wandering eye with its crazy look, his uncertain and swaying walk, his proud and haughty nose, the ridiculous expressions of his countenance, his uncontrolled and hysterical laughter, the way he jerked his head up and down for no reason, his halting and panting speech' (Gregory of Nazianzus, *Oration* 5.23). This is scarcely an objective description. It would be well to set beside it the words in which the historian Ammianus Marcellinus, who saw much of Julian a few years later, depicts him. 'He was of medium height, with a beard that ended in a point [at

Athens he was still clean shaven, in accordance with the etiquette of Constantius' court], with bright eyes of striking beauty. He had elegant eyebrows, a perfect straight nose, a rather large mouth with a loose lower lip, a neck somewhat bent, and large, broad shoulders' (Ammianus Marcellinus 25.422). Elsewhere Ammianus mentions his great strides as he hastened through the streets of Antioch. Both descriptions are evidently of the same man, though seen through very different eyes. Other observers describe him as below average height.

Looking back later, Julian saw these months in Athens as the happiest period of his life. But it was not to last. Suddenly in October, there arrived a courier with orders for Julian to present himself at the court in Milan without delay. The message brought a rude awakening and with it a cold fear. Julian prayed to the gods of Hellas and to the One whose servants they were for strength and guidance. In his dreams he saw his brother's headless body. He prayed to Athena, he tells us, to let him die rather than set out on this journey. His departure was no doubt accompanied by much ceremony, and we may be sure that he played his part as best he could. But it was with fear and foreboding that he saw the Acropolis, on which still stood the great statue of the goddess, fade into the autumn mists.

4 The Chance of Power

CONSTANTIUS HAD RECENTLY HAD much to disquiet him. Silvanus, his commander-in-chief in Gaul, had, as has already been told, been the victim of an elaborate plot. The man who had forged letters in his name implying that he was contemplating rebellion was a minor supply officer named Dynamius. Rumour had it that behind him stood Lampadius, the Praetorian Prefect, and other high officials, who were jealous of Silvanus. When the forged letters were shown to Constantius, he at once panicked and gave orders for the arrest of all those whose names were mentioned in them. Some of his counsellors felt that the whole story was too improbable and advised caution. At first they were ignored, but when they later pointed to traces of the underlying writing that had been erased – clear evidence that the letters were forgeries – even Constantius was convinced. Some of the officials involved were arrested and punished, but the prefect Lampadius, though his guilt was scarcely in doubt, had too many powerful friends and could not be touched.

In the meantime Silvanus in his headquarters at Cologne heard of the calumnies being spread against him at court. He knew Constantius, and had little hope of convincing him of his innocence. At first he thought of slipping across the frontier and taking refuge with the Franks, in present-day Holland and north-western Germany. Silvanus was himself of Frankish descent. His father Bonitus, a mercenary officer in the Roman service, had distinguished himself in Constantine's war against Licinius. The son, brought up in Roman culture and the Christian faith, had followed his father's profession. He was a senior army officer in Gaul when Magnentius was proclaimed emperor. And at the decisive battle of Mursa in 351 he had gone over to Constantius together with the troops he commanded, and made no small contribution to the crushing defeat of the usurper. It was as a reward for this service that he had been appointed commander-in-chief in Gaul. Now after a life-time as a Roman he recalled his Frankish origin. No doubt he had a powerful network of kindred among the Franks, whose position in their own society had been enhanced by the successful careers of Bonitus and Silvanus – and by the money and presents that they sent to their kinsman in free Germany. He could reasonably hope to be protected if he crossed the frontier. But another Frankish officer at headquarters at Cologne, who had been instructed by Silvanus to sound out the situation, assured him that if he returned to his native land he would certainly be either killed or handed over to the Romans. Silvanus now felt that he had no choice but to profit by his popularity among the soldiers. Purple cloth was hastily torn from flags and standards and made into a rough and ready imperial robe. On 11 August 355 Silvanus was proclaimed emperor at Cologne and acclaimed by the assembled soldiers.

The news of his proclamation reached Milan one evening about a week later. Constantius was thunderstruck. The very crime with which Silvanus had been falsely charged he had now committed. Who was Constantius to trust? An all-night meeting of the council of State was held, at which the name of Ursicinus was put forward as the only man capable of dealing with the situation. Ursicinus, a general of long experience and distinction, had been in disgrace since his name had been inconclusively linked with an abortive plot against the emperor. Constantius mistrusted him, but had little choice. Ursicinus was at once summoned to the palace and informed of what had happened. It was decided that Constantius would pretend not to have heard anything of Silvanus' proclamation as emperor, and that Ursicinus should be sent at once to Gaul, ostensibly as his normal replacement. Once at Cologne, he was to play it by ear. Ursicinus set off with only a few staff officers – among whom was the historian Ammianus Marcellinus – and made his way north by forced marches, hoping to reach Cologne before Silvanus learned that news of his proclamation had reached Milan. But rumour was speedier than the fastest horsemen. When Ursicinus reached Cologne it was already useless to pretend that he was an innocent successor to Silvanus. Instead he had to pretend to accept Silvanus as his sovereign, while secretly mounting a conspiracy against him among officers whom he knew. It was a delicate business. One approach to the wrong man and Ursicinus and his staff could expect little mercy. Yet speed was essential. The gamble came off. A hard core of officers and soldiers loyal to Constantius was formed. At dawn on 8 September a band of armed men burst into Silvanus' headquarters and hacked him to death as he tried to seek the refuge of a Christian chapel.

Constantius was overjoyed at the news from Cologne, and at once began to arrest and put to torture all of Silvanus' former friends and associates. He was finally convinced that there had been no deep-laid plot, but only a series of misunderstandings and failures of communication. This knowledge did nothing to set his mind at rest. What had happened once could happen again. In the meantime the various Germanic peoples on the right bank of the Rhine had been making the most of the disorganization of the leaderless Roman army. Franks, Alamanni and Saxons had seized many forts on the left bank, and made raids deep into Roman territory. Further east the news of Roman weakness led to attacks in force along the Danube frontier by the Germanic Quadi and the Iranian Sarmatians. From the east came disquieting reports of renewed activity by the Persian King Shapur II, who had penetrated the frontier in the mountains of Armenia and the desert plains of Mesopotamia. Constantius felt unable to trust any of his generals with command over a major military force. Yet he could not take the field himself at opposite ends of the empire. Nor could he sit in Milan and do nothing, without risking a rebellion on one or other of the frontiers.

The court *camarilla* of eunuchs and civilian officials, who had daily access to Constantius, advised him to keep power in his own hands. His superhuman qualities, they said, were enough to deal with any eventuality. They were inspired not so much by personal loyalty to Constantius as by the anxiety that no co-emperor should have a chance to look into the lucrative traffic in appointments and influence that they had long been carrying on. Other civilian officials and the military leaders urged upon Constantius, who was still childless, the need to appoint a colleague to relieve him of some of the burdens of empire. Inevitably Julian's name arose. He was devoted to scholarship and without experience in government. But he was Constantius' nearest male relative, better able to represent him than any stranger could have been, and his character and antecedents made it seem unlikely that the temptations of power would weigh much with him. At this point in the discussions the empress Eusebia offered strong support for Julian's claims. She knew Julian personally. Apart from a single stilted and formal audience, Constantius knew his cousin only from the police reports that he had been receiving for ten years. Eusebia persuaded her husband at least to see Julian. And so messengers were dispatched post-haste to Athens to fetch him. He was offered no information on the reason for the summons because at the time he was sent for no decisions had been taken. Constantius, as always, liked to keep his options open.

For a time after he arrived at Milan he was not admitted to court but was kept under surveillance on an estate outside the city. The emperor still hung in suspense between conflicting counsels. Those who wished to preserve things as they were reminded him of the dangers of appointing a Caesar to share his power, and pointed to what had happened with Gallus. Finally the empress Eusebia carried her point. Blood was thicker than water, she argued. And Julian's scholarly way of life was an assurance that he would not try to usurp Constantius' position: philosophers do not seek power. And in any case Julian had no political power-base, no network of friends and dependents, no army loyal to him. Julian was not wholly unprepared when his cousin suddenly summoned him to court and told him that he was to become his junior colleague in imperial power. Eusebia had been sending him messages of encouragement through a eunuch of her suite. Yet his first reaction was one of anxiety and depression. If only the empress had borne children, he could have gone home to Athens and his studies. But then he reflected that perhaps he was trying to set himself against the will of the gods. If they had chosen him to take on his shoulders the highest responsibilities, who was he to try to thwart their designs. And he consoled himself by reflecting on a famous passage in Plato's *Phaedo* in which Socrates argues that one must accept whatever is one's lot. For all his unworldliness, Julian had the resilience of a man of twenty-four and a more than usually well-developed sense of his own ability.

He was still wearing civilian clothes, the coarse mantle of the philosopher, and he had begun to let his beard grow. The court barbers shaved him, and the court tailors dressed him in military uniform, the silk tunic of a senior office. He made, he tells us, a comic soldier, with his downcast glance and unmilitary gait. As the hasty preparations for his formal inauguration went on, he had other thoughts to worry him than how to acquire a soldierly bearing. He was for the first time face to face with the problem of living under the same roof as the murderer of his family, who might well before long try to get rid of Julian himself. Once again it was his sense of being a man apart, the object of special care on the part of the gods, that enabled him to accept the unacceptable.

Constantius was in a hurry. On 6 November the ceremony of inauguration took place. We have a description of it by Ammianus Marcellinus, who was himself present. All the military units present in Milan were assembled. On a high tribunal, surrounded by legionary eagles and standards, stood Constantius and Julian, both in military costume and attended by all the high officers of State. Taking Julian's right hand, Constantius began:

We stand before you, valiant defenders of the State, to defend a cause which you all with one spirit regard as your own. I know that I plead my case before just judges, so I shall be brief in my explanation. After the destruction of the rebellious usurpers, who were driven by madness and infatuation to do what they did, the barbarians, as if offering to their impious shades a funeral sacrifice of Roman blood, have broken through the frontiers and are sweeping through Gaul. They are confident that pressing affairs keep us occupied in distant lands. If this disaster, which is already spreading beyond the border regions, is met in time by our decision and yours, those proud peoples will bend their necks and the boundaries of the empire will remain intact. It remains for you to confirm by your approval the hope which I cherish for the future. Here is my paternal cousin Julian, as dear to me for his modesty as for his kinship to me. He is rightly held in respect and is a young man of remarkable capacity. I wish to elevate him to the rank of Caesar. If you find it a good idea, support my initiative with your approval.

At this point the assembled soldiers interrupted the speaker with a murmur of approval. Waiting till silence was restored, he went on:

Since you have indicated your approval by your expression of joy, let this young man, whose quiet strength and balanced character it is better to imitate than to describe, rise to receive the honour which he already awaits. His remarkable talents have been strengthened by study. This I think I have made clear by the fact that I have chosen him. So, at the instigation of God in heaven, I put upon his shoulders the mantle of empire [Ammianus Marcellinus 15.8.3–10].

With these words he robed Julian in the purple that had been his grandfather's and his uncle's to the loud acclamations of the soldiery. Then turning to Julian, who stood lost in thought and a little sad, he addressed him:

My dearest brother, you have received in your youth the honour that belongs to you by birth. My own glory, I admit, is increased thereby, since I believe that I earn my exalted position better by conferring almost equal power on my noble kinsman, than by the mere exercise of my own power. Stand by me to share my toils and my perils; take over the care of Gaul and heal its devastation by your munificence. And should you be called upon to meet the enemy, stand firm among the standard-bearers, encourage your men, after due reflection, to display timely valour, inspire them as they fight by careful leadership, support them with reinforcements when their ranks are broken, rebuke discreetly the discouraged and bear true witness to deeds of bravery or of cowardice. Great is the need of the moment; go forth, a hero leading heroes. We shall sustain one another with strong and unshakeable affection, we shall fight side by side, and we shall rule with equal moderation and sense of responsibility a world to which – God grant our prayer – we have brought peace. Everywhere I shall see you before my eyes, and whatever you engage in, I shall not fail you. Go in haste, with the prayers of us all, and defend with unsleeping vigilance the post which the state itself has assigned to you [Ammianus Marcellinus 15.8.11–14].

At these words the soldiers began beating their shields against their knees and shouting their devotion to their new Caesar. As Julian, who had never before faced a crowd, stood motionless upon the tribune, the imperial purple hanging from his shoulders, a thousand eyes gazed upon his face, trying to read in the bright but fearful eyes, and the handsome features, now blushing, now pale, the secret of the man who was to lead them. As he felt himself the centre of attention, a momentary sense of power replaced the alarm and disgust with which he had first greeted his elevation. The gods had brought him thus far, and no doubt they had some great work for him to do. But the feeling did not last. He descended from the tribune, mounted the imperial carriage, side by side with Constantius, and drove to the palace through streets lined with cheering crowds. Only those closest to him could hear the words he occasionally muttered to himself under his breath. They were from Homer, from the account of the death of a hero, 'Purple death and mighty fate overwhelmed him'.

He had good reason to look on the future with foreboding. Constantius, well-intentioned only so long as his own interests were not involved, had learnt from the history of Gallus that a Caesar's functions must be representative and nothing else. Not only must the civil authority be kept out of his hands. He must exercise no real military command either. By restricting Julian in this way he hoped to preserve his own authority unimpaired. What he did not realize was that he was dealing with a much more intelligent man and a much stronger character than the irascible Gallus. Constantius could see no further into the future than most men, and less far than some.

Julian was theoretically Constantius' representative in Gaul, Britain and Spain. In fact civil authority in these provinces, together with the supply services of the army, was in the hands of the Praetorian Prefect Honoratus, a man who had been governor of Syria and later of all the eastern provinces during the Caesarship of Gallus. It was a measure of Constantius' lack of tact that he appointed to this post a man whose duty it had been to exercise surveillance over Gallus. He and Julian seem to have had a tacit agreement to keep out of each other's way. The military commander was at first the cautious and experienced Ursicinus, who had been one of Constantine's generals and had recently organized the overthrow of Silvanus. After a few months he was replaced by Marcellus, a mediocre officer who systematically refused to cooperate with Julian and made damaging secret reports on him to Constantius. From Constantius' point of view Marcellus was 'safe', since he was a Pannonian and hence unlikely to be proclaimed emperor by the mainly German soldiers of Gaul. Later Barbatio, an officer who had been with Gallus in the east, was sent with further troops. He was to prove thoroughly uncooperative. Ammianus Marcellinus, who knew him well, describes him as a man of boorish arrogance, disliked by all for his malicious scandal-mongering. These men all operated under Constantius' direct authority. Julian felt himself insulted by the situation in which he was put. His task, he said, was to parade the purple robe and the imperial image round the province. It may well occur to the modern reader that it was not unreasonable to leave affairs in the hands of men of experience rather than giving absolute power to an inexperienced man of twenty-four. But there was a contradiction between Constantius' words and his deeds that shocked contemporary observers. They felt that Julian was being needlessly humiliated.

Indeed he was. Constantius dismissed most of Julian's former personal attendants and replaced them by servants of his own, who could be counted upon to report to their former master. Only four of his old slaves were allowed to accompany him to Gaul. One of these, the African Euhemerus, was an initiate in the pagan mystery cults and shared with Julian the secret of his true religious faith. His personal physician, Oreibasios of Pergamum, a pagan of universal learning, who not only wrote an immense encyclo-

pedia of medicine at Julian's request – which survives in part – but kept a
diary of his life with Julian – which is lost – soon became his confidant and
friend, to whom Julian entrusted his personal papers. Concealed in the
mountain of Oreibasios' medical notes they were safe from the eyes of
Constantius' spies.

As well as these Julian had an unexpected companion on his journey to
his new post. A day or two after his inauguration he was married to
Constantius' sister Helena, just as his brother had been married to
Constantina. A spinister, and said to be devoutly religious, Helena must
have been at least six years older than Julian. Perhaps the difference in
their ages was much greater. Julian scarcely ever mentions her, and then in
a tone of complete detachment. He performed his marital duties; they had
a son, who did not survive birth. He was probably in his way a considerate
spouse. But she made no impression whatever upon him and had no
influence over him. His protectress at court Eusebia, on the other hand,
did what she could to make up for the meanness of her husband. In
particular she gave him a parting gift, which he remembered with warm
gratitude years later. He had brought only a few of his books from Athens
to Italy, and was now about to leave for a war-ravaged province of Latin
speech, where Greek literature would be hard to come by. Eusebia
presented him with a library of Greek poets, historians, orators and
philosophers to take on his journey. She seems to have been the only
person at Constantius' court who had a glimmering of understanding of
what kind of man Julian was. Constantius' parting gift was a set of minute
instructions, drawn up in his own hand, for Julian's conduct. It included
details of the money he was to be allowed to spend on various accounts,
and a number of model menus.

The two earliest surviving works of Julian belong to this period. Shortly
before leaving Milan for Gaul he composed a panegyric speech in praise of
Constantius. It may never have actually been delivered, but copies would
be circulated to high officers of State and read out at ceremonial gatherings.
Such encomiums were part of the traditional machinery for manipulating
public opinion, or at any rate the opinion of the upper classes, in the
ancient world. In an independent city state there was no room for such
exercises in propaganda. But with the imposition by Alexander the Great
and his successors of a super-state, standing outside and above the old
political units of Greece, the new rulers felt the need to project their
public personality and the new teachers of rhetoric devised rules for doing

it. By the beginning of the second century AD Roman consuls were delivering formal panegyrics on the emperor on the day they entered office. Many such compositions survive, both in Latin and in Greek. The handbooks of rhetoric lay down schemes for speeches in praise of a ruler, enumerating the topics to be dealt with, the order in which they should be treated, and the figures of speech and style appropriate to each. A good speaker who believed in what he was saying could breathe life into such a panegyric. Most of them are mere exercises in formal rhetoric.

Julian's panegyric on Constantius follows closely the rules laid down by Menander, a third-century rhetorician whose excellent textbook dominated the schools. We find the traditional topics of the emperor's native land and ancestors, an account of his early training and his accession to power, fulsome praise of his exploits in war and peace, decked out with the obligatory comparisons with the heroes of old, an analysis of his virtues in the framework set by Plato's ideal philosopher-king, a set piece on the happy state of the empire under his beneficent rule, and a concluding prayer for the long continuance of Constantius' life. Julian had been a diligent student of rhetoric, and the speech is competent in its technique and polished. But the reader has no feeling of meeting a powerful, idiosyncratic personality. Julian was more concerned to conceal than to reveal his thoughts about his cousin. Perhaps the description of the ideal monarch, to which Constantius is made to correspond, tells us something of his own thinking on the problem of power at the time when he became Caesar. But it is hard to distinguish much that is original and personal in this stereotyped piece of formal rhetoric.

About the same time he composed a similar panegyric on the empress Eusebia. She had befriended Julian on his previous visit to Milan, when he did not know whether he would leave the court alive, and she may well have had some influence on Constantius' decision to appoint Julian as Caesar. At any rate she was the one member of the imperial family in whom Julian detected some warmth and human sympathy, and he was grateful for her kindness. The handbooks of rhetoric gave no rules for encomiums on women. They did not display the martial virtues, indeed they rarely had 'exploits' at all. And the Platonic scheme of the qualities of an ideal ruler, in which 'manliness' (*andreia*) played a large part, was ill adapted to display the quieter virtues demanded of the female sex. Julian did his best to adapt the standard pattern to so difficult a subject. It is a *tour de force* of technique. Here and there he ventured to inject a personal motif, as in his veiled reference to Eusebia's intervention with Constantius when Julian was attacked by members of the court *camarilla* (inserted in a long passage of conventional praise of Constantius!), or his gratitude for her gift of a library of Greek books. It is interesting to observe how completely Greek in conception the whole speech is. The only reference to any Roman institution is a casual mention of the consulate of Eusebia's father Flavius Eusebius. Julian was at home in the world of philosophy and letters – which was a Greek world. The Roman world of political power was still strange to him.

On 1 December 355, three weeks after his proclamation as Caesar, Julian and his entourage set off in a convoy of carriages and baggage-carts and with an escort of 360 soldiers, 'the only army', he remarks ruefully, 'that I was allowed to command'. Constantius accompanied him to a point between Milan and Pavia. As he bade his cousin farewell, the emperor probably reflected whether it would be better for himself that Julian should win a series of resounding victories or that he should fail and be killed in battle.

The convoy rolled on through the plain of Lombardy into the hills of Piedmont. At Augusta Taurinorum (Turin) Julian learned that the great fortress of Cologne had been captured and sacked by the Chamavi, a tribe of Franks. Constantius had known of the disaster, but had concealed it from his junior colleague. The news launched Julian into a fit of depression, not so much because of its military implications, which were grave enough, but because it showed how little the devious Constantius trusted him. The first snow of winter was already falling in the Alps as Julian crossed the Mont Genèvre and descended into the valley of the Rhone. As he drove through the smiling countryside, untouched yet by winter, his spirits began to rise. The nightmare of the court at Milan was behind him. The role he had to play was a humiliating one, but at least he was to play it alone. When he reached the ancient city of Vienne, where the temple of Augustus and Livia still stood as a monument to the durability of the Roman empire, he found the streets beflagged and the whole population turned out to welcome him. They hailed him as the representative of legitimate power and imperial clemency, and as their saviour from the disasters that had befallen Gaul. Julian, who liked to be liked, was always susceptible to demonstrations of popular favour. Once again he began to feel that the gods were on his side and that he had been chosen by them to accomplish some great purpose. As he passed through the streets of the city, a blind old woman enquired who it was who had come. When told that it was the Caesar Julian, she cried out that he was the man who would restore the temples of the gods. His joy at this omen he could share only with a few, perhaps only with his slave Euhemerus and his doctor Oreibasios. But it was for a sure token that he was on the right path.

Settling in his palace by the banks of the Rhone for the remainder of the winter, Julian began to take stock of the situation. In a sense he was ignorant of public affairs. Yet he was widely read, and knew how to get at information, and his youth and his habit of study alike made it easy for him quickly to absorb a new body of knowledge. It is a reasonable assumption that the history of the Roman empire was familiar to him from his reading. He set himself to learn all he could about Gaul, its peoples, its cities, its fortresses. Though he was for the moment not allowed to command any troops but his own guard, he began to study the organization and training of the Roman army. He regularly attended parades and took part in military exercises, never allowing his rank to excuse him any of the hardships of his colleagues. This was partly a matter of youth and curiosity – a quality that Julian possessed in high measure. It stemmed in part from his slightly puritanical approach to life. But it was also a matter of calculation. If he was to survive the next few years and not end as his brother Gallus had done, he must establish a base of political power and win the loyal support of some effective pressure group. The army was an obvious choice. As a result of the collapse of the frontier defences there were now units of the frontier army stationed all over the interior of Gaul – where incidentally they were sometimes more of a scourge to the civil population than barbarian invaders would have been. In the immediate neighbourhood of Vienne there would be units of many different legions. By being seen by these, sharing their difficulties, making friends with officers and men, Julian could begin to build up the kind of network of loyalty among the troops on which he might well have to count later on.

Among the officials appointed by Constantius to accompany Julian to Gaul was a certain Saturninius Secundus Salutius, who has often been confused by historians, ancient and modern, with various contemporaries called Sallustius. Salutius' precise position in 356 is not clear. He may have been Julian's principal legal officer. He was a native of Gaul, by now past middle age. He had had a long career under Constans, including the governorships of Aquitania (south-western Gaul) and Africa. His career had probably begun under Constantine. Unlike most of the men who surrounded Julian in Gaul, he was a man of wide culture, both Greek and

Latin, thoroughly familiar with Neoplatonist thought. He was a friend of many Greek men of letters: Libanius' correspondence includes many letters addressed to him; Himerius dedicated one of his orations to him; Themistius, the pagan rhetorician and philosopher who became adviser to a series of Christian emperors in Constantinople, knew him well. Here was a man who could talk Julian's language, in the figurative as well as in the direct sense. Also, he was a pagan, whether or not he was an initiate of any of the half-secret mystery cults. A bond quickly developed between the two men that was broken only by Julian's death. Julian himself speaks of Salutius in the same tone as he had spoken of Mardonios, his tutor at Nicomedia. Clearly he felt some emotional dependence on the older man, who at this new stage in his life, when he had to make a fresh start with new problems, provided the kind of father figure that he needed. Julian was lucky, for Salutius seems to have been a man of integrity in a world where such men were rare. Even Gregory of Nazianzus, who attacks his paganism, praises his fair-mindedness towards the Christians. One can perhaps detect a certain wry critique of the popular ideas of the time in the story that later on he had pagans put to torture to determine whether they had more or less faith than Christians. It was under the growing influence of Salutius that Julian spent the winter and spring of 356, preparing himself for his new tasks. It is likely that the older man's caution and experience saved Julian from some of the mistakes into which his impetuosity would have led him. It certainly made easier his entry into the strange and dangerous world of imperial politics.

5 Julian in Gaul

WE DO NOT KNOW what was going on in Julian's mind during the first half of 356, since we have none of his writings from this period. Living in his palace in Vienne, studying history and State papers, taking part in military training and making sure he was seen so doing, having conversations that grew daily more confidential and intimate with Salutius, and presumably finding some time to spare for his newly married wife, he must have gradually come to terms with the reality of his new life. Since 1 January 365 he was joint consul with Constantius. The office was purely honorary. Gallus had held the consulship jointly with his cousin in 352, 353 and 354. Laws were promulgated in the names of Constantius and Julian. They had been issued in those of Constantius and Gallus. There was no comfort for Julian in his exalted position. It must have been clear to him that as the emperor's nearest kinsman and his junior colleague he might well be called upon to rule the Roman empire. But Constantius was still only thirty-eight. And the five men who had already been his colleagues had met with an untimely death. If Julian was sometimes buoyed up by a sense of divine protection, he was as frequently plunged in the depths of despair when he reflected on the peril of his position.

Power might come later. What mattered now was survival. To survive he must in the first place do nothing to offend Constantius or awaken his suspicions. And he must be alert to the certainty that others, for their own private reasons, would try to blacken his character in the eyes of Constantius. He must always be ready to defend himself, coolly and objectively; to lose his temper would be fatal. The restrictions Constantius had imposed on him were unworkable, as he knew, and some of Constantius' own officers were prepared to overlook violations of them. But he must be very cautious, and overstep the limits only a little at a time, always ready to draw back. In these ways he could avoid Gallus' errors. Or rather some of them. For Gallus had made errors of omission too. Julian realized that he must slowly build up a base of political support in the west, among the soldiers, among the western officials and among the common people of Gaul. If it later came to a confrontation between Constantius and himself, Constantius must be made uncertain how many in the western provinces would obey his orders, and hence hesitant to give any at all. So whatever the day-to-day changes in Julian's mood, the constants in his situation were on the one hand the need to keep on good terms with Constantius by a genuine or spurious appearance of subordination, on the other the constant search for support among influential elements in western Roman society, which might enable him one day to achieve parity with Constantius.

In the meantime, for all Julian's regularity in his military duties, strategic decisions belonged to Constantius and their tactical execution to his commanders in Gaul. There were two tasks facing the empire. The first was to defeat and if possible destroy the Alamanni, a well-organized confederation of Germanic tribes who dwelt in the region of Baden and Würtemberg. They had broken through the upper Rhine frontier at a number of points, and their raiding columns were penetrating ever deeper into the heart of the country. The loss of Cologne had enhanced their power. The Alamanni for the time being were after booty and slaves, not land. The second task was to drive back another Germanic people, the Franks, who lived as a loose union of tribes in what is now Belgium and Holland, who had for two generations been providing mercenary troops for the Romans, and were now infiltrating across the lower Rhine and the Meuse in search of lands for settlement. There could be no question of destroying them. They were not a confederation of peoples on the move like the Alamanni, but settled cultivators of the soil, impregnable behind their marshes and estuaries.

Constantius' plan for the campaigning season of 356 was that he himself would advance through Switzerland into the Black Forest, while the army of Gaul drove towards the Rhine. The plan was no doubt known to the senior military commanders in Gaul. It does not seem to have been divulged to Julian until it was about to be put into operation. The main body of the army of Gaul had orders to rendezvous at Remi (Reims) at the beginning of July. What prevented a campaign beginning earlier was not the weather in the theatre of war, but the need to supply the army in kind from the tax-contributions of southern Gaul. Marcellus, the commander-in-chief who had succeeded Ursicinus, issued the necessary orders. Only as a kind of after-thought was Julian told to make his way to Reims with his 'private army' of a few hundred horsemen, supplemented by a detachment of *balistarii*. These were technicians who operated the catapults and other artillery of the army, and were of little value in a fight without their cumbersome engines. In central Gaul in 356 one never knew where one might meet a flying column of German raiders. But the journey from Vienne to Reims was likely to be fairly safe. Just before his departure, however, Julian was told in Vienne of a raid on Augustodunum (Autun), about seventy miles north-west of Lyon, which had been repelled not by the tiny garrison of the walled city, but by the veterans settled in the surrounding countryside, who had spontaneously rallied and driven off the Germans. The incident probably fired Julian's imagination. At any rate he seems to have carried out his orders in the way most likely to lead him across the path of the marauders who had attacked Autun. First of all a forced march to Autun itself, where he arrived on 24 June. The local military and civilian authorities deliberated on what would be the safest route to the next major city, Autessiodurum (Auxerre). Julian decided to follow a route taken by Silvanus some years before – a difficult cross-country route that involved a passage through dense forests, instead of taking either of two safer routes that were proposed to him. It is difficult to avoid the conclusion that he was seeking an encounter with the enemy. If he did not realize his wish at once, he did on the next lap to Tricasini (Troyes), to which he pressed on after a brief rest. Germans fell on his column from both sides, and for a time Julian was afraid that he might be outnumbered. But the trained Roman troops took up strong positions on the flanks and the Germans, who did not want a pitched battle, fell back, leaving a few prisoners. And Julian then hastened on to Troyes. So surprised were the inhabitants that they at first took the small force of Roman soldiers – many of whom would be ethnically Germans – for a detachment of the invaders and refused to open the gates of their city to them. Again a short pause to rest his tired troops, and he continued his forced march to join Marcellus and the main body of the army at Reims.

In the course of this little exploit, which had no strategic significance, certain things had been accomplished. Firstly Julian had had his first experience of battle. Perhaps this was what he was seeking. Young men often feel the need to prove themselves in this way. Later in his life Julian always displayed great physical courage, particularly in battle. Was this because he lacked the close attachments that so often make men afraid to

die? Was it because he had early taught himself to maintain a steely
exterior that betrayed nothing of his feelings? Was it because in battle he
was swept on by an emotional enthusiasm that enabled him to act without
his usual reflection? We do not know. But whatever the true explanation,
the skirmish on the road from Auxerre to Troyes marked an important
stage in the development of Julian's character. Secondly he arrived at
headquarters already victorious in battle, with a group of German prisoners
in his train at a time when Marcellus and the main body of the army had
still not engaged the enemy. The psychological advantage this gave him
can be imagined. Whatever Constantius' instructions may have been,
Marcellus could no longer ignore Julian in his council of war. Thirdly and
perhaps most important of all, a victory had been won by one who wore
the imperial purple. The news would spread like wild-fire round the
soldiers. For many of them it would be an omen. For all it would be
something that raised their hopes and turned their attention towards the
unknown young co-emperor who was among them. Lastly Julian himself
felt filled with a new confidence. The gods were not defaulting on their
promise.

In the ensuing campaign Julian played more than a purely ornamental
role. During the advance eastward from Reims he was with the rearguard,
which came under heavy attack and was nearly cut off. As the army
approached the Rhine he was in command of the forces attacking Brotomagum (Brumath), and had his first experience of a pitched battle, albeit
a small one. The army continued down the left bank of the Rhine, driving
the Germans back across the river and recapturing fortress after fortress,
until in late summer they recovered Cologne itself. What part Julian
actually played in these operations is uncertain. Ammianus Marcellinus,
who himself took part in them and recounts them in detail, speaks as if
Julian were the effective commander-in-chief. This is clearly untrue. But
he did play a more conspicuous part than Constantius had intended when
he sent him to Gaul. And when the German leaders came to sue for peace
at Cologne in autumn it was Julian, as representative head of State, who
before the eyes of the army and the civil population set the seal on the
year's victories by imposing terms on the vanquished.

As winter drew on most of the army was withdrawn from the frontier to
winter quarters in the interior. It would have been impossible to feed and
maintain a large concentration of men and animals in the devastated
frontier zone. Julian settled for the winter at Senonae (Sens), where he
busied himself with administrative duties. Suddenly the Alamanni made

an unexpected winter attack on the walled city. They had booty in mind, naturally, but they were also anxious to strike a blow at Roman morale by capturing or killing the Caesar. For a month the enemy besieged Sens, while Julian and his troops – which did not include the élite units usually appointed to provide an imperial bodyguard – manned the walls, repaired damage, and fought off assaults. This time Julian was in effective command. His boundless energy and his impulsive eagerness to turn from passive defence to attack aroused the admiration of the soldiers. The unworldly scholar was not merely developing a taste for action – this happens often enough – but was being taken seriously by men who had spent all their lives in action. When the Germans finally withdrew because of shortage of supplies, there were some awkward questions to be answered. Why had Marcellus, who was not far off, and who had the main body of the army under his command, done nothing to relieve Sens? Was he in fact trying to deflate Julian's reputation by letting him be defeated, and perhaps captured or killed? Julian probably thought it wiser not to complain directly to Constantius himself. But he made sure that other officers did. The result was a peremptory order from the emperor to Marcellus to leave his command and return to his home at Sardica (Sofia). Julian had gained a point. But he knew that Marcellus would not accept passively the termination of his career and the ruin of his reputation. He would try to turn the tables by attacking Julian and accusing him of wanting to seize power. These were just the kind of charges that the frightened and suspicious Constantius was by temperament inclined to believe. So Julian sent an envoy of his own to Milan to refute, or if possible to anticipate, the accusations that Marcellus was bound to make. The man whom he chose for this delicate task was his chamberlain, the eunuch Eutherius. Eutherius was an Armenian, who had been captured and castrated as a child in the internal wars of his native lands. Sold as a slave in the Roman empire, he had eventually become a member of the private household of Constantine. There his intelligence, his learning, his judgement and his integrity attracted the emperor's notice. He was rapidly promoted, and after Constantine's death became chamberlain to his son Constans. Using his by-now-considerable authority he tried to persuade the weak and pleasure-loving emperor to take his responsibilities seriously. What happened to Eutherius after the murder of Constans by Magnentius we do not know. But by 356 he was a member of Julian's household. His long experience and his incorruptibility would in any case have recommended him to Julian. The fact that he was a pagan made him all the more acceptable. Eutherius, whom Constantius must have known since childhood, fulfilled his delicate mission with tact and skill, and not only persuaded Constantius that Julian was the victim of calumny by Marcellus, but also convinced him that the Caesar would never waver in his loyalty to his senior colleagues so long as he lived.

It must have been towards the end of 356 that Julian's wife Helena gave birth to a son, who died almost immediately. The birth might have taken place somewhere in southern Gaul. Helena would scarcely have accompanied her husband to the theatre of war. Rumour at the time attributed the death of the infant to mishandling by a midwife, who had been suborned by the empress Eusebia; childless herself so far, Eusebia could not bear her sister-in-law to give birth to an heir. As unverifiable then as it is today, this story is symptomatic of the way the man in the street saw the imperial family. As for Julian, he never mentions the birth or death of his son, and seems to have been untouched by it.

Marcellus' replacement was Severus, an officer of long experience and with little interest in intrigue. His situation was inevitably a weaker one vis-à-vis Julian, whom he found in effective command when he arrived in Gaul at the beginning of 357. In fact the two men seem to have collaborated easily and effectively. As the campaigning season opened Julian hastened to Reims. There he and Severus awaited the arrival of a force of 25,000 men under Barbatio, who had been sent from Italy by Constantius. This army marched through the Alps to Rauraci (Augst) and thence between the Jura and Vosges to Vesontio (Besançon). The object was to catch the Alamanni in a pincer movement – but one whose points never came within a hundred miles of one another. The Germans were in fact much disturbed, and the main body of their army moved westwards, pressing harder than ever on Gaul. Another Germanic group, the Laeti, slipped through between the two Roman armies as others had done on previous occasions, and made a lightning raid on Lugdunum (Lyon), deep in the interior and the greatest city of Gaul. They could not take the city, whose walls were in good order. But they did pillage and burn the surrounding countryside, with its many rich villas. Julian at once sent cavalry detachments to block the retreat routes of the invaders and called upon Barbatio to do the same. Most of the booty was recovered. But owing to a failure of communication or deliberate non-cooperation the raiders who withdrew through Barbatio's zone of command were able to do so safely. Barbatio put the blame on some of his subordinate officers, who were later cashiered.

Meanwhile the preparations for the main advance towards the Rhine went on. As the two armies met on the river there were fresh misunderstandings – or worse – about the use of river boats to dislodge the enemy from islands that they were occupying. Supply convoys coming from Italy through the zone controlled by Barbatio never reached Julian and Severus. The rumour spread in the army that Julian had been sent to Gaul in order to get rid of him and that Barbatio had secret instructions not to cooperate with him. All this helped to strengthen Julian's position among his troops, as did one or two dashing small-scale actions in which he took part. When later in the summer Barbatio's army was attacked by the Germans and driven all the way back to Augst in headlong flight, Julian and Severus were left alone in the field. Barbatio was ordered to withdraw to Italy by Constantius, who had sufficient tactical sense not to reinforce defeat. The Alamanni, who thought they had the Romans on the run, combined their forces in a single army commanded by Chnodomar and six other chiefs and offered battle before Argentoratum (Strasbourg). It was a difficult situation for the Romans, and at the same time their opportunity. They had only 13,000 fighting men left, while the Alamanni, flushed with victory, could muster several times that number. The enemy had concentrated their forces and risked a pitched battle. The rout of Barbatio's army had undermined Roman morale, and Julian was not sure how far he could depend on his men. Severus, probably on Constantius' instructions, seems to have yielded tactical command more and more to the energetic Julian, who was determined not to withdraw and let the Germans pour into Gaul, perhaps for good. His very willingness to take personal risks in the field had become a principle of strategy for him. But he kept a cool head. As the legions were marching from their camp to the enemy position he had them drawn up and addressed them. He praised their valour, reminded them that the impetuosity of youth sometimes needed the curb of prudence, and offered them a choice. Should they halt for the night or press on through difficult country and confront the enemy at once? Beating their shields with their spears the soldiers begged the Caesar to lead them against the enemy, who was already in sight. They were fighting under a general who was a favourite of fortune. Let him lead them to victory.

This was the first occasion on which Julian is reported to have made a speech to the army. It can scarcely be an accident that he waited so long. A general who addresses his assembled troops is in a curious position. He can exploit the emotion generated by the situation to call upon them to do things they would not otherwise do. Equally he can be forced by the pressure of his soldiers to say what he does not wish to say. It was when speaking to his troops that the unfortunate Silvanus had found himself willy-nilly proclaimed emperor. It is likely that Constantius had specifically forbidden Julian to address the soldiers. That he did so now was a measure of the degree of independence that he felt and of his assurance that he could count on the support of his troops. At the same time the occasion was carefully stage-managed so as not to appear a formal speech to the army. The soldiers were marching in column of route from their camp to the battle zone when they met their commander. What more natural than that he should have them drawn up in formation and take the opportunity of addressing them briefly. If his action was ever questioned, it could be represented as unpremeditated. Incidentally, this speech is evidence for the fluency of Julian's Latin, which has sometimes been doubted. At a moment of such tension a slight Greek accent could pass, inability to form readily correct Latin phrases could not.

The decision was taken to attack. It was supported, we are told, by Florentius, the Praetorian Prefect. But Florentius was not a soldier. The implication is clear that Julian joined battle without the approval of Severus. This need not mean that they disagreed. Severus may have been too far away to be consulted or not fully in touch with the tactical situation. Be that as it may, Julian was taking on himself a grave responsibility, which had certainly not been foreseen when Constantius sent him to Gaul. The Romans advanced to some high ground overlooking the Rhine. They found the Germans drawn up in a strong position on the left bank of the river, cavalry on the left, light troops in concealed positions on the right, the main body of the infantry in the centre. In command were the formidable King Chnodomar and his nephew Serapion, who had changed his name from Agenario when he became a devotee of an Egyptian mystery cult. Ironically, he and Julian shared a common attachment to the Neoplatonist syncretizing pagan religion of the late empire. On the Roman side Julian commanded on the left, Severus on the right. The battle began when Severus rode forward with a few men to try to get the Alamanni to reveal their concealed positions, and Julian on his side sent 200 cavalry against the enemy cavalry, trying to throw them into disorder before they could attack. Soon the *mêlée* became general. Julian was everywhere, in the thick of the fight, shouting orders, encouraging the timid, restraining the foolhardy, oblivious of personal danger. On the German side Chnodomar and the other leaders dismounted from their horses and fought side by side with their subjects. It was a hard-fought battle, mostly at close quarters, with little scope for manoeuvre. At one point the Roman cavalry on the right flank broke in disorder and turned and fled. But it could not get far or fast through the lines of its own infantry. The sight of Julian, conspicuous by the purple dragon pennant at the point of his long lance, shamed some of the officers into rallying their men, and soon the whole of the cavalry had wheeled round and resumed the attack. But it had been a close run thing. The infantry battle went on, with now one side and now the other gaining a little ground. It was a battle between equals, says Ammianus, who took part in it; the Alamanni were bigger and heavier men, the Romans better disciplined; the violence and disorder of the Germans was matched by the prudence and coolness of the Romans. These are of course clichés, but are not therefore necessarily untrue. Losses could be heavy on both sides, and the Germans had the advantage of numbers. Finally, however, they began to break in the face of Roman discipline. It is hard for the bravest man to hurl himself alone against a wall of shields. First one then another fell back, and soon the whole German army was in headlong flight, while the pursuing Romans hacked down the hindmost of them. The battlefield was littered with German dead. The Romans pursued the defeated enemy to the Rhine, in which many of the Germans drowned, while others succeeded in swimming to the other side. The river ran red with their blood. King Chnodomar and his entourage escaped on horseback up the left bank of the river, but were later surrounded in a wood by a Roman patrol. The Romans watched nervously, afraid of an ambush. Suddenly a huge figure emerged from the trees, alone and unarmed. It was Chnodomar. His companions surrendered soon after.

It was a tremendous victory, such as had not been seen on the Rhine for generations. The Romans lost 243 men and four senior officers. There were 6000 Alaman corpses lying on the field of battle, and no one knew how many being swept down the Rhine. The Alamanni had been destroyed as a military force and their leader captured. When Julian, calm after the heat of battle, fully realized what had happened, he was filled with quiet confidence. He had Chnodomar brought before him. The old king, who a few days before had been the terror of Gaul, grovelled on the ground before Julian, begging forgiveness in his native German. Julian coldly bade him be of good cheer and sent him off to Constantius in Milan. Later Chnodomar died of a lingering disease in Rome, where he was held prisoner in the Castra Peregrina on the Caelian hill.

In accordance with long-standing Roman practice Constantius sent letters bound with laurel leaves to every province, announcing that he had drawn up the army, led the combat, and received the surrender of Chnodomar. Julian's name was not mentioned in these official dispatches, but his fame spread throughout the empire. Some at court, trying to make trouble for him, nicknamed him Victorinus; the reference was ostensibly to the victories that he mentioned in his reports, but also to a rebel called Victorinus who had been proclaimed emperor in Gaul a century earlier. But by now it would have been dangerous to make trouble for Julian. He was the idol of the Rhine army, the hero of the Gaulish population, and his exploits were being discussed from one end of the empire to the other. The battle of Strasbourg had changed irreversibly the relations between Julian and Constantius.

Julian was determined to exploit the victory both to deter the Alamanni from further incursions and to raise the morale of his own troops, who had been too long used to defeats or indecisive victories. After burying the dead and falling back to Tres Tabernae (Saverne) to rest his troops, he announced his intention of leading a punitive expedition across the Rhine and deep into German territory. The soldiers grumbled and protested, fearful as they were of venturing into the homeland of the enemy. But Julian tirelessly went round the units haranguing the assembled soldiers, arguing individually with those whom he knew, and convinced them that now was the moment to strike. A bridge was built across the river, and the Roman legions set foot on the German bank for the first time in many years. At the first sign of German resistance, parties of Roman soldiers were sent up and down the river by boat at night with orders to land and set fire to every building they found. As the sun rose the great columns of smoke to north and south were a warning to the Germans of Roman intentions and Roman power. The army marched further up country, systematically pillaging and destroying the wretched huts of the peasants and the luxurious villas in the Roman style that the chiefs had built for themselves. It was a deliberate policy of terror, designed to convince the Alamanni of the futility of resistance. Julian had no qualms about the use of force to carry out State policy against outsiders, and it is unlikely that he had ever read Tacitus' characterization of Roman expansion – 'They made a desert, and call it peace;' As they pressed on the country grew wilder, the forests more impassable and the great tree-trunks with which the Germans blocked their path grew harder to move. And it became colder as the end of September came and passed. Soon the first snow lay on the ground. In fact, of course, the climate is much the same on the one bank of the Rhine as on the other. But the stereotype of the harsh German winter developed in Mediterranean thought over the centuries paralysed men's minds long before the cold froze their limbs. Even an army composed of half-Romanized Franks from northern Gaul was uneasy at the onset of winter. But Julian was in no mood to halt yet. He pushed on until they reached a ruined fort built by Trajan in the heart of German territory 250 years earlier. They set to work to repair this fort, and Julian sent back to base for artillery and other heavy equipment to install in it. Food and forage for its garrison was obtained simply enough by taking it from the surrounding Germans. When they saw the Roman standards flying from the turrets of the reconstructed fort, the neighbouring German chiefs realized that there had been a radical change in the balance of forces. Three of them arrived to offer their submission. Julian granted them a truce of ten months, on condition that they undertook to supply the garrison of Trajan's fort.

The main body of the army now returned to Gaul, to be dispersed in winter quarters. A body of 600 Franks had profited by the absence of the Roman army to cross the lower Rhine and Meuse and plunder extensively in northern Gaul. As Julian and his forces returned from Germany the Franks took fright and withdrew to two abandoned Roman forts on the bank of the Meuse, where they soon found themselves besieged. The forts were not to be taken by assault, and the Franks had no shortage of supplies. As winter wore on and January succeeded February, things became difficult for the besiegers. The river was now freezing, and it would be easy for the Franks to slip across on the ice by night and make their way home. This seemed to some Romans the best solution to the problem. But Julian was determined not to let them go. Every night he had boats rowed up and down the Meuse from dusk till dawn to prevent the ice forming. Finally both forts surrendered, and the prisoners were dispatched to Constantius in Milan. The emperor was delighted to receive 600 such sturdy soldiers, and at once enrolled them in the Roman army. Julian at last withdrew to his winter quarters at Lutetia (Paris) – now reduced to the Ile de la Cité, the old centre on the left bank having been given up in the troubles of the third century. It was nearly the end of January 358.

During a long campaigning season Julian had displayed untiring energy – marching, fighting, talking, planning and communicating something of his own enthusiasm to others. He struck observers as moved by a kind of manic drive, unable to rest. Some said that he had decided that it was

better to die gloriously in battle than to meet the miserable fate of his
brother Gallus. Maybe they were right. We have no direct testimony to
Julian's state of mind at the time. Though he took risks, he never seems
to have taken foolish risks, and his tactics and strategy scarcely look like
the exteriorization of a death-wish. Whatever the true explanation may be,
these occasional periods of almost superhuman activity were a part of
Julian's make-up. They do not seem to have been accompanied by any
impairment of his judgement.

The Paris that Julian knew was a shadow of what it had been. The old
tribal capital of the Parisii had flourished under Roman rule, and become
one of the larger cities of northern Gaul. Its centre had moved from the
old site on the island in the Seine where the Parisii had first built their
fortified camp in the third century BC. The new city lay mostly on the
left bank, and occupied much of the present Latin quarter. The forum was
on the site of the present rue Soufflot. There was a theatre at the corner of
the boulevard Saint-Michel and the rue Racine, an amphitheatre for
gladiatorial shows and beast-fights in the rue Monge, and baths at Cluny,
in the rue des Écoles where the Collège de France now stands, and a little
further south in the rue Gay-Lussac. North of the river a temple of
Mercury stood on the dominating height of Montmartre, near the present
church of the Sacré Coeur. As well as being a centre of gracious living for
its citizens – or at any rate for some of them – the city was an important
river port, with extensive wharves lining the Seine.

All this, however, had been destroyed in the civil wars and the ensuing
peasant revolts of the middle of the third century. The city had been
sacked and burned, and most of its inhabitants dispersed. What Julian
found a century later was a much smaller settlement, largely confined to
the Ile-de-la-Cité, and perhaps the neighbouring Ile-St-Louis, and connected by bridges to the banks, on which the ruins of the monumental
city of the High Empire, overgrown with grass and scrub, provided raw
materials for the more modest constructions of a later age. There was a
palace on the island, and doubtless other dwellings suitable for high
officials, and barracks. The civilian population must have been small, and
largely devoted to satisfying the needs of the soldiers and administrators.
The civic organization of the past, with its councillors and magistrates
appointed or elected from those who owned landed-estates in the city
territory, had probably long ago collapsed. The previous city had become
a garrison town, very different from Vienne.

Yet it was a pleasant enough place in its way. The site was picturesque. The varied countryside of the Paris basin, not yet transformed by intensive cultivation, began a few hundred yards from the Palace gates. The society over which Julian presided was a small and undemanding one, in which he had many friends, and of which he was the undisputed leader. His writings make it clear that he enjoyed his winters on the island city and looked back to them later with nostalgia.

The Alamanni had been defeated, the flower of their young men killed in battle, and their leaders humiliated in the eyes of their people. The Franks on the lower Rhine and the Meuse, whose political unity was much looser than that of the Alamanni, had so far faced only isolated reverses. Northern Gaul still lay open to their raids. It was essential to make a display of Roman power that would discourage the Frankish chiefs from hostile action, and to re-establish the chain of forts from the Channel coast to Cologne by which they had formerly been kept in check. This would not only put an end to Frankish attacks, but would also prevent the Alamanni, when they recovered their strength, from turning the flank of the Roman defences on the upper Rhine and invading Gaul through present day Belgium – a strategy that was to be applied more than once in modern times.

But there was more involved than strategy. The aim of Constantius and his court, which Julian fully shared, was to re-establish peaceful life, centred upon cities, each with its surrounding territory, in northern and eastern Gaul. The region had been terribly devastated during the invasions and civil wars of the third century, many of its cities had been destroyed, the population of the countryside had fled, abandoning the neat villas and vineyards to be overgrown by scrub and woodland. From the reign of Constantine there had been the beginnings of a timid return to the area, but the events of recent years had sent the new settlers scurrying to the doubtful safety of Lyons or Vienne, when they had not been taken captive and enslaved by the Germans. Much of the territory had become waste land. And waste land it would remain until the frontier could be securely re-established. Then there would be other problems, such as finding men to settle on the land and bring it back to cultivation. But in the meantime security was the first consideration.

In setting themselves such a goal, both Julian and Constantius, and indeed all those concerned with determination of Roman policy, were animated by a variety of motives. In part they were pursuing the dream of turning the clock of history backwards and restoring the rich, self-assured Roman empire of the Antonines and the Severi. This was a dream that haunted all of late antiquity and coloured its approach to problems often very different from those of the High Roman Empire. That it was only a dream took a long time to dawn upon men, even when in fact they had succeeded in creating relatively stable societies of their own quite distinct in character from that of the second century AD. Julian's emotional commitment to the Hellenic past and his sense of alienation from the world about him may have made him more sensitive to this kind of appeal than a more down-to-earth man would have been. Then at a different level there was the question of State revenue. Lands that were untilled and cities that were uninhabited produced no revenue, whether in money or in kind. The ever-growing cost of administering the centralized State of late antiquity, in which more and more persons were removed from directly productive activity and engaged in service occupations the economic and social benefit of which was doubtful, called for a corresponding rise in the revenues of the State. Uncultivated land meant that someone somewhere else had to pay higher taxes, the collection of which involved more people in unproductive activity. And so the vicious spiral went on. Whatever the true economic analysis may have been, men were conscious of a shortage of tax payers. They were conscious too of a shortage of soldiers, and had to make up for it by employing more and more half-romanized foreigners from beyond the frontier, whose level of technical attainment was low and whose loyalty was doubtful. The settlement of northern and eastern Gaul would rehabilitate one of the old recruiting areas of the Roman legions. Lastly purely humanitarian considerations played a part, especially with Julian. The number of homeless, landless, hopeless men was great, their misery a constant challenge to that *philanthropia* – love of one's fellow men – which was part of the heritage of ancient ethical thought.

It was impossible to pursue any of these lines of thought or action very far without running into one of the crucial difficulties of Julian's position. Though he had been military commander-in-chief since the recall of Marcellus, he still had no authority at all in civil affairs. The assessment and levying of taxation, the supply of the army, not only with food, forage and munitions, but even with pay, were in the hands of the Praetorian Prefect Florentius, who reported to Constantius, not to Julian, whom he need not even inform of what he was doing. Florentius was a reasonable man and does not appear to have been deliberately obstructive. But he had to look after his own interests and those of his department and carry out the orders he received from the emperor. Julian had all the time to walk a dangerous tightrope. On the one side lay military failure, inevitable if he tried to fight a campaign with too small resources, on the other side lay accusations of interfering in Constantius' affairs. It was not merely a matter of military supplies. Julian well realized that no army can fight well with a sullen and disaffected civil population in its rear, and least of all when that civil population included the soldiers' own families.

There were two special difficulties in mounting a campaign against the Franks. The first was the obvious one that the bulk of the soldiers in the Gaulish legions were themselves Franks or of Frankish decent, and thus pulled by divided loyalties. The only way to surmount this difficulty was to make life in the Roman empire as attractive as possible for the soldiers and their families, and then to win one's battles. The other difficulty was that the food and forage for the army had to come from the taxes in kind of south-western France. By the time they were delivered at Reims, it was too late in the season to fight a long campaign in a region where winter came early and where the autumn rains flooded the flat countryside. The way round this problem was to supply the army from nearby Britain, bringing the corn and feeding stuff up the Meuse and the Scheldt to the forward positions of the army. Florentius, in whose area of responsibility this matter lay, was quite willing to help. All that was needed, he said, was to bribe the Franks who now controlled those waterways to let the convoys through. This was a short-term accountant's solution, and not at all acceptable to Julian. What he wanted to do was to expel the Franks by force from these areas and keep them out by a network of fortifications. Here was an immediate source of conflict.

In the end Julian got his way. Making his soldiers carry three weeks' ration of biscuit in their knapsacks he set off in early summer 358 against the Salian Franks, who had infiltrated over the former border and now occupied Toxandria (Hainault and Brabant, the region between the Meuse and the Scheldt). Catching them unprepared and defeating them in a series of minor engagements he forced them to sign a treaty accepting Roman sovereignty and undertaking to provide men for the Roman army. Then he moved eastwards to attack another Frankish people, the Chamavi, who had been foremost in the capture of Cologne. They too were defeated, many prisoners taken, and members of the leading families handed over to the Romans as hostages. A series of forts were built or rebuilt to control the territory of the conquered Franks, and Julian returned to his winter quarters in Paris, well pleased with his summer's work.

During the winter port installations were put into shape on both sides of the channel and a fleet of several hundred ships, most of which had been lying abandoned in British harbours, was made seaworthy. In early summer 359 Julian led his army into the field once again, confident that supplies would soon begin to reach him from Britain. This year the Alamanni were again his target, particularly those tribes that had escaped the punitive operations of 357. All seemed to go well till they neared the Rhine. Then his troops suddenly mutinied, refusing to go any further. The immediate cause of the mutiny was shortage of supplies. They had finished what they took with them from their winter quarters, the convoys from Britain had not arrived, and in the fields all round them they saw nothing but unripe corn. But there were deeper reasons too. A Roman soldier was paid a regular salary, proportionate to his rank, which he received at long intervals, sometimes of several years. In addition he expected to receive donatives from his commander, especially after a victory. These donatives, which replaced the old right to a share in the booty of a war, could be a powerful means of influencing the loyalty of troops. They could only be given on the authority of the emperor and in his name. Constantius had neither authorized donatives for Julian's army nor provided the money for them, and the soldiers felt they had been cheated. This was not all. Julian had no treasury of his own. When he needed money he had to go to the *praepositus thesaurorum* of Gaul and ask for it. The *praepositus* had authority from his superior, the Count of the Sacred Largesses at Constantius' court, to meet Julian's demands. But in fact the money was not always available when it was needed, and many of the soldiers' pay was in arrears.

It was an alarming experience for Julian to see how quickly the idol of the troops could become the object of their vilification. As he rode through the ranks men called him 'Asian', 'little Greek', 'cheat', 'fool got up as a philosopher'. What was the use of defeating the enemy, they cried, if they were to die of starvation themselves? Was this the reward for all the dangers and hardships they had endured? But Julian did not lose his nerve. And his faith in reason was vindicated this time. He convinced the soldiers that it was through no fault of his that they had not been paid, assured them that rations were on the way, and by a combination of frank explanation, promises and flattery succeeded in nipping in the bud what could have turned into a full-scale military revolt. A bridge of boats was thrown across the Rhine and the army set foot once again on German soil. Things were made more difficult by Severus' sudden failure of nerve. He had loyally supported Julian during the last two years, but he was an old man, and it seems that his last illness was already upon him. At any rate, from now on Julian had to carry the burden of command alone. Suomarius, one of the Alaman chiefs, submitted of his own accord. The other, Hortarius, had to be brought to a sense of reality by the burning and pillaging of his tribal land. Finally, both agreed to sign a treaty of non-aggression and to hand over all the Roman civilians whom they held as slaves. By careful interrogation of the survivors in every city and village the Romans had prepared a list of all those taken off by the Germans to captivity, with their names and places of origin. That such records could be available had probably never occurred to the Germans, whose own society was still illiterate. At first they produced only a few prisoners, saying there were no others. Julian flared into anger, real or feigned, and declared that he would not let his German hostages go until the last prisoners had returned. Soon they came pouring out of every German village and hamlet to be checked against the lists held by Julian's officers. The Alamanni were further ordered to provide timber and other building material for the restoration of the cities they had destroyed, and to furnish supplies for Julian's army. In the autumn Julian once again quartered his troops about the countryside and withdrew to his winter headquarters in Paris.

At Constantius' court there were many who did their best to denigrate Julian's successes, whether out of mere flattery for Constantius or because they feared that Julian, if he gained influence, might put a stop to their own particular lucrative illegalities. 'This billy-goat is becoming a bore with his victories', said some, alluding to Julian's unfashionable beard. Others called him a loquacious mole (a joke whose precise point escapes us), an ape in purple, or, playing on the anti-Greek feeling at Constantius' predominantly western court, a Greek bookworm. Julian was a coward, they said, an ivory-tower theoretician, who dressed up his mediocre accomplishments in fine words. Others no doubt made more serious innuendoes, suggesting that Julian wanted to share power with Constantius. These latter were more dangerous because of the element of truth in what they said. However, Constantius did not let himself be unduly influenced by the slander and tittle-tattle of Julian's enemies at court. Julian had on the whole remained within the terms of reference that he had been given. And the empress Eusebia continued to speak up for him to her husband. Julian's name continued to appear beside that of Constantius on official documents and inscriptions. Thus on a fort in Cilicia, repaired probably in 359, appears the inscription:

> *Iussu dd.nn. Constantii triumfatoris Augusti et Iuliani nob. Caesaris castellum diu ante a latronibus possessum et provinciis perniciosum Bassidius Lauricus v.c. com. et praeses occupavit adque ad perpetuam quietis firmitatem militum praesidio munitum Antiochiam nuncupavit*

(By order of our Lords Constantius the triumphant Augustus and Julian the most noble Caesar, Bassidius Lauricus, count and governor captured this fort long held by brigands and dangerous to the provinces, manned it with a military garrison as a permanent reinforcement of peace, and named it Antiochia)

This may be the work of a provincial governor out of touch with the imperial court. But the inscription placed about the same time on the rebuilt baths at Spoleto, with its graceful compliment to Julian, must represent the views of the emperor himself:

> *Reparatores orbis adque urbium restitutores dd. nn. Fl. Iul. Constantius p.f. semper Aug. et Julianus nobilissimus ac victoriosissimus Caes. ad aeternam divini nominis propagationem thermas Spoletinas in praeteritum igne consumptas sua largitate restituerunt.*

(The regenerators of the world and restorers of cities, our Lords Flavius Julius Constantius, pious, fortunate, ever Augustus and Julian the most noble and victorious Caesar by their munificence restored the baths at Spoleto destroyed by fire in the past, to the eternal renown of the divine name)

There were however sources of tension between the imperial cousins. Florentius, the Praetorian Prefect of Gaul, was involved in corrupt practices, and as some of these became common knowledge he was openly criticized and attacked. Something had to be done, and Florentius asked Julian to hear the charges against him in private, assuming that Julian would be willing to cooperate in covering up his illegalities. But Julian would not play. He refused to hear the case, claiming insufficient legal knowledge, and handed it over to his Council of State. We have a letter that he wrote to a friend at the time in which he asks whether a pupil of Plato and Aristotle can allow the unfortunate to become the prey of robbers. It would be outrageous, he wrote, to condemn to death officers who fled in the face of the enemy, and to play the coward himself at such a moment as this. God, who had put him in his high office, would be dishonoured by such conduct. Florentius, seeing that Julian would not help him, went over to the attack, and complained to Constantius that Salutius, Julian's closest personal friend among his officers of State was a trouble-maker and was causing hostility between the Caesar and his Praetorian Prefect. Julian's enemies at court made the most of the occasion, and Salutius was peremptorily recalled by Constantius. It was a hard blow for Julian to lose the counsellor whose advice he valued most and who shared his ideals of justice and his pagan faith. And at the same time it was a danger signal to Julian, reminding him that the long arm of his enemies could reach out and strike those closest to him. He exteriorized some of his grief and chagrin at the loss of Salutius by composing a fictitious address of farewell to him. It was probably about the same time that he also wrote a second oration in praise of Constantius, perhaps in an attempt to bridge the growing gap between his cousin and himself. It is a cold, technically competent piece of work. Constantius had gained no fresh laurels since Julian had last addressed him. What was to be said that had not been said before? Julian found a way out by launching into a series of comparisons between Constantius and various Homeric heroes, in which Constantius naturally always comes off best.

In 359 the empress Eusebia died. She had constantly protected Julian and used her influence on the side of reason and humanity in the intrigue-ridden hothouse that was Constantius' court. From this point Julian's enemies seem to have had a free hand with the emperor. Julian himself must have realized that his scope for manoeuvre and compromise had been disastrously reduced, and that he must now prepare himself for a trial of strength with Constantius. He had long hoped to avoid such a confrontation. But as he grew surer of his own ability and saw the success of his policy in Gaul he began more and more to prepare for confrontation and even to welcome it. Perhaps it was to this that the gods had called him. In a letter to the doctor Oreibasios, his pagan confidant, he recounts a dream in which he saw a great oak falling, while a green sapling standing beside it, remained firmly rooted in the ground and flourished. 'Heaven knows what it means', he writes, and goes on to complain of the squalid intrigues against him by Eusebius, Constantius' eunuch chamberlain. It was clear enough to Julian and Oreibasios that the mighty oak was the house of Constantine, while the sapling was himself. This was the direction in which his thoughts were turning in 359.

He had many other things to do, however, during these years. Forts and supply depots in the frontier zone, now firmly in Roman hands, had to be rebuilt. Permanent arrangements had to be made for supplies from Britain. Seven towns were taken from the enemy and had to be made defensible. They were Castra Herculis (somewhere on the road from Leiden to Nijmegen in Holland), Quadriburgium (Qualburg), Tricensima near Xanten, Novaesium (Neuss), Bonna (Bonn), Antennacum (Andernach) and Vingo (Bingen). Their situation suggests that Julian was anxious to make the lower Rhine safe for shipping, particularly that bringing military supplies from Britain. After an intelligence mission by a bilingual Roman officer revealed that some of the German chiefs were chafing at the terms imposed by the Romans, Julian once again crossed the Rhine after a skilful night attack. The punitive expedition he led soon brought the German leaders to his camp to sue for peace, which was granted to them on the usual terms. At the end of 359 he had to deal with trouble in Britain. The Scots (who lived in Northern Ireland and the Western Isles) and Picts had been renewing their raids in the northern regions of the Roman province and causing disquiet even in the south, since they possessed ships and could strike far behind the frontier. Julian was unwilling to leave Gaul himself. He was fully involved in the rehabilitation of the frontier zone, and was afraid that the Alamanni might seize the opportunity of his absence to break the peace terms and undo all the work of the last few years. At the same time the growing tension between himself and Constantius made it imprudent for him to leave Gaul, which was the centre of his support. It was decided to send several units of light infantry, suitable for operations in broken country, under the command of Lupicinus. Lupicinus had replaced Severus as Julian's military deputy. He was a Christian, a competent enough soldier but arrogant and haughty. Men who knew him debated whether his greed or his cruelty was the greater. The expeditionary force reached Bononia (Boulogne) before the end of winter and crossed to Richborough and set off on the long march through London to the north. Julian was probably glad to be rid of Lupicinus.

During 358 Julian had been maintaining and developing his contacts with friends in the Greek east. A number of letters survive that he wrote at this period to eastern friends. Many philosophers and men of letters came to visit him. From these he learned that the fame of his exploits and the rumour that he was well-disposed to pagan religion was winning him support in Greek lands. Men began to wonder whether the young Caesar who had saved Gaul from the Germans might not also save Hellenism from the Christians. A kind of whispering campaign spread through the limited circles of Neoplatonist initiates. At the same time the news from the imperial capital was hardly reassuring. The sneers of the court *camarilla* were matched by the threats of those who urged on Constantius the need to put a stop to Julian's growing power and influence. At the same time Persian pressure had been increasing in the east, and Constantius had finally decided to take command himself in major operations against the Persians. From late summer of 357 he had been concerned with the security of the Danube frontier and his court had been established at Sirmium (Sremska Mitrovica). By the autumn of 359 it had been transferred to Constantinople. The emperor planned to move to Mesopotamia as soon as the roads across Asia Minor became passable again. For Julian this new development had several implications. First of all there was a power vacuum created in the west by the withdrawal of the central administration of the empire to Syria. Not that the everyday apparatus of the State did not continue to function. But everyone in the west knew that in an emergency the Caesar Julian and the army of Gaul was nearer than the emperor Constantius and the eastern army. Then the possibility that Constantius might be crushingly defeated, or even captured or killed in battle must have been present to Julian's mind. He might have to act quickly to take over power and preserve the unity of the empire. Thirdly he might be called upon by Constantius to transfer some of his Gaulish troops to the eastern front. This would not only risk undoing his work of reconquest and resettlement, but might destroy the loyalty and support that he had won from the men under his command. What would he do if such an order came? Julian was a man with the habit of examining his conscience. We may be sure that he pondered this and related questions, and had worked out what his conduct should be in various hypothetical situations. The historian Eunapius, who is not always to be trusted in such matters, recounts that Julian performed some secret rites with his pagan friends Oreibasios and Euhemerus, as a result of which he resolved to overthrow the 'tyranny' of Constantius. Be that as it may, Julian can have been in no doubt at the end of 360 that the moment of choice was not far off. What its occasion might be, only the gods knew.

He had not long to wait. In January 360 the tribune Decentius arrived in Paris with orders to withdraw four of Julian's best regiments and 300 men from each of his other units, and to dispatch them all with haste to the East. The orders were addressed to Lupicinus and another general,

Sintula. All that Julian received from his senior colleague was a letter ordering him not to interfere. Julian himself, writing a year later, claims that these orders were the result of pressure by his enemies at court, who were determined to ruin him. Their hostility to the Caesar is not in doubt. But it must be borne in mind that Constantius had just lost six legions at Amida (Diyarbakir) when the Persians took the city after seventy-three days of siege. He really needed reinforcements if he was to pursue the war in the east. Yet the insulting manner in which the orders were given suggests that Constantius had decided to humiliate Julian. He hoped no doubt that the whole operation could be carried out before Julian had time to react. Julian at first agreed to the demands. But he pointed out that Lupicinus was at the time in charge of operations some- where on the Scottish border and could not possibly comply with Constantius' orders at once, and that the Praetorian Prefect Florentius, on whom arrangements for supply of the troops depended, was at Vienne. He at once sent a dispatch to Florentius requesting him – he could not command him – to join him in Paris. Florentius, who suspected that Julian held him partly resonsible for Constantius' decision, refused to comply with the request. Julian sent a second message, hinting that the prefect was guilty of a grave dereliction of duty in leaving his post at so delicate a juncture, and declaring that if he failed to come to Paris and carry out his duties he, Julian, would of his own accord lay down the insignia of Caesar, since he preferred an honourable death to being responsible for the ruin of Gaul. This message only strengthened Florentius' resolve to stay in the south and keep out of trouble. Perhaps it was meant to.

Julian had gained time to think what to do. Sintula was already making arrangements for the departure of some of the troops. Julian sent warning orders to the other units to get ready to leave. It would be naive to suppose that he did not take the opportunity of obtaining reports on the state of their morale from the officers who conveyed his orders. The orders to move set off a chain reaction among the soldiers. Most of the Gaulish army were locally recruited men, often Germans by race, from one side or the other of the frontier. They had married local women, and their wives and families lived in the cities and villages of northern and eastern Gaul. Some of them, particularly the Germans from beyond the frontier, had been recruited under the terms of an agreement with their tribal leaders that they would not be called upon to serve beyond the Alps. A move to distant Mesopotamia would mean that few of them would ever again see their families, who would be left destitute in Gaul, and that men who still depended on close links with an extensive kindred would be isolated in a distant land. Leaflets began to circulate among the troops. One, which was brought to Julian, complained that the soldiers were being driven to the ends of the earth like condemned criminals, while their families would be enslaved once again by the Alamanni, after being freed through bloody battles from their former servitude. Julian observed that in his view their complaints were justified, and announced that the men's families would be allowed to accompany them to the east, and would be transported by the imperial wagon service. But the soldiers' resentment was much deeper rooted. They felt betrayed by Constantius, who had given no recognition to their hard won victories and who was now sending them to fresh battles against an enemy with whom his own troops could not deal. The ferment of disaffection went on working among them.

In the absence of Lupicinus, who was in Britain, Florentius, who was sulking in Vienne, and Sintula, who had set out with the first contingents of troops for the east, Julian was obliged to take the lead in a matter in which Constantius had brusquely told him not to interfere. Arrangements had to be made for routing the troops, for the selection of camp sites, mustering areas and so on. A kind of *ad hoc* committee was formed, consisting of Julian, Nebridius, an Etrurian who was Julian's quaestor, Pentadius, the Master of Offices, a man who had been involved in the downfall and execution of Gallus and whom Julian could not stand, and the tribune Decentius, who had brought the orders from Constantius. Of the four, only Julian had any military experience. Julian argued that they must wait for the arrival of Lupicinus and Florentius. The others pressed for immediate action, and hinted that if their advice was not taken Julian would be held responsible by Constantius. They forced him to write to Constantius promising to send the troops at once. Then the question arose of the routes to be followed by the units. Julian was for keeping them away from centres of population, since he knew that the civilian population shared their feelings. Decentius, with the unerring misjudgement of the chairborne administrator, proposed that they should be concentrated around Paris because it was easier. His proposal was supported by the majority, and Julian had to acquiesce. But from that moment he knew that he would be lucky if he was not drawn into a military rebellion. What course events would take he could not know, but he realized that as far as the exercise of his own choice was concerned he had reached the point of no return.

As each unit arrived in the neighbourhood of Paris Julian went out to meet it, inspected the troops, spoke to those whom he knew from his campaigns, urged them to join Constantius in the east, where opportunities and rewards awaited them commensurate with their merits. The sight of the young commander under whom they had won so many victories only made them more unwilling to leave Gaul. By February when all the units were encamped round the city Julian invited the officers to a banquet in the palace, where he called upon them to speak their minds freely. They repeated what he already knew, explaining at length how the morale of their troops could not be worse, how bitterly they resented this sudden order to abandon their native land and a commander whom they admired and respected. Julian replied that he too had to carry out his orders and that he could offer them no comfort. When the officers left the palace to rejoin their units it was with a new feeling of solidarity and resolution, since each now realized that other units felt exactly as did his own.

After the officers withdrew Julian went to his wife's apartments on the upper floor of the palace to rest. His mind was in a turmoil. Writing a little later, he says that he did not know at that moment what the soldiers had in mind. This is literally true: they might proclaim him emperor or they might kill him. But he can have been in little doubt that they would not meekly carry out Constantius' orders. As the sun set, terrified courtiers brought the news that the legions were marching to the palace. Within minutes they had surrounded the building and cries could be heard by those within. 'Iulianus Augustus' – 'Julian for emperor' was the slogan they chanted. Julian's moment of choice had come, and he did not know what to do. Desperately he prayed to Zeus to vouchsafe him a sign, looking out through the open window at the planet Jupiter in the evening sky. A man who needs a sign from heaven usually gets one, and Julian got his, whatever it was. Indeed on the previous night, before he had spoken with the assembled officers, the spirit of the Roman people had appeared to him in a dream and warned him that if he did not seize this opportunity to improve his position she would abandon him for ever. The new divine sign too told him not to oppose the will of the army. Those who believe that the gods usually tell us to do what we most want to do ourselves will draw their own conclusions.

The soldiers called on Julian to appear, but throughout the night he remained within the palace, uncertain how to meet the situation. As soon as it was light he appeared on the steps before the building, to be greeted by redoubled cheers and rhythmic cries of 'Iulianus Augustus'. Julian's

gestures of refusal and of supplication could be seen, but against the din
no one could hear his words as he begged the soldiers not to spoil their
record after so many glorious victories and not to let their enthusiasm
carry them towards civil war. Finally silence was imposed, and Julian
addressed the troops in the crisp morning air.

> Calm your anger a little, and what you ask for will easily be obtained
> without dispute or revolt. You are held back from leaving by love for
> your native land and your fear of the strangeness of foreign lands. Very
> well, go back to your quarters and you will not set foot beyond the
> Alps, since such is your desire. I will explain this to the emperor, who
> is a reasonable and prudent man and I am sure that I will convince him.

Julian and the soldiers alike knew that they were playing out a ritual, and
that there was no going back. His words were greeted with a fresh outburst
of shouts in which insults addressed to Constantius were mingled with
acclamations of Julian as emperor. At last he yielded. Some soldiers
stepped forward with a shield on which they raised him shoulder high in
the old Germanic ritual that had become traditional in the Roman army.
A herald solemnly proclaimed him 'Imperator Caesar dominus noster Flavius
Claudius Iulianus pius felix victor ac triumphator semper Augustus'. The
cheer that rang out echoed through the city. Next someone suggested that
he be invested with the diadem or tiara which since Diocletian had been
the emblem of imperial power. Julian protested that he did not have such a
thing. Someone else suggested that there must be a necklace or tiara
among his wife's jewels that would suffice. But Julian answered that it
would be a poor omen for an an emperor to wear a woman's baubles on so
auspicious an occasion. Then someone was sent to look for a brass horse
trapping, until it was pointed out that that too would be an inauspicious
way to inaugurate a reign. The spirit of the moment was almost playful,
now that the die was cast. Finally a standard-bearer named Maurus took
off the brass collar that he wore as a badge of rank and put it on Julian's
head, to the renewed acclamations of the assembled troops. Julian, who
had studied Roman history, knew what the next move was. Standing
before the palace, in purple cloak and with the metal collar precariously
balanced on his head, he made a short speech promising to every soldier a
donative of five gold pieces and a pound of silver. Then, emotionally
exhausted by his sleepless night and the events of the morning he retired
into the palace to rest and to think through the implications of what had
happened.

The troops were still uneasy, though most of them had withdrawn to their camps outside the city walls. Not everyone was pleased with the turn events had taken. There were still officers and civilian officials who were loyal to Constantius. Some of these began secretly to offer money to soldiers and tried to mount a counter-demonstration, in the hope of breaking the unity of the army or even of turning it against Julian. An officer in his wife's suite found out what was going on and rushed to inform Julian. The new emperor dismissed the matter as of no account. But soon the words spread among the soldiers that a plot was afoot to kill Julian. Some even said that he was already dead. Once again the troops poured into the city, surrounded the palace, threatened the guards and ushers and demanded to see Julian. Seeing that all was quiet in the palace they stood uncertain and confused. Then once again the cry rang out that Julian must appear. Instead they were taken into the audience-chamber in the palace, where Julian awaited them, resplendent in imperial garb, and calmly collected. Delirious with joy they raised him shoulder high and carried him in procession through the streets of Paris, as soldier and citizen alike joined in wishing long life and victory to the new emperor.

6 From Rebel to Emperor

WHEN THE HEADY EXCITEMENTS of the first days were over, Julian had a number of difficult problems to face. Though his position in Gaul was strong enough, could he afford to challenge Constantius in battle for the empire as a whole? Constantius had already defeated half a dozen rival emperors, some of them, like Magnentius, very formidable indeed. He was a good commander, and his habitual indecision left him on the field of battle. Julian had little support outside Gaul and three-quarters of the military resources of the empire were still in Constantius' hands. In an all-out confrontation Constantius was likely to win. These considerations suggested that Julian should try to negotiate with his cousin for a division of power, and avoid provoking a military clash. On the other hand it could be argued that Constantius was already committed to a war with Persia, from which he could not easily extricate his forces without losing both territory and face. This was the moment for Julian to strike, when his adversary's hands were tied. Why wait for Constantius to reach a settlement with the Persians and then move westwards with vastly superior forces? The choice before Julian was not in fact a clear-cut one between all-out hostility and passive negotiation. He could try to strengthen the basis from which he negotiated by taking control of further territory. Italy was of little account and had scarcely any military forces. But the Danubian provinces, from Noricum (roughly present-day Austria) to the Black Sea were heavily garrisoned, and the man who controlled them could easily bring pressure on the imperial capital at Constantinople. Should Julian advance down the Danube while Constantius was busy in the East? If he succeeded, he would establish a much stronger bargaining position. But if the Danube legions stood by Constantius and resisted, he would be involved in the very civil war that he was trying to avoid. There was a further complication. Lupicinus was in Britain with a substantial detachment of the army of Gaul. If he declared for Constantius, as he well might, since he and Julian did not usually see eye to eye, he could leave the Picts and Scots to their own devices and attack Julian in the rear with the army of Britain. Should he make overtures to Lupicinus? At any rate he could not make any kind of military move until the position of Lupicinus became clear.

Julian decided to try to avoid a conflict with Constantius. An officer was stationed at the port of Bononia (Boulogne) to prevent the departure for Britain of any unauthorized persons who might tell Lupicinus what had happened in Gaul. The manoeuvre worked, surprisingly enough. The authorities in Britain remained totally unaware that Julian had been proclaimed emperor. And when in the course of summer 360 Lupicinus returned to the Continent he was arrested as he disembarked and his force was taken over by an officer appointed by Julian.

Two emissaries were sent to Constantius with letters from Julian. One was Pentadius, the Master of Offices, who was Constantius' *homme de confiance* at Julian's court. He could not be accused by Constantius of being partial to Julian, who was in any case glad to be rid of him. The other was Eutherius, the eunuch chamberlain, who had previously undertaken a confidential mission from Julian to Constantius. His diplomatic skill and known integrity made him an ideal negotiator. The envoys bore two letters for Constantius. One was for public circulation. It explained that Julian had always faithfully carried out his obligations towards Constantius, that his troops had never received the rewards they deserved for their victories, but had been treated with total lack of consideration, and that he himself had been faced with a *fait accompli*: he could not assuage the anger of the soldiers as he had hoped but had to allow himself to be proclaimed emperor to prevent someone worse being proclaimed. Constantius was adjured not to listen to idle gossips or mischief-makers who put another interpretation on events. He then went on to state his conditions. He would send horses from Spain and reinforcements from the Laeti, units raised from German communities settled in Roman territory, to strengthen Constantius' forces. He would accept a Praetorian Prefect nominated by Constantius, who would thereby maintain theoretical supremacy in civil affairs, but all other officials, civil and military alike, were to be appointed by Julian himself. He repeated that it was quite impracticable to try to send Gaulish troops or Germans recruited from beyond the frontier, to fight in the east, especially when the security of Gaul itself was not firmly guaranteed. He ended by reminding Constantius that division of imperial power had often been practised to good effect by members of their family. The other letter, which was for Constantius' eyes alone, was allegedly much sharper in tone and spelt out in detail Julian's charges against his colleague and cousin.

Julian can scarcely have expected Constantius to accept his terms, which were tantamount to a claim to equality in standing and power. But his messages were a signal to Constantius that he did not intend in the meantime to seek to overthrow him by force. They could serve as an overture to negotiations, and Julian was confident that the indecisive Constantius, who had trouble enough on his hands already, would remain in hesitant uncertainty and thereby leave the initiative in his own hands.

The envoys had the greatest difficulty in pursuing their journey through Italy and Illyricum. No public authority was willing to take the risk of appearing to assist the agents of a rebel. In the end they reached Constantinople and went on to Constantius' headquarters at Caesarea in Cappadocia, near where Julian had spent six years of forced residence. Constantius had already learned what had happened from financial officials returning from the west, and possibly from Julian's hapless Praetorian Prefect Florentius, who had gone straight from Vienne to join Constantius when he heard of Julian's proclamation by the troops. But Julian's intentions were still unknown to him. When the envoys were introduced to his presence and read their messages he flew into such a rage that for a moment Pentadius and Eutherius were afraid for their lives, then dismissed them without a word. But as Julian had calculated he decided after some hesitation to pursue his campaign against Persia and sent a senior official named Leonas to Paris with orders to Julian to remain in his former position of subordination. By way of assertion of his authority he promoted Nebridius, Julian's quaestor, to the post of Praetorian Prefect in Gaul in replacement of Florentius and made a number of other appointments to Julian's staff.

Julian was ready for Leonas when he arrived about the beginning of May. He first heard him in private audience. Leonas, it seems, was tactless enough to observe that Constantius had elevated a penniless orphan to the highest rank in the empire after himself. 'What,' cried Julian, 'does my father's murderer reproach me with being an orphan?' On the next day Julian invited Leonas to read out his message before an assemblage of the soldiers and the citizens of Paris. As soon as the envoy reached the passage calling upon Julian to restrict himself to his former duties as Caesar, the crowd broke into shouts of *'Iuliane Auguste'*. The rest of Constantius' message was left unread. The lesson of the demonstration was not lost on Leonas. He realized that Julian was not merely the candidate of the legions, but that he enjoyed the massive support of the civil population. He was sent back to Constantius bearing Julian's reply, the contents of which we know only vaguely. The essential point was that negotiations had begun which might well end in a division of power more in keeping with the realities of the situation. Nebridius, the new Praetorian Prefect, was recognized by Julian, in accordance with the terms he had set out in his first message to Constantius. The other appointments made by Constantius were quietly ignored.

The dialogue between Julian and Constantius went on all through 360 without any kind of settlement coming into view. Both parties were content to keep communications open while they got on with more pressing tasks. In the east Constantius moved down to Edessa, thence to Amida, whose ruins he inspected, besieged in vain Bezabde, on an island in the Tigris, and withdrew for the winter to Antioch to prepare for the next year's campaign against Persia. In Gaul Julian crossed the Rhine once again and invaded the homeland of the Attuarii, a Frankish tribe living near Xanten, who had been making minor raids into Gaul, thinking themselves safe in their land of forests and marshes. After burning and pillaging the Frankish villages and taking many prisoners – who would later be embodied into the Roman army – he made a tour of inspection of the Rhine fortresses as far upstream as Basle, and returned to winter at Vienne. His move to Vienne from Paris suggests that he was more interested in watching the Alpine passes than the crossings of the Meuse and Rhine. In spite of the continuing negotiations – or perhaps because of them – Julian distrusted Constantius.

On 6 November occurred the fifth anniversary of Julian's inauguration as Caesar, his *Quinquennalia*, which in accordance with Roman custom he celebrated with a military parade and a distribution of gifts to the soldiers. The ceremony, which took place in Vienne, was made the occasion for a public assertion of Julian's power. Observers noted that for the first time he wore a diadem studded with precious stones. It was probably on this occasion that he issued his first edict of toleration. Its precise terms are unknown, but it seems to have accorded freedom of public worship to adherents of pagan cults, without withdrawing from the Christian Church its substantial State subsidies, its taxation exemptions, the privilege accorded to its bishops of travelling by the public post, and other rights that made Christianity in effect the religion of the Roman State. At the same time Julian himself took no part in public celebration of pagan rights. On the contrary he continued to attend the services of the Christian Church, and on Epiphany (6 January) 361 he took part in a special service in the episcopal church of Vienne.

Julian had long ago broken completely with Christianity himself. And he was convinced that he had been chosen by the power that ruled the universe to play some very special role. What that role was, he was not yet certain, though the events of 360 had done much to clear up his conception of his future. Among the tasks that would face him if and when he became ruler of the Roman empire would be that of reversing the course of events since his uncle Constantine had given Christianity a privileged position. It is unlikely that he had thought the problem through in 360 or had a very clear idea of how to tackle it. His political power extended only to a group of western provinces in which Christians were thin on the ground. And Julian knew better than most of his recent predecessors that the strength of the Greco-Roman world lay in the east. He had, like many others in the fourth century, been living a kind of double life, outwardly a member of the Christian Church, privately taking part in the rites of the syncretistic pagan mystery religions of late antiquity. This meant that he had no experience of actual public controversy with Christians. Basically he supposed that it was a matter of explanation. If the absurdities of Christian doctrine and the duplicity and hypocrisy of Christian practice were pointed out, people could not fail to be impressed by them and would return to the religion of their ancestors in some form. There was no question of mass adherence to the secret mystery cults, which required philosophical training and wide learning. These were only for the minority. For the mass of the people Julian probably thought in terms of a combination of what remained of traditional local cults with some simple monotheistic religion, like the worship of *Sol Invictus* or its close congener the worship of Mithras. In any case there would be no obligatory theology and no professions of faith. There were many roads to the great mystery.

What stood in the way of an impartial presentation of the facts was the special position of the Christian Church. It had material resources and a virtual monopoly of public communication. And above all it had a tough and flexible organization, which the pagans had always lacked. Later on Julian tried to deal with these problems. In the meantime, confined as he was to Gaul, he could only recognize them.

A man who believes that he has been chosen by Heaven to fulfil a special mission is peculiarly liable to make errors of judgement. Julian made many. But he combined his sense of mission with a strong grasp of the distinction between the possible and the impossible in any given situation. His own keen intellect and his long experience of situations in which his scope for action was extremely limited had taught him this. In a fragment of a lost work he writes: 'To fail to foresee what is possible and what impossible in affairs is a sign of the utmost folly.' In the situation in which he found himself in Gaul in 360 he had much need to exercise his sense of the possible. In particular he realized that the soldiers who had called him to power could as easily bring him down again. And some of those soldiers were Christians. Not theologically knowledgeable Christians eager to argue about subtle points of doctrine, of whom there were many in all strata of society in the Greek east. But simple men, who accepted uncritically and often without full understanding what their priest told them and who clung to it with the fervour of converts; for converts most of them must have been. Any public sign of rejection of the Christian religion, any slight to the Christian Church, risked provoking the unreasoning hostility of the soldiers upon whom his power rested. Hence Julian was obliged to continue his policy of outward conformity even after being proclaimed emperor. If he did at this time make it easier for non-Christians to perform public religious ceremonies – and it is not certain that he did – he had himself to continue to wear the outward aspect of a devout Christian.

Julian seems during 360 to have extended the circle of those admitted to share in his pagan worship. No longer was it a secret between Oreibasius, Euhemerus and himself. Many of his old friends had come from the east, perhaps even Priscus, the pupil of Aidesios, who had first initiated him in the secret rites of the pagan Neoplatonists. And he had sent for the chief priest of the temple of Demeter at Eleusis. His devotion to pagan religion cannot have been the deep secret it once had been. Yet it was probably unknown to the mass of soldiers and citizens. That his conduct exposed him to the very charge of hypocrisy that he levelled at the Christians cannot have escaped Julian's notice. It must have made him ill at ease. But he was by now accustomed to move on two different planes. And he fully realized that it would be suicide for him to have an open confrontation with the Christian Church, so long as Constantius was alive and in control of the greater part of the empire.

As the winter of 360 to 361 wore on, the façade of negotiation between Julian and Constantius grew thinner, though envoys, including an Arian bishop, continued to go to and fro between Gaul and the east. The reasons for the growing tension were many. First of all Julian's wife Helena, who was Constantius' sister, died in the summer of 360. There were rumours that she had been poisoned, but they do not seem to have been widely believed. Any sudden or unexpected death tended to be attributed to poison or sorcery. Julian sent her remains to Rome, where they were buried beside those of her sister Constantia, the wife of Julian's brother Gallus, in the magnificent domed sepulchre built by Constantine by the Via Nomentana, now the church of Santa Costanza.

Another factor was the persistent rumour that Constantius was bribing some of the Alaman tribes to renew their attacks across the Rhine. If successful in this, Constantius would not only have tied Julian down in Gaul. He might have undone all that Julian had accomplished in five years as Caesar. For the support that Julian certainly enjoyed from the soldiers and the citizens depended largely on their confidence that a stable peace had been assured. In fact a band of Alamanni under their chief Vadomar, who had not taken part in the alliance headed by Chnodomar, raided the neighbouring province of Raetia (eastern Switzerland and Vorarlberg). And when Julian sent a punitive expedition against them the Roman force was defeated and its commader, a staff officer named Libino, killed. A little later Julian's forces captured a messenger bearing a letter from Vadomar to Constantius. In the letter Vadomar referred slightingly to Julian as 'your disobedient Caesar', though in his correspondence with Julian he always scrupulously addressed him as Augustus. This was little enough evidence. The ruler of a small state caught between two great powers must always keep communications open with both if he hopes to retain any freedom, and Vadomar seems merely to have been following this rule. Julian had no doubt more evidence than we have, and perhaps some of it was more conclusive. And Vadomar, it seems, had a reputation for double-dealing. At any rate Julian sent an officer to the frontier with sealed orders, to be opened only if he found Vadomar on the Roman bank of the Rhine. Vadomar, who like many others among the Alaman leaders had adopted Roman ways, crossed over unsuspectingly to dine with the commander of a Roman frontier post.

Julian's emissary opened his sealed orders, which were to arrest Vadomar at once, and carried them out to the letter. Vadomar was brought before Julian, where he learned that his correspondence with Constantius had been intercepted. Julian did not deign to rebuke him, but sent him off under a military guard to Spain. Curiously enough Vadomar ended his days commanding Roman troops in Syria. In this revealing anecdote of Roman frontier policy there is one element omitted by our sources. Surely the commander of the frontier post had received secret instructions to invite Vadomar to visit him.

Finally in spring 361 there reached Julian reports of ominous troop movements in Constantius' territory. All these factors together made it more and more clear to Julian that the time he had gained by negotiating with Constantius was running out. Conflict could not be avoided. It was too late for Julian to submit to Constantius, even if he had wanted to. For too many people had committed themselves to his cause. It could not now be abandoned by its leader. The question for Julian was whether he should wait and let Constantius attack him in Gaul where he was strongest, or whether he should make a pre-emptive attack himself and try to gain control of the Danube region, or as much of it as he could. Julian, as always at such moments, anxiously prayed to the gods of Greece, and through them to the One, that a sign be vouchsafed to him. Several were. In particular a luminous vision appeared to him one night and proclaimed in Homeric verse that when Jupiter entered Aquarius and Saturn reached the twenty-fifth degree in the Virgin, then Constantius would meet his end in Asia. Such lack of ambiguity was unusual in a communication from the beyond, and Julian was heartened. His astrologers apparently calculated the date referred to as falling in the summer of 361.

In the spring of that year the information reaching Julian from the east was more disquieting than ever. Constantius was recruiting fresh troops. He was establishing supply dumps on the shores of Lake Constance and along the approaches to the passes through the western Alps. Gaudentius, an officer who had a few years earlier been sent by Constantius to Gaul to spy on Julian, was now reported to be in Africa with a special mission to strengthen the coastal defences and make sure that none of the corn surplus of that province went to Gaul. On 19 May Constantius issued a law in his own name alone, a clear recognition of the breach with Julian. As summer came on reports began arriving that the Persian king was withdrawing his forces from the frontier zone, and that Constantius had returned from the Euphrates to Antioch in the middle of summer. There could no longer be any doubt that Constantius was preparing to attack Julian with all the forces under his command.

Fortified by the omens he had received and following his bent for rapid and decisive action, Julian resolved to move at once, before Constantius could march his lumbering army across Asia Minor and into Europe. Before announcing his decision he took part, we are told, in a secret rite of the Roman goddess Bellona, the personification of war. It is likely that this secret ceremony was a *taurobolium*, in which the beneficiary sat in a trench over which a bull was slaughtered, and so was bathed in its blood. The rite, which was originally part of the worship of the Asiatic goddess Cybele, the Great Mother, had been taken over by the Mithraic religion and by a Celtic or Germanic cult of three female deities popular in the Rhine army before Christianity took its hold. We have a detailed, but of course contemptuous, description of a *taurobolium* by the Christian poet Prudentius. The ceremony, which was probably preceded by ritual purification, cleansed the recipient of all previous pollution. He was reborn to a new life, which might be everlasting. In the days immediately after the *taurobolium* he was fed on milk, like a newly born child. Some of those who benefited by a *taurobolium* – and only the rich could afford one – describe themselves as *in aeternum renatus*, 'reborn to life everlasting'. Others preferred to hedge their bets and repeated the ceremony every twenty years. We cannot be certain, but it is likely that this was the secret rite in which Julian participated on the eve of setting off to meet Constantius in a battle for which the Roman empire would be the prize.

Something of what was afoot had no doubt filtered down to the soldiers. Indeed from all we know of Julian it is likely that he sounded their opinion in various ways. Finally, after his ritual rebirth he assembled the troops at Vienne and addressed them. For what it is worth, our sources tell us that he looked more self-assured than he had lately been. He told them:

I am sure that you have long been awaiting a statement from me, so that you may judge what lies ahead of you and prepare to meet it. Battle-tired soldiers listen rather than talk, and a commander of proven probity dare propose nothing but what is honourable. This is what I have to say to you. The will of heaven brought me to you in my first youth. Together we broke the power of the Alamanni and the Franks and crossed the Rhine whenever we wished. Gaul, restored to peace after so much devastation and death, will bear eternal witness to your valour. It was by your authority that I was raised to imperial power. God and yourselves willing I now aim higher, for it is my boast that an army whose courage and fair-mindedness are famous always found in me a calm and reasonable commander in peace and a cautious and careful leader in the many wars which we have fought together. Let us anticipate our adversary's designs in the same community of spirit. Follow me now, while we have freedom of action to match our resolution. While there are still no major bodies of troops in Illyricum let us press on with all haste to the furthest limits of Dacia. Once there, our success will enable us to do what has next to be done. As befits a general who trusts his men, I call on you to swear an oath of undying loyalty. I for my part will take the utmost care that there be no rashness or slackness and I will guarantee, if you wish, that I shall attempt nothing that is not for our common good. I beg of you that in the ardour of your onset none of you inflict any harm on private citizens. For we owe our reputation no less to the security and prosperity of our province than to the countless enemies we have slain [Ammianus Marcellinus 21.5.2–8].

This speech was greeted with effusive demonstrations of enthusiasm as the soldiers beat upon their shields and cheered their commander. Then all of them, holding their swords to their necks, repeated after their officers an oath to stand by Julian, if need be to death. The civilian officials, who had also been assembled on the parade ground, took the same oath – all except the prefect Nebridius, who courageously declared that he could do nothing against Constantius, his benefactor and emperor. Some nearby soldiers rushed forward, bent on lynching him. But Julian threw his cloak around Nebridius and escorted him to the palace. There Nebridius fell to the ground and beseeched Julian to give him his hand to reassure him. 'If I give my hand to you,' replied Julian, 'what will I have left for my friends? Go in peace wherever you wish.' Nebridius returned unharmed to his home in Tuscany.

The forces at Julian's disposal were negligible compared with those of Constantius. A regular battle would be risky for Julian, and a battle at a time and place chosen by Constantius would be fatal. Julian's sole advantage was speed of movement. If he could gain control of the Danubian provinces and Italy before Constantius completed the transfer of his army from the east, then it would be harder for Constantius to attack him. And he would be in a position to negotiate from strength, since some of the major recruiting grounds would be in his hands. But he must move quickly to realize his advantage. This was the kind of situation that brought out the best in Julian. By now he was an experienced commander. He fully realized the danger of his situation, but was sure that God – or the gods – was on his side. He knew that if he did not act now it might be too late. As in his first campaign on the Rhine, or that which culminated in the great victory at Strasbourg, Julian combined almost demonic energy with cool judgement.

He had only about 23,000 fighting troops to take with him, for a garrison had to be left in Gaul, and he did not to wish to risk withdrawing units from hard pressed Britain. He divided them into three columns, both in order to avoid straining the resources of the territories through which he passed and to give the impression that his army was larger than it really was. One force of 10,000 men was to cross the Alps, march through northern Italy, then into the valley of the Sava and so down to the Danube. It was put under the command of Jovinus, a *magister equitum*, a Christian general who later built the church of St Agricola at Reims. A second force of the same size was sent through Raetia and Noricum, to march between the Alps and the Danube. Julian himself took command of a small force of 3000 men which crossed the southern end of the Black Forest and proceeded down the Danube. The three columns had orders to rendezvous at Sirmium, the great fortress and imperial residence on the Sava guarding the entrance to the Balkans. Its site is now occupied by the small town of Sremska Mitrovica, about twenty-five miles north-west of Belgrade. The first two armies were to make what haste they could while observing the principles of security. Julian with his smaller force pressed on regardless of danger, making forced marches through difficult mountainous and forested territory until it reached the head of navigation on the Danube, probably near Ulm. There they found boats assembled to convey them. There would always be some vessels waiting at the point where portage began during the navigational season. But that there were enough to carry 3000 men, even with the minimum of equipment, suggests that Julian had made arrangements in advance, even though Ammianus Marcellinus (21.9.2) speaks of the boats as there 'by chance'. Boats descend the upper Danube quickly, but can only move very slowly against the current, even with good pilots. Julian must therefore have ordered the fleet to be assembled some time – say several weeks – earlier. The decision to march against Constantius at the end of the campaigning season of 361 was less hasty than our sources make it appear. It is noteworthy that the troops whose unwillingness to leave have been so manifest a year earlier made no difficulties about marching east under Julian's command. Their earlier reluctance had probably been exaggerated by Julian.

Sailing down the river, to the acclamations, we are told, of the populace on the banks, and stopping only to bivouac for the night, Julian made very good time. By about 10 October he had reached Bononia, the nearest point on the Danube to Sirmium. It is probably near the modern Beocin, west of Novi Sad. So far he had encountered no resistance. In Sirmium Lucilianus, the military commander of Pannonia, had received disquieting reports of Julian's activity in Gaul, and had concentrated his troops in the fortress and was preparing to resist an expected attack. He was an experienced soldier and his preparations were no doubt in accordance with the best military practice of the day. Julian had arrived at Bononia in the evening. He at once sent a small force under the command of Dagalaifus, his *comes domesticorum*, to march by night across the Fruška Gora to Sirmium – the distance was nineteen miles – and seize Lucilianus. Whether the gates of the fortress had been left open, or Dagalaifus and his men had deceived the guards, we shall never know. But the first sign Lucilianus received that anything was wrong was when he was rudely awakened and found unknown soldiers standing round his bed. He was at once brought to Julian. On looking round and realizing that Julian had only a handful of men he remarked that it was very rash of him to venture into someone else's territory with so few troops. 'Keep your advice for Constantius', replied Julian with a bitter smile, 'if I permit you to offer me your respects, it is not because I need your counsel, but to put an end to your fear.'

On the next morning Julian and his men marched to Sirmium. The leaderless garrison, superior in numbers though it was, offered no resistance, and townsmen and soldiers poured out of the gates to greet Julian, showering him with flowers, acclaiming him as Augustus, and escorting him to the palace. Without losing a man Julian had won possession of the key to the Balkans. On the next day he presided at a chariot race in the hippodrome of the city, sitting in the imperial box in diadem and purple cloak and receiving the rhythmical acclamations of the assembled citizens. But there was no time for symbolic displays of imperial power. On the following morning Julian was again on the move with the bulk of his 3000 men, down the great military highway to Constantinople, the line of which is followed closely by the railway from Belgrade to Sofia and Istanbul. By forced marches he pressed on to Naissus (Nis), where he stopped to await the arrival of the rest of his forces and to

1 Julian. Miniature chalcedony bust, now in Leningrad. A metal diadem was originally fixed to the groove in the head, and the eyes were of a different material.

2 Opposite top Julian sacrificing. This miniature, in a ninth century manuscript of Gregory of Nazianzus now in Paris, is a medieval composition firmly based on classical models.

3 Bottom Ivory pyxis with relief of Christ in the pose and dress of a pagan teacher, flanked by Apostles, now in Berlin. An example of the adoption by Christianity in the fourth century of the iconography and style of classical art.

4 Below Reliefs on the sarcophagus of Junius Bassus, Prefect of the City of Rome, who died in 359, showing Biblical scenes executed in the classical manner.

5 *Opposite* Julian. An idealized portrait of the emperor, wearing a diadem and in the garb of a philosopher or pagan priest. Now in the Louvre.

6 *Below* A Persian king hunting wild boar. Silver bowl, now in Washington.

7 *Opposite* Constantine. This colossal head, now in the Museo dei Conservatori, probably originally stood in his Basilica in Rome.

8 *Left* Constantius II. Amethyst cameo now in the British Museum.

9 Gold medallion showing Julian beardless, in military uniform. Struck at Constantinople, probably early in 362.

10 Coin portrait of Julian bearded and wearing diadem, probably struck in 363.

11 The north front of the Porta Nigra at Trier, probably built under Constantius I.
12 Antioch. In the foreground the river Orontes, in the background Mount Silpius.

pass the winter. Nevitta and his column soon caught up with him. The other column had run into difficulties. When they first appeared in northern Italy fortune seemed to smile on them. Taurus, the Praetorian Prefect and principal civilian official, panicked and fled as fast as he could change horses across the Julian Alps and down the road to Constantinople. He infected with the same panic his colleague Florentius, the Praetorian Prefect of Illyricum, who in any case had reason to be afraid of Julian since he had deserted him in Gaul. There were no combatant troops in Italy, which appeared to have fallen to Julian without a drop of blood being shed. However the former garrison of Sirmium, whose loyalty Julian suspected, had been ordered by him to march to Gaul. Disgruntled at their humiliation and unwilling to go to a distant and unknown province, the troops mutinied *en route* and seized Aquileia, the fortress guarding the approaches to Italy from the north-east. There they blocked communications between Italy and Illyricum. The citizens of Aquileia supported the mutineers, more out of fear than out of loyalty to Constantius, and many of the Italian cities, seeing the turn that events were taking, declared themselves in favour of Constantius. Julian had entertained no fears for his rear, and was disconcerted by the news. Aquileia had the reputation of being impregnable. And while the military danger was negligeable, it would be politically very awkward for Julian to leave in his rear a hostile Italy, to which troops might eventually be transferred from Africa. Jovinus, who was by now in the neighbourhood of Ljubljana, was ordered to return at once and besiege Aquileia, and other units were dispatched to reinforce him. The result was that the force remaining with Julian at Naissus was considerably reduced in strength.

By now it was getting a little late in the year to press on into Thrace. In any case it would have been rash. Thrace, the hinterland of the new capital of Constantinople, was defended by the great fortresses of Philoppopolis (Plovdiv) and Adrianopolis (Edirne). Though the main body of Constantius' army was still in Syria, there were considerable forces in Thrace likely to be loyal to him. If Julian were to descend into Thrace, the most likely outcome for him would be defeat in battle. Even if he were not at once defeated, he would be unable to withdraw from Thrace. The fortress in his rear, which he could not hope to capture, would block his exit. And in any case from December onwards the passes between Thrace and Illyricum were likely to be blocked by snow. Quick to seize the initiative, Julian sent on a small force under Nevitta to occupy the most important of these passes, that of Succi, between Sofia and Plovdiv.

E.J.—5

As the winter wore on, the difficulty of his situation and the disparity between his forces and those of Constantius preyed on Julian's mind. He had gone as far as dash and good logistics would take him, and he was in a strong position to defend himself, should Constantius attack. But in the long run his strategic position could be outflanked through Italy. And if there was a long break in his run of success, he risked the disaffection of the civilian population and ultimately of his own troops. Like Moses, he was poised at the gateway of a promised land on which he might never set foot. The uncertainty of his situation was reflected in his unceasing search for a divine sign, and in the frenzied activity with which he filled the autumn and early winter of 361. Though he waited for a token of the gods' favour, yet he saw what had to be done and did it. If he could not increase his military strength, then he must obtain the loyalty and support of the citizens of the territories that he controlled. So on the one hand he issued a stream of open letters to the authorities of the various cities, setting out the rights of his case and depicting Constantius' conduct in the worst possible light. This propaganda, which Julian drafted himself, had a mixed reception. The letter addressed to the Roman Senate was rejected by that august body because of the violence of the attacks against Constantius. Tense and anxious, Julian had miscalculated. The only one of these open letters that survives is that to the Athenians, with whom Julian felt himself to have a particularly close connection. It is a long and skilfully composed document in which the writer recounts his own life story with less than complete candour. He claims that he did everything in his power to avoid being acclaimed as emperor by the troops, and shifts the whole blame for the breach between the two rulers on to Constantius' shoulders. In the face of Constantius' cruelty and perfidy, Julian appeals not only to the Athenians' sense of justice but also to their feelings of pity. He also takes up an openly pagan position, expressing himself entirely in terms of the gods of classical and post-classical Greek religion. Athens, of course, may have been a particular case. It was a university town, living on the traditions of the classical past, allusions to which would be appropriate in a letter addressed to its citizens. Perhaps Julian did not adopt so overtly pagan a tone in his communications to other cities. The only other fragment of this extensive propaganda that we possess – a sentence or two from his letter to the Corinthians – is inconclusive. It is important to bear in mind that the letter to the Athenians is not in any sense anti-Christian, it is merely couched in pagan terms and implies that its author saw the world through pagan eyes.

Along with propaganda went action. A supplementary tax imposed on Illyricum by Constantius was withdrawn. The price paid by the government for compulsory purchase of produce and animals, which had been a kind of concealed tax tending to limit production, was raised to a more realistic level. Measures were probably announced for increasing the membership of city councils and giving them more real power in the administration of city affairs, though these could hardly have immediate effect.

Julian's 'Hellenic' picture of the empire was of an agglomeration of cities, each with its dependent agricultural territory, responsible for their own internal affairs, including both commerce and arts and letters, while the imperial government provided security from external aggression and certain minimal common services. It was a concept shared by many of the inhabitants of the eastern part of the empire and particularly by its urban upper classses. It probably had less appeal in the Latin west, where urban institutions were less deeply rooted and where the power of the great landowner with his network of dependents was more firmly established. It had never been the whole truth about the relation between city and empire, and it certainly corresponded less with reality in the fourth century than, say, in the second. Julian himself recognized the incapacity of the cities to conduct their own affairs in complete autonomy by setting on foot schemes of public works in many cities at the expense of the imperial government. It was probably during his stay at Naissus in autumn of 361 that a beginning was made of programmes for public works in Athens, at Eleusis, at Nicopolis in Epirus and elsewhere. Ruined public buildings were repaired or rebuilt, new aqueducts installed, and so on.

Now that Julian was in effective control of Italy and Illyricum, he appointed a number of civilian officials in these dioceses to replace those of Constantius, many of whom had fled eastwards. Though some of his own old adherents were rewarded by office, Julian seems to have taken care in general to appoint men of standing and distinction, who enjoyed the respect of the urban upper and middle classes, the only groups in society whose opinions normally had political effect. Claudius Mamertinus, perhaps a professional rhetorician, perhaps a wealthy man of letters, but at any rate a man who counted in intellectual circles in the Latin west, was appointed Count of the Sacred Largesses (effectively minister of finance) and a little later Praetorian Prefect of Illyricum. He and Julian's general

Nevitta were nominated consuls for the following year 362. Sextus Aurelius Victor, whose Latin history of the Roman empire had probably just been published, was one of those who met Julian when he halted briefly at Sirmium. Julian later summoned him to Naissus, appointed him governor of Pannonia Secunda, and then or later caused a gilded statue of him with an honorific inscription to be set up in Rome. A Roman senator called Maximus, who arrived at Naissus on his return from a mission to Constantius, was appointed prefect of the city of Rome. It is recorded that his period of office was marked by cheap food and absence of civil discord.

All this argues a serious attempt by Julian to gain solid support in the new territories that had fallen to him. Probably he still hoped to negotiate with Constantius. There is a story that he offered to let the combined armies choose between Constantius and himself. If the offer was ever really made, it was not meant to be accepted. To march his own forces into Thrace to join those of Constantius would have been suicide. During all this time Julian exteriorized his own anxiety by pestering the gods to vouchsafe him a sign. He was in the awkward position of being sure that he had been chosen by heaven for some great purpose and not quite knowing what it was. And he had the intellectual's incapacity for inaction. He was not good at waiting, especially when the longer he waited the less likely did a successful outcome become. Had the gods forgotten him? Had he misunderstood their signs? As the weeks passed, the tension built up within him.

One day towards the end of November a small group of weary horsemen reached Naissus from the pass of Succi. They had with them two officers from Constantius' court, Theolaifus and Aligildus, who brought the news that Constantius was dead and that the armies of the east and the Asian provinces had sworn allegiance to Julian. When the travel-worn messengers were brought into Julian's presence and delivered their message, Julian's iron self-control broke at last, and he burst into tears. The gods had not deceived him, he had not misread their message. What no man could have foreseen had happened, for Constantius was only forty-four and had always enjoyed excellent health. The despised and mistrusted orphan, the bookish philosopher, the Caesar who was to have been an empty symbol of another's power, was now undisputed ruler of the Roman world, from the Forth to the Euphrates.

When in mid-summer 361 it became clear that the Persian King Piroz was withdrawing his main striking force from the frontier area, Constantius had decided to move against Julian. He fell back from Hierapolis on the

Euphrates to Antioch and began preparations for the move north-westwards. The decision was not an easy one to make. He had always had a guilty conscience about Julian and his family, and would have liked to avoid a confrontation if it could be done at no cost to his personal power. Even after the decision was made he was uneasy, nervous and strained. He told his closest companions that he no longer felt the presence of the guardian angel who had so long stood by his side. He was a demoralized man. He may well have been a sick man. In the middle of October he set off from Antioch towards Constantinople. Three miles outside of the city he came on a headless corpse lying by the roadside. Terrified by what he took to be an omen he pressed on to Tarsus. There he began to suffer from a low fever. He was not a valetudinarian, and decided that the best treatment for his illness was to continue his journey. But it was to no avail. By the time he reached Mopsucrenae, a few miles further on the way to the Cilician gates, his fever had grown worse, and he was in a state of collapse. The convoy halted. His fever grew and his breathing became shallow. Medicine was of no avail. The approach of death frightened him, for his conscience was not light. After a long agony he died on 3 November 361. It was later said by some that with his dying breath he named Julian as his successor. This seems highly unlikely, particularly since his third wife Faustina was pregnant and might bear him a son – in fact the child turned out to be a girl. And in any case it would have added nothing to the strength of Julian's position, for the imperial power did not pass by inheritance. It was probably a piece of clumsy propaganda by supporters of Julian.

The soldiers who had escorted the living Constantius to Mopsucrenae accompanied his remains on the long journey to Constantinople. It was noted by observers that as the cortège passed through the defiles of the Taurus mountains, the voices of angelic choirs could be heard. Meanwhile Julian marched with all haste down the military highway through Sardica, Philippopolis and Perinthus to Constantinople. He reached the capital on 11 December to be greeted with loyal acclamations by Senate and people, acclamations that were all the more sincere since they were addressed to an emperor born in the city, whom many could remember seeing there as a young man. It was like a dream come true, says Ammianus Marcellinus, to see his youthful figure walking through the city, as if he had dropped from the skies. What Julian's thoughts and feelings were on returning as emperor to his native city we can only guess. He had ordered mourning on receiving the news of Constantius' death, wore mourning himself, and showed no sign of joy that the cousin whom he had feared had died of natural causes. When Constantius' remains reached the Bosphorus, Julian himself went down to the quayside to greet the cortège, and stood bareheaded and weeping as the coffin was unloaded from the galley. And he marched himself at the head of the funeral procession to the Church of the Holy Apostles, where Constantius was laid to rest by the side of his father Constantine. He was probably genuinely moved by the solemnities of the funeral. He certainly did not take seriously the decree, which he graciously permitted the Constantinopolitan Senate to pass, formally recognizing the deification of the late emperor, in accordance with an ancient Roman custom which Christianity had not changed.

7 Constantinople

WHEN HE FOUND HIMSELF suddenly sole ruler of the Roman world, Julian was brought face to face with a number of problems, some of which were to remain with him throughout his brief reign. During the months he spent at Naissus he had doubtless reflected on the tasks that faced him. But everything had been too uncertain then, the apparent choice had been between coming to terms with Constantius and risking an armed conflict with him, and Julian himself had been in such tension that he could not coolly weigh one hypothesis against another. His correspondence written immediately after receiving the news of Constantius' death is full of anxiety for the fate of his friends, relief at the unexpected solution of his problems, and the conviction that he enjoyed the special protection of heaven.

The first problem was what to do about Constantius and his government. Julian had learnt from the bad reception of his letter to the Senate and people of Rome not to attack Constantius personally. Loyalty towards him was still strong in Italy and in the East. And in particular the eastern armies, which had fought under Constantius' direct command, would have felt themselves humiliated and insulted if he were depicted as a murderer and a traitor. In any case these eastern troops were probably mistrustful of Julian's Gaulish army, and had to be treated with circumspection. So Julian permitted the traditional apotheosis of his deceased cousin, and took part in his funeral ceremonies with every mark of respect. Neither in his own declarations nor in official pronouncements such as the address to Julian by the consul Claudius Mamertinus is there any word of criticism of Constantius. Consequently both Julian's proclamation as Augustus and his decision to march east had to be depicted as not involving hostility to

Constantius. Much had already been done in this direction. The letter to
the Athenians protests that Julian had only accepted the proclamation by
the soldiers in Paris against his will and as a last resort, and this is the
general line taken by most contemporary sources. The decision to march
east was more difficult to explain. One line taken by Julian himself was
that it was due to Constantius' treacherous conspiracy with Vadomar and
the Alamans, and that Julian acted only in self-defence. As we have seen,
this is a somewhat tendentious presentation of the facts. Another explanation offered by Julian and reflected in our sources was that he wished the
combined armies of east and west to choose between himself and Constantius. This would be addressed particularly to the eastern armies. It is
unlikely that such a project was ever seriously entertained by Julian before
Constantius' death, though it may have been put forward as a diplomatic
manoeuvre. A third explanation, mentioned this time by Gregory of
Nazianzus, a hostile witness, is that Julian was going to meet Constantius
in order to defend himself against the charge of usurpation. The currency
of so many different explanations suggests the difficulty in which Julian
and his advisers found themselves when he became ruler of an empire of
which the greater part had been loyal to Constantius.

Constantius' ministers were another matter. Among them were some of
Julian's bitterest enemies, men who had constantly poisoned Constantius'
mind against him. Julian had old scores to settle with them, and in any
case they were far too dangerous and experienced intriguers to be left in
positions of power. Fortunately for Julian, he was not alone in his hostility
to the court *camarilla*. The military leaders in the east were jealous of its
influence over Constantius, and anxious to humiliate it and punish its
leaders. Julian seized the opportunity offered by this situation. In the first
days after his arrival he set up a tribunal with wide powers to arrest and
try those guilty of crimes under the previous régime. The court was
primarily a military one, including Julian's two generals Nevitta and
Jovinus, and the two chief commanders of the eastern armies, Arbetio and
Agilo. The two civilian members were the Praetorian Prefects Mamertinus,
who had accompanied Julian from Gaul, and Salutius, who presided over
the meetings. Arbetio and Agilo, Constantius' chief generals, could hardly
be suspected of pursuing Julian's grudges. In order to detach the new
emperor even further from the proceedings of the tribunal, it sat, not in
Constantinople, but across the Bosphorus at Chalcedon (Kadiköy). The
officers of two of the guard regiments, the Jovii and the Herculii, were
invited to attend the sessions. In this way Julian succeeded in winning the

good will of the eastern armies, getting rid of some at least of his enemies, and establishing his own lack of vindictiveness.

Whatever may have been the legal authority of the tribunal – the lawyers probably brought it under the general rubric of *coercitio*, the right of a Roman magistrate to do what was necessary for the conduct of the essential business of the State – it was in fact an instrument of vengeance, such as almost inevitably follows upon a civil war. It got to work with military promptitude, and does not seem to have been over-delicate on such matters as rules of evidence or natural justice. The first to be condemned were two men who had organized Constantius' pervasive network of espionage, directed as much against his own officers as against his enemies. They were Paul 'the Chain' and Apodemius. Both were condemned to be buried alive. The eunuch chamberlain Eusebius, who had been as much a thorn in the side of Constantius' generals as of Julian, was also condemned to death. All these three had been deeply involved in the death of Julian's brother Gallus. Florentius and Taurus, formerly Praetorian Prefects of Illyricum and Italy, were found guilty of dereliction of duty, and received mild sentences of forced residence. Pentadius, who had been one of the principal agents in the condemnation of Gallus, and whom Julian had attacked virulently in his letter to the Athenians, convinced the tribunal of his innocence. However Ursulus, who had been Julian's minister of finance in Gaul and rendered him loyal service, was condemned to death because of disparaging remarks he had made about the efficiency of the army. Ursulus' life was part of the price paid by Julian for the support of the eastern generals. By January 362 the businesslike tribunal had completed its work and was dissolved. It had served its purpose of cleaning the air, and of establishing that those responsible for the misfortunes of the empire were to be found among the officials of the imperial palace.

It followed naturally that there must be some kind of purge of Constantius' hypertrophied court. Since the time of Diocletian the emperor had lived a life apart, surrounded by a vast army of chamberlains, body-guards, major-domos, gentlemen of the bed-chamber and so on, whose duty it was to protect his sacred person. A great many of these posts were virtual sinecures. And all of them enabled their holders to engage in a lucrative traffic in influence, real or imaginary. The life-style of the court was marked by luxury rather than refinement. Rarity and high cost were the marks of distinction. Not only the emperor and his family, but all those in contact with him, must eat the rarest dishes, drink the scarcest wines, dress in the most expensive materials, enjoy snow in summer and roses in winter. Julian's genuine simplicity of taste was revolted by this tasteless display of wealth and by the astute courtiers who battened on it. More than that, he was anxious to inaugurate a new kind of relation between emperor and subjects, to abandon or reduce the endless ceremonial that separated ruler and ruled – and which in point of fact was modelled on the ceremonial of the Sassanid court of Persia – and to return to a simpler, more open life-style, in which the emperor was accessible and shared the way of life of at any rate the better off of his subjects. His ideal emperor was not Diocletian but Marcus Aurelius.

The story goes that during his first days in the great palace at Constanti-nople Julian wanted a haircut and asked for a barber. When a gentleman in splendid attire presented himself, the emperor remarked that there must have been a mistake, he wanted a barber, not a councillor of State. The newcomer explained that he was indeed the imperial barber. To Julian's further questions he replied that he received daily rations for twenty men and twenty horses as well as a substantial salary, and gained a great deal in addition by forwarding petitions. On another occasion he found an imperial cook dressed in the most magnificent garb. He sent for his own cook, and made the two men stand side by side. He then asked his entourage which of the two they thought was a cook. When they pointed to the more plainly dressed of the two he dismissed the other as obviously ill-adapted to his post.

The purge was rapid and radical. Thousands who thought they had a secure situation for life were summarily dismissed, many of them, re-marked an observer, honourable men who deserved better. But Julian was not concerned with the merits of individuals, but with a system that he believed led to corruption and inefficiency and sometimes to cold-blooded murder. There was a direct political element in the purge. The whole establishment of eunuchs, which from their intimate association with the imperial family was believed to be a hotbed of intrigue and of power without responsibility, was dismissed. Julian remarked dryly that he had no need of them, as he was a widower and had no intention of remarrying. The *agentes in rebus*, officials under the Master of Offices, who were widely used as spies upon other departments of State, were drastically reduced in number. Only seventeen were retained as members of the emperor's personal staff.

New appointments had to be made to many offices of State, both in the territories previously controlled by Julian and in those he had inherited from Constantius. The military commands in the east were left intact; it would have been dangerous for Julian to try to replace men like Agilo and Arbetio by nominees of his own. But he appointed his most trusted adviser Salutius Secundus to the key position of Praetorian Prefect of the east. Claudius Mamertinus, a cultured Gaul, perhaps a rhetorician by profession, who was already Praetorian Prefect of Illyricum, was appointed to one of the consulates for 362. The other went to Nevitta, Julian's faithful general. The consuls, of course, had no longer any part to play as such in the government of the empire. But the office still carried enormous prestige. Julian's close friend Anatolius, who had been his Master of Offices since 360, continued to hold this position in Constantinople. Iovius continued to hold the office of *Quaestor Sacri Palatii*. Felix, whom Constantius had appointed to be Julian's Master of Offices in 360 and whom Julian had refused to accept, was now made Count of the Sacred Largesses. He had been an adherent of Constantius, but became a close associate of Julian and was later converted by him to paganism. Nymphidianus, brother of Maximus of Ephesus, and a rhetorician by profession, was made *Magister epistularum graecarum* (secretary of State of the Greek-speaking portion of the empire). Ecdicius Olympus, probably to be identified with a friend of Libanius, became prefect of Egypt. Julian's maternal uncle Iulianus, with whom he was on the closest of terms, was given the key post of *comes Orientis*. Another Iulianus, a friend of Libanius and Themistius, became governor of Phoenicia. Atarbius, another friend of Libanius, was appointed governor of the frontier province of Euphratensis, while Celsus, a pupil of Libanius, a philosopher and rhetorician, was governor of Syria. Leontius, a fellow student of Libanius and a teacher – presumably of rhetoric – governed Palestine. Vettius Agorius Praetextatus, son-in-law of Symmachus and one of the leaders of the pagan wing of the Roman Senate, who was in Constantinople on private business, was appointed to the politically unimportant but prestigious post of proconsul of Achaea.

We know of only a few of Julian's appointments. But certain features of his policy emerge with clarity. First, military appointments are made and prolonged on grounds of proven competence, and not of influence or political attachments. Second Julian's appointments to civilian office are all eminently serious; there are no incompetents owing their place to wealth or family influence. Third and perhaps most important, Julian tried to appoint professional men and intellectuals to high government office.

Other emperors had done so before him and would do so after him. This was no longer the world of the early second century, when Juvenal could laugh at the idea of a rhetorician becoming consul. But none pursued this policy so systematically as Julian. He made overtures to other men of letters and science that were not taken up. Julian of course felt himself at ease with men of education, as he did, in a different way, with soldiers. But there is more to it than that. On the whole the educated classes of the Greek cities of the empire, the men who taught, who wrote books, who influenced opinion, had traditionally held themselves aloof from the empire and its affairs since the chaotic years of the third century. Their world was that of the cities, the city councils, the provincial assemblies, the declamations of rhetoricians, the disputes of philosophers. They often knew no Latin and did not want to know any. The defence of the frontiers, and the levying of taxes could be left to men of a different kind, often rude soldiers from the northern provinces, speaking Latin, boorish in their habits and limited in their interests, who held the ring, as it were, while the men of letters – who were usually also men of substance on a local scale – pursued their *dolce vita* of local politics, intellectual excitement and exquisite good taste.

The swollen central bureaucracy created by Diocletian needed men to run it, and the eastern intellectuals had opted out. Office, promotion and influence went to men whose qualifications were often minimal and whose sense of tradition was limited. In the middle of the fourth century a knowledge of shorthand could be the passport to a meteoric career in the civil service. Men like Libanius, who were the very embodiment of Hellenic tradition, met this situation by turning in on themselves. They deplored the nobodies who were reaching office, but they did not suggest to their own pupils and sons that they transfer their activities from the limited area of city and provincial life to the larger one of the central government, where the risks as well as the prizes were greater. Yet the transference of the capital from Rome to Constantinople had made this a question of burning urgency for the upper classes of the eastern cities. Previously the centre of imperial power, where large-scale decisions were taken, had been far away, and the sphere in which imperial power was exercised had been limited. Now a new imperial capital had been planted in the midst of the Greek cities. And the central government now acted in a multitude of spheres that had previously been left largely to local civic initiative. The Greek urban upper classes, who prided themselves on their Hellenic culture, were still largely pagan in an empire whose rulers were

Christian. This added to their isolation and their sense of defending a threatened cause. Yet if a society whose primary unit of organization was the city was going to survive, the leading citizens must in some way be drawn into the process of decision-making which so closely affected the fortunes of their own communities. A few men of letters and science elected to work in the larger world of the empire rather than in the smaller one of city and province.

Such a man was Themistius (*c.* 317–388). A native of northern Asia Minor, he taught rhetoric and philosophy in the new capital of Constantinople from 345 until his death. He is the author of a series of commentaries on Plato and Aristotle. But he also took part in the public life of the capital and soon attracted the attention of Constantius, who in promoting him to the Senate spoke of exchanging '*sophia Hellēnikē*' (Greek learning) for '*axiōma Romaikon*' (Roman dignity). He held high State office under every emperor from Constantius to Theodosius, and, in a long series of panegyric speeches, addresses to emperors and so on, contributed to the formulation and dissemination of the political ideals that they put into practice. Unlike the Neoplatonists, who saw the chief end of philosophy in personal enlightenment, Themistius took a pragmatic, more Aristotelian view. For him practical action in city and State was one of the main aims of philosophy. A convinced pagan, he loyally served a series of Christian emperors. He was not a philosopher of originality, and as a statesman he inclined to blur outlines and make vague compromises. But he did express at the imperial court some of the aspirations of his class throughout the empire. Though Julian's philosophical position was very different from that of Themistius, they were linked by their paganism and by their understanding of the folly of boycotting the centre of imperial power.

Julian's eagerness to draw the best representatives of the Hellenic intellectual world into active participation in the government of the empire may owe something to Themistius' example. For the two men had long been in correspondence. But an exchange of letters between them in the first weeks after Constantius' death reveals the deep gulf that divided them, and throws light on some of the contradictions of Julian's position. Themistius' letter is lost, but the gist of it can be reconstructed from Julian's reply, the date and circumstances of which give it the character of a public manifesto. In form the argument is about the interpretation of certain philosophical texts. In reality it is a dispute about the relation between Greek city and Roman empire. Themistius had argued that the philosopher must play a full part in the life of the Roman empire, holding office in the new capital, and concerning himself with the large-scale problems of government. Julian, who treats Themistius with the utmost respect, declares that the true task of the philosopher is to teach a few pupils, that he cannot and should not involve himself in affairs of State. This is an ultra-reactionary Hellenic position – aloofness from the Roman empire while enjoying its protection, and cultivation of an élitist Greek culture in the small circle of leading cities in the east. It is also typical of Neoplatonism, which 'was interested in the individual rather than the community, in the contemplative rather than the active life' (A. D. Nook). Why then did Julian invite members of the Greek pagan intellectual class to accept office under him? To understand his motives we must look at the other side of his character.

Julian was by choice and upbringing a Greek and a philosopher. But birth and chance had made him also a Roman emperor. In his younger days he seems to have been little interested in Rome and its traditions. But since he became Caesar, and above all since he became a rival to Constantius, he had begun to study and reflect upon Roman history. It is no accident that he sent for the historian Aurelius Victor when he was at Naissus, appointed him governor of Pannonia and had a gilded statue of him set up. His main guide in Roman matters was probably Salutius Secundus. It is clear from Julian's own later writings that the Roman emperors whom he took as models were Antoninus Pius and Marcus Aurelius. In outlining the ideal emperor in his first panegyric on Constantius he described him as dealing with people and magistrates like a citizen subject to the laws and not like a monarch who is above them. This ideal of government under the law is echoed again and again by Julian's friend Libanius who opposes it to the unbridled authority of an autocrat. Julian was seeking to turn back the clock of history and recreate the style of government of two centuries earlier, before the chaos of the third century and the centralization and bureaucratization that had ensued under Diocletian, and before Plotinus had broken the old bond between philosophy and politics. His ideal was an imperial government that interfered as little as possible with the economic, political and cultural life of the cities, headed by an enlightened emperor who was not a remote god incarnate but a reasonable and approachable *primus inter pares*. That a certain roseate glow of falsification had already been cast over the age of the Antonines is neither here nor there. Any illusions Julian may have had about the world of Antoninus Pius and Marcus Aurelius were

shared by his contemporaries. Now the age of the Antonines saw the cul-
mination of the so-called Second Sophistic, this curious backward-looking
Greek cultural renaissance that accompanied the economic upsurge of the
Greek cities of the east. And one of the features of the Second Sophistic
was precisely the role played by the sophist. These men, whose base was
in the cities of Asia Minor, often became the confidants, the counsellors,
the critics of Roman emperors, and in this way served as a kind of pressure-
group representing the interests of the urban upper classes of the east.
But they did not usually hold government office, and they never became a
permanent part of the State apparatus of the empire. Their true habitat
was always the Greek world of the cities. This was the kind of role that
Julian envisaged for the philosophers and sophists whom he invited to his
court. It is to the credit of the many who refused the invitation that they
perceived the anachronistic assumptions on which it was based. In the
second half of the fourth century the pagan Greek intellectuals were faced
with the choice between total participation in the affairs of the empire,
like Themistius, or total withdrawal from them, like Libanius. The
delicate balance of the Antonine age had long ago been upset.

Julian, then, when he found himself sole emperor, was faced with a
personal dilemma that he never really succeeded in resolving. It concerned
his own attitude to the Constantinian empire, which had so changed the
balance between east and west, between Latin and Greek. His own
personal attitude was probably strongly coloured by the experiences of his
youth and young manhood, and the extraordinary isolation in which he
found himself. It was perhaps the very strength of his emotions that made
it difficult for him – intelligent and sincere as he certainly was – to think
through this complex of problems rationally. Instead he took refuge in a
return to a past which, like so many historical pasts, was in part mythical.
These considerations will be of importance in due course in assessing
Julian's religious policy. In the meantime, however, there remain some
points to be emphasized concerning his political and legislative measures
at the beginning of his reign.

On the first of January 362 the new consuls Mamertinus and Nevitta
began their year of office. Julian used the occasion to underline the new
imperial style. When Mamertinus paid his official morning call at the
palace, the emperor rose to his feet to greet him. And instead of summon-
ing the Senate to the palace, as Constantine and Constantius had done,
he went himself, and on foot, to the Senate House, where he listened to a

speech from Mamertinus in praise of himself. This break with the protocol of the past was not to everyone's taste. Many felt that Julian demeaned himself by behaving like an ordinary citizen. To secure the unthinking, emotional loyalty of his subjects, perhaps an emperor had to create a certain distance between himself and them. Julian of course wanted rational acceptance, not unthinking, emotional loyalty. Throughout his reign there was a conflict between the role of 'democratic prince', which he wished to play, and that of a remote half-divine ruler, which the mass of his subjects expected, and which may have been what the situation called for.

Mamertinus, the general tone of whose speech must have been approved by Julian, refers disparagingly to a disagreeable past that is over and done with, but makes no attack on Constantius, whose funeral in the church of the Holy Apostles had taken place only a few days earlier. He dwells mainly on Julian's military exploits, and on the care that he has always shown for the people over whom he ruled, and reminds the citizens of Constantinople that in the preceding autumn Julian had allowed a fleet carrying grain from Africa to reach the city, although at that time it was still in the hands of Constantius. A day or two later Julian himself wrote to the authorities in Egypt to hasten the delivery of an obelisk to Constantinople. His action was doubtless made known in the city.

His first surviving legal enactment, promulgated on 6 January 362, was a technical regulation concerning the provision of forage for army horses, the precise purport of which cannot now be determined. A law of 17 January tightens up control of fraud by civic officials, one of 1 February rejects claims by persons who have bribed officials to get their money back. Later in the same month an edict was issued severely restricting the use of the imperial post for non-official purposes. Even honest officials had been subject to intolerable pressure to grant authority to travel by vehicles of the post, while the dishonest had openly trafficked in permits. Now each official from Praetorian Prefect to provincial governor was to have a fixed allocation of permits. Further permits could be issued only on the authority of the emperor himself. And some of the less essential services, like that to Sardinia, were cancelled altogether. A series of laws issued in March aimed at strengthening the financial and political position of cities: city land taken over by the imperial government was to be returned to the cities, so that the rent it brought in might swell their revenues; no fresh taxes or corvées were to be imposed without his authority; members of city councils who had been excused on various grounds were to be recalled to their civic duties; the immunity from taxation which lessees of imperial estates had enjoyed was revoked. A series of measures were aimed at reducing the intolerable delays in the judicial process. In March Julian laid down that the *aurum coronarium*, the tribute in gold paid principally by city dwellers, was to be regarded as a voluntary contribution and not as a tax. At the same time there was a general cancellation of arrears of the land-tax, and possibly a reduction in the rate of tax for the ensuing year. These of course are only fragments of a much more widespread legislative activity. But they indicate certain lines of Julian's political thought – the elimination of irregularities and abuses (though it may in fact be the irregularities and abuses that make a system of government workable), the separation of the central government from the affairs of individual citizens, the restoration of the cities as near-autonomous organs of local administration (though the flight of councillors from their duties and the interference of the central government in civic affairs were features of long standing, and indications that the cities of the empire were no longer able to perform their old functions). In the capital itself work was begun on a new harbour. We hear also of the building of a portico and a public library, and of arrangements to bring an obelisk from Egypt, which may be in fact that still standing in the centre of the Hippodrome, where it was erected by Theodosius.

It would be a gross mistake to suppose that Julian was a kind of antique liberal. His aim was not the suppression of the centralized bureaucracy, but its rationalization. In the same way his abandonment of the trappings of autocracy did not mean that he favoured a real devolution of power. Government was, if anything, more autocratic under Julian than under Constantius. But it probably was in some ways more just. And justice, the attribution to each citizen of a status commensurate with his capacity and a reward commensurate with his status, was the goal of the Platonic philosopher-king. Behind all the democratic gestures, which doubtless corresponded to a genuine simplicity and directness in Julian's character, stood the austere and forbidding Platonic ruler, lost in contemplation of the transcendant world of the Forms. The true ruler, he says in his letter to Themistius, 'even if he is actually human by nature, must be divine by his rule of life, expelling all that is mortal and animal from his soul, except what is necessary for the preservation of his body'. The point was taken by his contemporaries. A Latin inscription from Pergamum calls him 'lord of the world, teacher of philosophy, reverend ruler, pious emperor, ever-victorious Augustus, spreader of republican liberty' (H. Dessau, *Inscriptiones Latinae Selectae* 751) and a Greek inscription from Iasus in Caria speaks of his rule as based on philosophy, 'as he guided the whole world by justice and the other virtues' (*Orientis Graecae Inscriptiones Selectae* 520). Julian's character was riddled with inconsistencies and conflicts, often arising from his conscientious endeavours to find a rational basis for his own intuitions and emotions. Were he not inconsistent, he would have been a dull man and a dull emperor, a shortcoming of which not even his severest critics accuse him.

Good Platonist that he was, he could not conceive a genuine political community without a State religion. This is a point of view which he shared with most Christians of his time, but which would have appeared perverse to his heroes Antoninus Pius and Marcus Aurelius. His objections to Christianity as a State religion were many: the gross discrepancy between what the Church preached and what most Christians practised, of which he himself had had particularly bitter experience; the internal strife of the Christians, which he saw pursued without scruple by many of the leaders of the Church; its preoccupation with corpses – from Christ himself to the martyrs, genuine or spurious, who were worshipped in every city or village; and more than anything else, perhaps, its moral softness – it did not appear to him to make sufficient demands, and the greatest scoundrel could have his slate wiped clean by repenting. This was not the justice that the good community and the good man must alike embody, but a kind of moral free-gift scheme that sapped men's ability to distinguish between right and wrong. It opened a path to heaven not through consistent practice of virtue but through periodical orgies of lachrymose confession. It was a religion for children, not for grown men. One could go on cataloguing Julian's accusations against the Christians, and some of them will be discussed in greater detail later on. But perhaps his greatest ground for hatred of Christianity was precisely its novelty. Like many men of initiative, Julian had a fundamentally conservative nature. 'Innovation', he writes, 'I abominate above all things, especially as concerns the gods, and I hold that we ought to maintain intact the laws which we have inherited from the past, since it is evident that they are god-given' (*Letter* 20).

Julian's adherence to Neoplatonist paganism had been kept secret. In practice it must have been something of an open secret. But so long as he conformed outwardly to the requirements of Christianity this was good enough for Constantius and for the public opinion of the age. There were plenty of public Christians and secret pagans since the days of Constantine. Even after his proclamation as emperor in February 360 he avoided any open display of pagan ritual, and took part as custom required in Christian ceremonies, such as the Easter service at Vienne on 8 April 361. It would have been dangerous to provoke a predominantly Christian civilian population and an army in which there were many Christians. It was on his march through Thrace from Naissus to Constantinople that Julian first openly performed pagan sacrifices, as he joyfully recounts in his letter to Maximus, his former teacher and initiator: 'We worship the gods openly and the majority of the troops accompanying me is devout [=pagan]. I myself sacrifice oxen in public. I have offered many hecatombs to the gods in gratitude for what they have done for me. The gods bid me purify everything as far as I can, and I eagerly obey them. They say they will repay my labours with a great reward, if I do not slacken off.' It is interesting to note that these soldiers, who are now for the most part pagan, are the very soldiers in deference to whom Julian attended church at Vienne a few months earlier. They were largely Franks and Alamans and other Germans, and it is likely that their true religious beliefs, in so far as they had preserved any, were as far from Julian's intellectualizing Hellenism as they were from Christianity. But they had learnt when in Rome to do as the Romans do. News of Julian's public sacrifices of oxen and the like must have spread quickly to Constantinople. Yet no one found it odd that he took a leading part in the Christian funeral service for Constantius.

Religion, however, could not for Julian be a purely personal matter. Like his Christian contemporaries he believed that right belief and action in regard to the deity was essential for the welfare of the State. At the same time his own inclinations and the rarefied intellectualism of the pagan conventicles to which he belonged forbade the use of force. Men must be shown the truth, and sooner or later they would recognize it. What was needed was to let the truth be seen to equal advantage with falsehood. So within a few days of his arrival at Constantinople he issued a decree – the text unfortunately does not survive – offering the restoration to its original owners of all temple property confiscated since Constantine. The same decree, or others accompanying it, expressly permitted the public performance of all religious ceremonies, and withdrew the subsidies that the Christian clergy had received from the government since the days of Constantine. There was to be a fresh start, and no one was to have a handicap. At the same time or a day or two later a further decree ordered the recall of all Christian clergy exiled for heresy or schism. This could be defended as a further instance of the policy of non-discrimination. As there was to be no distinction between pagan and Christian, so there was to be none between one Christian and another. In fact, of course, the return to office of those banished for heresy would create immense problems for the semi-Arian hierarchy that dominated the Church, and Julian was well aware of this. He hoped that the Christian Church might tear itself to pieces. He probably had his tongue in his cheek when he summoned an assembly of bishops and their followers, orthodox and heretic alike, to the palace and enjoined them to give up their disagreements so that each might practise his religion in freedom and without fear. As for the restoration of temple property, it turned out to be a complicated matter, productive of much bad blood in the property-owning classes. Many temples were rebuilt or restored. In other cases indemnities were paid. But in many others endless lawsuits ensued, as third parties who had bought former temple property in good faith sought to avoid the responsibilities laid upon them by the law. In spite of Julian's reminder that Christians were not to be harmed or forced to offer sacrifice, there were instances of public disorder. At Alexandria the Bishop, Julian's old neighbour George of Cappadocia, was lynched by a mixed pagan and Christian crowd. George was an opportunist and a scoundrel, whose only saving feature was his love of book-collecting. But neither mass violence nor the use of force by the State authorities was desired or welcomed by Julian, who reprimanded the people of Alexandria for their crime, and instructed the prefect of Egypt to get hold of George's library and send it to Constantinople. In Arethusa in Syria Bishop Mark, who had been in the habit of forcing pagans to profess Christianity, was attacked by a mob and killed with great cruelty – the schoolboys, the sons of the largely pagan upper classes, stabbed him with their styluses. The local governor, though himself a pagan, submitted a report to Julian strongly condemning the action of the citizens and observing that they were making themselves ridiculous. There were Christians who sought martyrdom, like the three Phrygian youths who knocked down the statues in a newly reopened temple and then gave themselves up to the authorities. And there were horror stories, often with sexual overtones, such as often gain currency on such occasions. One concerned nuns in Heliopolis in Lebanon, who were allegedly forced to display themselves in the nude, had their hair shaven, and were finally butchered and their entrails fed to pigs. The story occurs first in a fifth-century source, but is not mentioned by any of Julian's contemporaries. Violence, when it occurred, was the product of local circumstances. The emperor had at this time neither the desire nor the intention to force anyone to change his views. The story of his encounter with Maris, Bishop of Chalcedon, is revealing. Maris, who was elderly and had a double cataract, had an audience with Julian, apparently at his own request, at which he called the emperor traitor and atheist. Julian replied that Maris could not see the truth because he was blind, and added: 'Your Galilean God will not cure you', to which Maris retorted that he thanked God he was blind and did not have to look on the face of a turncoat emperor. There the interview seems to have ended. The ecclesiastical historian who tells the tale remarks that Julian, having seen how earlier martyrs were glorified, decided to punish the Christians by not allowing any more martyrdoms.

In fact the effect of these measures depended very much on local officials. There were places with a large Christian majority where virtually nothing was done. There were others where the law was applied with malicious vexatiousness. Whole houses were demolished because part of the masonry from a temple had been used in their construction. But on the whole the legislation was put into effect without disturbance. A great many temples, cult-sites and oracles began to be frequented again. Pagan priests who had been reduced to indigence found themselves once again in affluence and honour. Processions and ceremonies long abandoned were celebrated once again. An inscription from a village near Bostra of February or March 362 records that the temple there had been rebuilt and reconsecrated. Julian had sent as governor of the desert frontier province of Arabia Petraea a former professor of rhetoric, by name Belaeus, who applied Julian's edicts to the letter. Titus, the Bishop of Bostra wrote to Julian explaining that the Christian population, though enraged, was obeying its bishop's instructions and remaining quiet. We have Julian's letter to the citizens in which he emphasizes that no one is to be made to participate in pagan rites against his will, that the clergy and others who so wish are at liberty to carry on Christian worship. But there must be no disturbance of the peace. He goes on to invite the citizens to expel Bishop Titus from their city, since the Bishop had attributed their own reasonable behaviour to his own influence. The letter dates from late in 362, when Julian's policy towards the Christians had changed somewhat, and there was an attempt on his part to separate the Christian laity from their clergy. In general the restoration of the freedom of pagan worship, the recall of exiles, and the return to city councils of clergymen who had been exempted from service were short-term inconveniences to the Christian communities of most cities. What was much more serious, and permanent in its effects, was the withdrawal of State subsidies to the Church, both direct and indirect by way of fiscal immunities. This threatened the whole structure of charitable works carried out by bishops, and weakened the already established position of the Church as a property-owner.

Julian was no doubt satisfied with the early results of his policy of equality of opportunity for all religions. But his satisfaction did not last long. There was no mass falling away of Christians, though individual conversions were not infrequent. And the pagans who began once again to worship in public were not much interested in the sophisticated Neo-platonist religion of Julian and his philosophical friends. Traditional local cults flourished. So did the cult of Mithras the Sun God, of which Julian was himself an initiate. He had indeed installed a Mithraeum in the palace by the Sea of Marmara, and celebrated a *taurobolium* there, perhaps his second. But there was little in common between the dualistic, militant Mithraism of the Roman soldier and the man in the street and the complex, and perhaps slightly muddled, metaphysics set out in Julian's *Hymn to the Sun God*, a prose work probably written in the first months of his rule as emperor. The original dualism, which made Mithraism so attractive to the combative, is here replaced by a process of emanation from higher to lower. Mithras, the Sun God, is an emanation of the true sun in the world of ideas, and in his turn gives rise to the visible sun of the material world. He demands from his worshipper, and particularly from those called to high positions, paternal kindness towards subordinates, strict self-control, loyalty to allies and friends, reverence for the gods. He offers no longer bodily resurrection but rebirth into a higher and spiritual world. He is the same as Apollo and Dionysos and Serapis and a multitude of other gods, Greek and foreign. What Julian and those like him are doing is to fuse Mithraic ritual and morality with the metaphysics of the new synthetic mystery religion of the Neoplatonists. All this was too rarefied for the man in the street.

Moreover it was theological. And ancient religion in general managed to do without theology, in the sense of a body of doctrine about divine beings, belief in which is demanded of their adherents. The ancient religions of the Greeks and Romans, and all the various syncretistic fusions of them with one another and with the religions of various eastern peoples, were essentially religions of action. If a man performed the proper acts in the proper way he would satisfy the gods and obtain their favour. What he believed was neither here nor there. Moral demands might be made of the practitioner of religion, so that the sacrifices and prayers of a scoundrel, even though performed with ritual correctness, might be of no avail. A man had not only to perform the right ceremonies but to be a good man to win the protection of the gods. Mithraism is an example of a late Roman religion that made moral demands of its adherents. Or secret information about divine beings might be imparted to worshippers in an initiation ceremony or otherwise, as in most so-called mystery religions. But the worshipper was not asked if he believed what had been revealed to him. Or again the possession of secret information might be essential to successful intercession with the gods, or god, or to full enjoyment of the salvation they offered. Such was the position of the Gnostics, both pagan and Christian. Worshippers of Isis, or Manichaean dualists, put a large body of information concerning the gods and their relation with the universe and with mankind at the disposal of their adherents: in the case of the Manichaeans this was in the form of sacred books. But no profession of faith seems to have been demanded, and we hear of no Isiac or Manichaean – or for that matter Mithraic – heretics. A bewildering variety of doctrine and ritual was the rule. And the tests, where tests were imposed, were of action, not of belief. Christians could avoid legal prosecution not by reciting a Mithraic or Isiac or Hermetic creed, but by offering a pinch of incense on an altar, more often than not the altar of the reigning emperor's Genius, whom no one seriously supposed to be a deity of any consequence.

Brought up as a Christian in an age of sharp doctrinal dispute, Julian was familiar with theological definition and argument. And his metaphysical approach to what for most people was essentially a matter of feeling encouraged systematization, lists, clearly formulated doctrines. He hoped that he would make pagan monotheism, in which he fervently believed, more acceptable to those outside the restricted circles of intellectual initiates, by setting out its theology. He also hoped that it would better bear comparison with Christianity. The project had probably formed itself slowly in his mind, in the course of his discussions with his intimates in Gaul and at Naissus. One of the principal among these was his friend Salutius Secundus, now Praetorian Prefect of the east. It was Salutius, a man of culture and standing, respected even by Christians, who was charged with composing this manual of pagan theology. Entitled *On the Gods and the Universe* it is a short work, occupying no more than twenty printed pages. It was probably published – in the sense that copies were distributed to key figures, including booksellers – between March and

June of 362, while Julian was in Constantinople. It is likely that the text was discussed with Julian as it was written.

Salutius' handbook discusses, briefly and without digression, such topics as the immortal, immaterial, unspatial nature of gods, the value of myths, which though false lead us towards the truth, the nature of the universe, of the human soul, of providence and destiny, the origin of evil, why we offer sacrifices to gods who are in need of nothing, rewards and punishments, the necessity of the transmigration of souls, the necessary happiness of the good. Not overtly polemical this little work was yet clearly intended to answer the objections made by Christians to traditional paganism. It draws largely on Plato's thought, though probably usually at second or third hand, but sets it out in a systematic, expository way. It is not an intellectually impressive work, since its arguments are often question-begging and it avoids some of the major problems that have preoccupied theologians. Yet it is important as the first – and the last – attempt to provide a rational and philosophical basis for the confused welter of beliefs and practices that constituted the paganism of late antiquity. Salutius, and behind him Julian, are concerned not merely to preserve the past in an antiquarian sense, but to breath new life into it and to fit its religious heritage to compete with Christianity – organized, articulate and polemical. The work is addressed to the educated, who have some grounding in philosophy, and its concluding chapters presuppose acceptance of late Neoplatonist doctrines. The mass of the uneducated were to be left to their traditional religious rites and beliefs. The battle was for the minds of the urban upper classes, who were more and more turning to Christianity. Christian preachers and the Christian Church could now talk their language. The great fourth-century fathers were men of education, who did not reject wholesale the traditional culture. The days were long past when Tertullian could exclaim 'What has Athens to do with Jerusalem?' Salutius' handbook of pagan theology is a first step towards meeting this intellectual challenge of Christianity, and is an interesting indication of the direction Julian's thoughts were taking in the early months of 362. There was to be no violence, no force. The tide of Christianity, that threatened to overwhelm a culture already more than a thousand years old would be turned. But it would be turned by rational argument. And what mattered was to win the assent of the educated upper classes of the cities. The others would follow their natural leaders.

To these same early months in Constantinople belong two of Julian's own works, which throw some light on his attitude to religious problems. The Cynics, who traced back their intellectual pedigree to that Diogenes, who told Alexander the Great to get out of his light, had not taken part in the fusion of the schools of philosophy in late antiquity. They continued to be the anarchistic drop-outs of ancient society, mockingly critical of all its values and institutions, ostentatiously simple in their style of life, with nothing positive to offer in place of what they demolished, and by now politically and socially ineffectual. In a sense they provided a safety valve for the intellectual discontents of an age of transition. Their destructive criticism of traditional religion made them up to a point the natural allies of the Christians, and Christian leaders like Gregory of Nazianzus treat with considerable respect some of these rather exhibitionist critics of established order. One such was Herakleios, who had already made something of a name for himself at Constantius' court in Milan. Early in 362 he presented himself at Constantinople and asked permission to give a lecture in the presence of Julian, who was not at all eager to listen to him. However in due course he yielded to Herakleios' importunities and attended his lecture. Julian was shocked by the blasphemy of Herakleios' style and the negative conclusions of his paradoxical arguments. That was only to be expected. What was unexpected was that he shortly afterwards gave a public lecture himself in which he refuted Herakleios' views and expounded his own. The gesture was typical of Julian's intensity of purpose, his neglect of protocol, and his almost overpowering need to communicate. It was the first of a series of such public lectures on controversial topics that he gave. Some contemporaries felt that he was demeaning the imperial dignity and so hindering the proper functioning of the State by his conduct. Others found his directness and sincerity appealing, and a welcome change from the hypocrisy of official communication under his predecessors.

The text of Herakleios' lecture is lost, that of Julian's reply survives. It is quite a long work, and goes much further than merely replying to Herakleios. Julian's contemporaries noted his great ability in controversy, and his ability to make his adversary's position appear ridiculous. So it would be unwise to reconstruct Herakleios' arguments in any detail from Julian's critique. What Julian objects to, apart from the blasphemous tone, is the dismissal as ridiculous of the traditional myths about the gods, the confusion that the Cynics cause in society – an interesting testimony from a hostile source – and the discrepancy between their moral pretensions and their conduct. He goes on to give his own interpretations of some of the myths, which were probably those current in Neoplatonist circles, and to outline his own intellectual and moral development as a kind of allegory of the descent of the divine to man and the corresponding ascent of the soul to God. The Cynics he compares with the monks who were just beginning to appear among the Christians, men who for the most part have nothing to lose and who gain many material advantages from their pretended asceticism. His own rise to power he saw as the work of the gods; he was a man of destiny. But the power they had given him was one based on reason, not on force. He was to treat his friends as friends, and not as servants, and his subjects as children, passing on to them the love given him by the gods, and sure of their present help at every moment. He goes on to pay a compliment to Maximus, the teacher who had initiated him into the mystery-religion of the Neoplatonists, and who had recently joined the court at Constantinople. And he finishes by reminding Herakleios that Diogenes himself was a devout servant of the gods. What emerges most strikingly from this curious work is Julian's powerful sense of mission, which keeps uneasy company with his natural kindness and unaggressiveness.

A little later, probably shortly before 21 March 362, Julian composed, in the course of a single night, his treatise on the Mother of the Gods. Whether it was publicly recited we do not know. But it would certainly be circulated widely among the emperor's friends and associates. What Julian does is to set out the Neoplatonist interpretation of the strange oriental myth of Attis, the youth who was loved by Cybele, the mother of the gods. Cybele keeps him to herself. But Attis falls in love with a nymph, runs away, and lives with her in a cave in the mountains. After a time he is struck by remorse at what he has done, castrates himself, leaves his genital organs with the nymph and returns contrite to the Mother Goddess, who in due course makes him whole again. It was probably in origin a fertility myth. But it had already been subject to accretions and distortions of all kinds. And it had been allegorically explained by generations of commentators of Stoic background, who gave it a physical or moral interpretation. Julian takes this curious story, which centuries earlier had provided Catullus with the starting-point for one of his most powerful poems, and gives it a Neoplatonist metaphysical interpretation. For him it is an oblique description of the descent of creative intelligence from the transcendent world to the world of matter and its return towards the intelligible god from which it took its being. If Julian emphasizes that this is not something that happened once, in history, but something that has always been happening and will continue to happen for all eternity, the universe being indestructable, it is probably in order to emphasize his opposition to the Christian historical account of the descent of God to earth. The treatise involves much allegorical interpretation of details of the story, and presupposes a philosophical understanding that only the most highly educated possessed. Julian lays down in the treatise some principles of ritual abstinence for the pious pagan. No root vegetables, no pomegranates, no fish except on special occasions, no pork. All these prohibitions are found in one cult or another. What Julian and his Neoplatonist friends are doing is to pool them together to provide the kind of dietary prohibition that would give a sense of unity to the Neoplatonist pagans and satisfy certain traits in the mental make-up of most men.

Finally in early June 362 Julian published a third treatise on philosophy, occasioned by the lecture of a Cynic on Diogenes, who had been for centuries the type specimen of the Cynic. Most of the treatise, entitled *On the Ignorant Cynics*, is devoted to an examination of Diogenes' life, as traditionally recounted. His immediate object is to show that Diogenes was in fact a devout man, animated by the same principles as Plato, with whom he was traditionally contrasted, and that the fourth-century Cynics were hypocrites and charlatans who had misunderstood and distorted the heritage of their great master. What emerges from his argument is his belief in the fundamental unity of all Hellenic philosophy, with the exception of the now virtually extinct Epicureans and the Pseudo-Cynics, of whom the lecturer he is attacking was one. Julian is not a tough-minded philosopher. Few of the fourth-century Neoplatonists were. Like them Julian likes to paper over fundamental differences and to represent everything in the roseate glow of a unity in which outlines are blurred. He was anxious that defenders of pagan Hellenism should present a united front against the main enemy in Christianity. His treatise *On the Ignorant Cynics* is best interpreted as a contribution to that end, and an attempt to rally to Neoplatonist mysticism what he probably regarded as the moderate wing of the Cynics. It is a tribute to the strength of radical criticism of established order. Its impact, however, must have been limited to the highly literate, whose political importance Julian always exaggerates. Compulsive communicator though he was, he had not found a way to speak to the common man and win his allegiance. Or rather, the only situation in which he could do this was on the parade-ground and the field of battle.

A few days after publishing, or himself delivering, this address, he was *en route* for Antioch and the Persian front.

8 Antioch

THE EMPEROR and his party lost little time in traversing Asia Minor. The Roman military road followed a natural route used by the Persians 900 years earlier and by the Hittites before them. From Chalcedon, across the Bosphorus from Constantinople, it led through Nicomedia (Izmit), Nicaea (Iznik), and thence eastwards to Ancyra (Ankara). Before reaching Ancyra Julian made a detour to the south to visit the ancient temple of Cybele at Pessinus (near modern Sivrihisar), in the foothills of Mount Dindymus. At Ancyra there seems to have been a hostile demonstration by local Christians, as a result of which a priest named Basil was sentenced to death. Julian soon pressed on, probably taking the road that skirts the glittering salt flats of the Tuz Gölü, avoiding the double crossing of the River Halys (Kízílírmak), to reach Tyana (Kíz Hísar), between Niğde and Ereğli, at the southern border of Cappadocia. From there began the only good road across the formidable barrier of the Taurus Mountains, over the pass known as the Cilician Gates, to Tarsus in the smiling fertile plain of Eastern Cilicia, where the emperor made a brief halt. From Tarsus onwards it was easy going, through Adana and Mopsuestia (Ceyhan) to the coast at Aegae (Yumurbalik), then round the head of the gulf of Iskenderun, past Issus, where Alexander the Great had defeated Darius almost 700 years earlier, and over an easy pass through the Amanus mountains. As he emerged from the pass on 18 July, Julian saw for the first time the walls and towers of Antioch, gleaming in the summer sun. He had marched 700 miles from Constantinople and entered what was for him a new world.

Lying astride the river Orontes below its sharp bend to the south-west, Antioch vied with Alexandria for the title of third city of the empire.

Founded in 300 BC by Alexander's general Seleukos, it was by the fourth century AD a major centre of industry and trade, as well as of Greek culture, the administrative key point of the Roman east, and the base for military operations against Persia both in Mesopotamia and in Armenia.

The site is eye-catching. About twenty miles from the sea, the city itself lay on level ground, its centre on an island in the Orontes. But immediately to the south-east Mount Casius rose steeply to a height of some 5000 feet. The city walls ran up and down two of its precipitous spurs, high above the habitations in the valley below. About five miles to the north-west rose the heights of Mount Amanus, an offshoot of the Taurus Mountains. The city was linked with Cilicia and Asia Minor through a pass in this mountain range. The plain in which the city lay, ten miles long and five broad, was very fertile and intensively cultivated. The lower slopes of the mountains were terraced for vines and dotted with the summer residences of the well-to-do citizens. Their higher slopes were the domain of shepherds, whose solitude was only now being invaded by Christian hermits.

Like all ancient cities, Antioch controlled an extensive rural territory, extending nearly to Beroea (Aleppo) in the east, and for some twenty-five miles to the south. Its area has been estimated at some 2500 square miles. Any estimate of the population of Antioch is largely guess-work for us, as it was for contemporaries of Julian. A recent study puts the population of the city itself in the fourth century at about 150,000, while another 400,000 may have lived in the city territory (J. H. W. G. Liebeschütz, *Antioch: City and Imperial Administration in the Later Roman Empire* (1972, 41, 92–100)). And it was a population that was growing, as the smaller cities of the Roman east decayed and their citizens moved to the flourishing capital of the region.

Yet Antioch was essentially an agrarian community. By far the greater part of the wealth of its citizens came from the cultivation of land in the city territory. The share of industry and commerce was small. And the political and social importance of manufacturers and traders was negligible. A closer look at the various groups within the population of the city will make clearer what the possibilities open to Julian were, and what avenues were closed to him.

At the head of Antiochene society stood an upper class of landlords, owners of larger or smaller estates in the territory of the city. They were not in general agricultural entrepreneurs. Most of their land was leased to peasant cultivators, while the landlords lived from rents rather than profits. The principal exception to this rule would be the 'home farm' from which a landlord would get fresh fruit and vegetables in season. A landlord might engage in quite large-scale commercial transactions. But these would arise out of his ownership of property. They would not be ends in themselves. Libanius, for instance, sent an agent to Apamea to sell produce from his land near Antioch, and he sold wine in nearby Cilicia, from which he bought timber for building on his property in the city. Landlords lived in the city, and rarely visited their estates, even in the heat of summer. They preferred to build villas in the cool suburb of Daphne, only a few miles from Antioch. In this respect they were very different from their counterparts in Italy and the west, who lived on their estates as well as from their estates.

On the whole the rich had no occupation. Their lives must have been spent largely in idleness or in factitious activities. They did, however, provide recruits for the learned professions, above all rhetoric and law. The practitioners of these arts enjoyed high social status, and their professional emoluments could be considerable. Their skills, too, were useful to their colleagues among the landowning class. A case in point is Libanius, himself among the wealthiest of Antiochene landowners, who taught rhetoric in his native city and was by the 360s recognized as the most distinguished man of letters in the Greek world. The imperial civil service also drew many recruits from the landowning upper class of such cities as Antioch. The less wealthy became *officiales*, pursuing a career in one or other of the local or central departments. The wealthy and influential had no career; they went straight to provincial governorships or more elevated posts. Civil servants enjoyed rich emoluments, security and extremely high social status. They also avoided some of the burdens that fell upon their colleagues at home. For it was from this class that the city council was recruited.

Far more numerous than the landowners were the city tradesmen. In most cases they made the goods that they sold; there was no distinction between manufacture and selling. These tradesmen-manufacturers were small men, working with the aid of their families and perhaps one or two slaves. For all the importance of Antioch as an industrial centre, there were no captains of industry among its citizens. Indeed there were probably no industrial buildings as such. Men worked where they lived, and lived where they worked. Workshops, booths and shops were found all over the city. The concentration of trade in a bazaar was a much later development. Among this section of the population must be counted also the bankers and money-lenders. They too were relatively small men. And their main function was not the provision of credit. Antioch, like other ancient cities, had no equivalent of the merchant prince or the wealthy banker of the towns of medieval Europe. The social status and political influence of this whole class was low. They were separated from the landlords by the great divide of late Roman society between *honestiores* and *humiliores*. A merchant, shop-keeper or banker was a *humilior*, and as such subject to degrading – and dangerous – physical punishments.

The labour force on the land was provided by peasants. If Antioch was a Greek city, those who cultivated its fields were not Greek. Syriac was the language of the villagers, most of whom knew no Greek at all. In fact Syriac was also widely spoken and understood within the city walls. As a recent writer puts it, there was much 'shame-faced bilingualism'. Even the great Libanius on at least one occasion betrays his knowledge of Syriac. The peasantry had of course to visit the city to sell their produce and to buy such few manufactured goods as they needed. But their visits were clearly rare, and were discouraged by the authorities. Men might spend their lives tilling the soil within sight of the walls of Antioch and have no point of contact at all with the life of the city. The precise legal situation of the peasants is not clear. They probably held their plots of land on leases, often share-cropping leases, the terms of which might include the provision of labour services on the landlord's home farm. They do not seem to have been legally tied to the soil, as were their counterparts in some other provinces of the empire. But custom can be as powerful as law, and it seems to have been very unusual for a landlord to evict a tenant or for a tenant to leave of his own accord. In the plain of Antioch the life of the peasants was probably poverty-stricken and squalid, and their homes may have been no more than huts of reeds. Further east, on the limestone uplands, we find large villages with substantial stone houses. These villages owed their prosperity to the monoculture of the olive, which was in part destined for distant markets.

Some of the long-distance trade routes to the east – to India and China – passed through Antioch, and we hear of Antiochene exports to the west, particularly textiles and glass-ware. But there is no sign of substantial merchants engaged in import and export. The caravan trade across the desert to Persia was probably in the hands of the largely Arabic-speaking nomad herdsmen. Long distance trade to the west would be carried on as an incidental activity by the *navicularii*, substantial landowners who were obliged to provide a ship to ensure the corn supply for the capital.

The government of the city was in the hands of a small hereditary oligarchy of the richer landowners, who formed the council. This was all that remained of the civic constitution of the early empire, with its assembly of the people, council and elected magistrates. The assembly had withered away – or been destroyed – in most cities by the end of the first century AD. Even its electoral functions had been taken over by the council. Such magistrates as survived became mere members of the council, appointed to carry out its decisions. The chaos of the third century was brought to an end by greatly strengthening the central government, which took over many of the functions formerly performed by city authorities. By the middle of the fourth century the old balance between local initiative and central policy had been irreversibly changed. The role of the council at Antioch was reduced to collecting taxes, spending money made available to it by the central authorities, and advising the governor. It was the governor – either the *consularis Syriae* or his superior the *comes Orientis*, both resident at Antioch – who made decisions. The council was expected to carry out these decisions in so far as they concerned the internal affairs of the city. If things went wrong, its members were individually and collectively responsible. When in 387 a riotous crowd tore down some statues of the emperor, everyone in Antioch expected that members of the Council would be arrested and executed. In 303 when the citizens of Antioch fought and defeated a mutinous military unit, Diocletian executed a number of the leading councillors, though there was no suggestion that they were responsible either for the mutiny or for the resistance to it. Things were bound to go wrong often, as the Council had no real coercive power. There was a small police force armed with cudgels, and a body of archers. But they were not effectively controlled by the council. And it had no bureaucracy to carry out its decisions, as had the central government. The situation of the council was one of responsibility without power. It is not surprising that those rich enough or poor enough often tried to avoid the dangerous obligations of membership. Yet there were still rich pickings to be made, and membership of the council carried great social prestige.

The revenues of the city came mainly from the rents of civic land, that is to say land in the territory of the city that was not in individual ownership but belonged to the city, as a legal personality. This land was taken over by the imperial government in the first half of the fourth century as part of the process of centralization of power. No doubt it was alleged, and perhaps rightly, that the civic lands were being misused by councils composed of local landowners. This did not mean, it seems, that the council was wholly deprived of its main source of revenue. But the governor and his civil servants decided how much they received, and when, and for what purposes. Thus the initiative of the city authorities was still further limited. It is significant that most public works seem to have been undertaken by the central government rather than by city authorities. One of Julian's early measures as emperor had been to restore the civic lands to the city authorities.

Some vestige of the earlier democratic set up remained in the sixteen tribes into which the population of the city was divided. Despite their name, these were probably local subdivisions. They had minor powers to deal with such matters as street lighting, obstruction of the highway and the like. And they may well still have had elected officers. But they counted for nothing.

Such was the city in which Julian established his court and his military headquarters in the summer of 362.

Julian expected much from Antioch. It was a flourishing Hellenic city of ancient tradition, with an apparatus of self-government, unlike Constantinople, which was a new foundation with a large Latin-speaking element in its population and governed directly by an imperial official. It was a centre of art and letters, to which young men came from all over the Greek world to pursue an education in literature. It was the home of Libanius, the most distinguished man of letters of the age and a pagan, whom Julian had admired as a young man in Nicomedia and whom he was to meet face to face. Here, if anywhere, he would find that vigorous traditional civic life without which the government of the empire was doomed to become a tyranny. Here he would find in full flower that combination of religious observance, philosophical speculation and literary culture that he yearned for. Refreshed and inspired by Antioch he would march east like a new Alexander to conquer the age-old enemy. At the same time he would be following in the footsteps of a long line of Roman commanders, from Lucullus to Trajan, from Aurelian to Constantius, who had marched out from the firm bastion of Antioch to defend or enlarge the frontiers of the empire. He may also have been eager to win the support of the large and influential Jewish community of the city as part of his campaign against Christianity. Gamaliel, the son of the Jewish patriarch Hillel II and later patriarch himself, was a friend of Libanius.

E.J.—6

In the outcome Julian found nothing in Antioch but frustration and disappointment, and was glad to shake the dust of the city from his feet eight months later. Historians have spoken about unbridgeable differences in temper between the austere young emperor and the frivolous Antiochenes. This kind of explanation, in which there is probably an undertone of western contempt for the 'oriental', will not do. Julian may have formed a slightly idealized picture of Antioch. But on the whole he must have been well informed about a city in which he had many friends. And a man who had succeeded in keeping on good terms with the citizens of Athens, Vienne, Paris and Constantinople was not prevented by any defect of character from establishing friendly relations with those of Antioch. He had already appointed his maternal uncle and close friend Julian as *comes Orientis*, and is likely to have been informed by him of the situation in the city.

The reasons for the failure of Julian in Antioch lay deeper. In the first place Antioch was not only a Greek city, it was a Christian city. The origins of the Christian community there could be traced to apostolic times. By the middle of the fourth century the Christians were perhaps a majority of the inhabitants of the city itself. John Chrysostom, preaching in Antioch some twenty years after Julian's death, speaks of the city as containing 100,000 Christians. This may have been guess-work or wishful thinking: but when he tells his congregation that the Christian Church maintained 3000 indigent persons in the city he is likely to have had reliable figures to work from. In Julian's time the proportion of Christians will not have been much less. Many of the leading families in the city had been Christian for generations. Thalassius was one of the wealthiest citizens of Antioch. His estates were spread over a number of provinces of the Roman east from Asia to Egypt. His daughter was married to a wealthy landowner of Cyrrhus. His son Bassianus was an imperial notary and a man of power and influence in Constantinople. His mother-in-law Bassiana was an aunt of Libanius. Thalassius himself had held an exalted position in Constantius' court, and had been Praetorian Prefect of the East from 351–353, during which period he sent unfavourable reports to Constantius on Julian's brother Gallus. Thalassius was dead by the time Julian came to Antioch. But his son, also called Thalassius, had inherited his estates and his influence on the city. The family was Christian, and had probably been Christian for generations. Its case is typical enough. There was probably no major city in the empire in which Christianity had made so much headway among the leaders of society, as at Antioch, and had so profoundly affected the life-style of the society as a whole. The younger Thalassius was obliged by Julian to rebuild a temple which the family had converted for use as a house, and forced to enter the city council, from which his father had successfully escaped.

Here, then, was one source of Julian's inability to come to terms with the situation in the city. His own Antiochene friends were mainly pagan, whether Neoplatonist enthusiasts like Julian's fellow-student at Athens, Celsus, now governor of Syria, or traditionalists for whom religion was a part of their ancestral culture, like Libanius. They may well have given him a somewhat one-sided view of the life and interests of their fellow-citizens.

Julian's acquaintance with civic organization in the empire was limited to Constantinople, which had virtually no civic government, and the cities of Gaul, where it had never recovered from the devastations of the previous century, and was in any case something of an alien growth. He knew of the lively local political life of the Greek cities of the east largely from literature. The speeches of Dio Chrysostom and Aelius Aristides reflected an age in which the division of responsibility between city government and imperial government was fairly clear. Neither could function without the other. A man could have a distinguished and satisfying career in either. And some men, in particular the so-called sophists, moved in both worlds, representing the views of their cities and provinces before the emperor and explaining to their fellow-citizens the problems that faced the holders of imperial power. Though Julian was well aware of the changes that had taken place since then, he probably hoped to find in the council of Antioch a body of men still retaining a spark of the old fire. In fact he did not. The position of the council was weakened by the presence in Antioch not only of the provincial governor of Syria but also of his superior the Count of the East, whose sphere of responsibility extended to the whole eastern sector of the empire. These powerful officers, with their establishment of civil servants, not only overawed the local council; they often overruled it. And within the council itself a process of differentiation had set in. The wealthier families were withdrawing from their civic responsibilities by one means or another and transferring their activities to the larger theatre of imperial affairs. Thalassius is a case in point. There were many more. Thus the very men who in the past had been the leaders of local political life were turning their backs on it. At the same time the poorest landowning families were finding it more and more difficult to meet the obligations of council membership, and were escaping, some to the minor ranks of the civil service, some to the law, some to the Church. Theoretically these escape routes were blocked. In practice many used them. So the council that Julian found, and the men who composed it had limited initiative, and limited prestige in their own society, and were faced with constant defections at top and bottom. It was all very unlike the world of Dio Chrysostom and Aelius Aristides.

A more immediate source of trouble was economic. Since Constantius began his operations against Persia in 360 the city had been the principal Roman military base. The main body of the army was stationed outside the city, nearer the frontier. But Antioch itself was full of soldiers and civilian officials. In a speech made in 360 Libanius graphically describes the new situation:

> There flowed into it [that is to say the city], as rivers flow into the sea, all the infantrymen, all the archers and cavalry, chargers and pack horses, camels and artificers. The ground was hidden by them as they stood or sat, the walls were covered with suspended shields, spears and helmets were to be seen everywhere, on all sides was noise and confusion and the neighing of horses. So many were the regiments stationed in the city that their officers alone would have been no mean addition to the population. So great was the assembled host that anywhere else it would have exhausted the water supply by what it drunk. But every citizen welcomed the soldiers as if they had been long absent kinsmen. Every dwelling-house became a kind of natural cave of refuge. There was an abundance of food, as if it were not produced by human design and labour, but made ready by the divine power of the gods [Libanius, Oration 11.178].

Behind the flowery periods of what was essentially an exercise in public relations there can be discerned the disquiet of the citizens with billeting and requisition. Ancient armies were not, as their modern counterparts sometimes are, big spenders. They were supplied with food and fodder largely by compulsory purchase at prices fixed by the government. When one bears in mind the high cost of transport over even very short distances by land, it becomes clear that there must have been a shortage of basic foodstuffs on the market at Antioch and a consequent rise in prices. When Julian came to power at the end of 361 a delegation from Antioch came to Constantinople to pay its respects to the new ruler. We do not know what requests or complaints it made. But we do know that Julian responded by enrolling 200 additional citizens in the council and by granting a special remission of taxation to Antioch over and above the general cancellation of arrears of tax with which he marked his accession to power. The former step would spread the financial burdens of council membership wide and would draw more citizens into such decision-making as was possible under the watchful eye of the Count of the Orient and governor of Syria. The latter suggests that the Antiochenes had special economic problems over and above those of the rest of the empire. We cannot today estimate the seriousness of the situation. Men always tend to exaggerate their misfortunes. But it is clear that by the time Julian arrived in Antioch in July 362 the citizens were edgy and discontented, mistrustful of the authorities and obsessed by their grievances. A local drought at the end of 361 had affected the crop of winter-sown wheat, and the harvest of May and June 362 had been a poor one.

When, on the day after his arrival the emperor appeared in the theatre he was greeted by cries of 'everything plentiful, everything dear'. The city landowners, the very stratum from which the Council was selected, had been hoarding their crops rather than putting them on the market in the hope of a further rise in corn prices. Their barns were overflowing with grain, while daily the cost of food went up. It was a familiar picture in the ancient world. On the day after the demonstrations in the theatre Julian summoned a meeting of the leading citizens, as well as of certain artisans and retail traders. An undertaking seems to have been given that the city authorities would take measures to get the corn on to the market and force prices down. At the same time the emperor undertook to reduce the establishment of his court. A measure dated 18 August 362 (C.Th.6.21.4) orders all functionaries not actually on duty to cease drawing rations and to return to their homes.

Julian recalled from his readings in the literature of the Antonine age how the councils of cities had regarded themselves as responsible for ensuring stable food prices. This was part of the system of social distribution that marked the ancient city. He hoped that the Antiochenes, now that their council had been strengthened, would cope with the situation themselves and leave him to get on with his preparations for war.

Whether the crisis was one that could have been dealt with by the authorities of a single city is open to doubt. But the leading men of Antioch did not even try to deal with it. They had lost the sense of civic responsibility of their ancestors. And there was too sharp a conflict between their interest as landowners and their duty as councillors. Nothing happened for three months. As winter approached Julian decided that he would have to take action himself. He imported grain from outside the city territory, beginning with 400,000 'measures' from the rich agricultural land between Antioch and the Euphrates, around the cities of Chalcis (Kennisrin, near Aleppo) and Hierapolis (Membidj). This probably involved the use of the army supply organization and army transport. Later he supplemented this local grain by three successive deliveries from imperial estates in Asia Minor, and finally had supplies brought from Egypt, supplies that had probably been originally earmarked for Constantinople. At the same time as augmenting the supply Julian fixed the selling price of bread grains as two-thirds of what it had been. But price control of durables without rationing is ineffective, and the organization for public distribution of cheap or free corn or bread that had once existed in Antioch had collapsed in the chaotic years of the third century. Speculators – who were often enough agents for the councillors and other well-to-do landlords – bought up corn at the fixed price in the city markets and either held it back in the hope that price-control would fail or sold it in the countryside where it was impossible to enforce the controlled price. Some of the corn merchants complained that they were caught between the rising price charged by the landowners for corn and the fixed selling price, and went out of business. The council was uniformly hostile to the whole project of a controlled market, and Libanius, for all his friendship and admiration for Julian, declares that only the inspiration of an evil demon can have led him to take so shocking a step.

The problem was not one of general inflation, such as had occurred in the late third century. It was the much simpler one of food prices rising in a situation of shortage, with the inevitable accompanying hoarding. It had often enough been solved by the cities of the empire in the past. But in the fourth century there was neither the will nor the means to stabilize grain prices. It seems to have been impossible in Antioch to distribute cheap food in the form of bread – which cannot be hoarded – rather than as grain – which can – though this was the principle applied in Constantinople. By the end of February 363 prices were still high, food was still scarce, and tempers on both sides were growing more and more frayed.

The enlargement of the council, which Julian had ordered when he first came to power, had not worked as he expected. We hear of men of substance evading membership, of speculators and other doubtful characters being appointed. It is difficult to know how seriously to take such charges.

But Julian took them seriously, and repeated them in his writings. By a decree of 28 August 362 he tried to enrol as council members all those whose fathers or grandfathers had been councillors. Nothing much seems to have come of this. The scope for prevarication was too great. But the mutual distrust and dislike between the young emperor and the upper class of Antioch grew more violent and unbridgeable. That very order in Antiochene society to which he had looked for collaboration and understanding proved the least able to comprehend his purposes and the least willing to work with him for their realization.

Meanwhile the economic crisis dragged on, impoverishing still further the urban poor and enriching at any rate many among the city landlords. A further 20 per cent reduction was made in the land-tax payable by Antioch, in the vain hope that it would lead to a reduction in prices. And 3000 lots of land that since Constantius' time had been held by the imperial government and apparently lay uncultivated were distributed to the leading citizens, so that the revenues from them might be used to provide chariot races. They would also presumably contribute to the city's food supply. This step, Julian tells us, was taken in response to popular requests. It may therefore have won him some sympathy, if only from the cultivators of the new allotments. But as a remedy for the city's economic problems it could have only a long-term effect.

In general Julian's relations with the citizens and council of Antioch on economic matters led only to tension and recrimination on both sides. The kind of solution that would have challenged the position of the city landowners could have only been carried out by a use of force such as Julian was not prepared to make, and would have destroyed the very class to which he looked for support in turning back the clock and restoring the glories of the past. Julian was caught on the horns of a dilemma.

The unpopularity caused by his economic measures reinforced that which his militant paganism brought him in a city so largely Christian. It is probably no accident that his imposition of price control was almost immediately followed by the burning down of the temple of Apollo in nearby Daphne. This was thought by many at the time to be the work of the Christians and an act of revenge for the disinterment of the remains of the martyr Babylas, which had been transferred to Daphne by Julian's brother Gallus. It certainly exacerbated feeling between the emperor and the mass of the citizens and drove Julian to take up a more intransigent position than he might otherwise have wished. The story will be recounted in detail in the following chapter.

One of the factors that aggravated the economic situation was the absence of any intermediate coins between the stable and valuable gold pieces – *solidus*, half-*solidus* and third-*solidus* – and the practically valueless bronze or copper small change. The unit among these was the *nummus*, a squalid and minute piece of metal of which 6000 theoretically went to the *solidus*, though often the exchange rate was less favourable. There were also coins of ten *nummi* and twenty-five *nummi*, whose value also tended to fall against gold. Julian while he was in Antioch began to issue a new coin of silvered bronze probably equal to a hundred *nummi*, as an attempt to bridge the gap between the gold money of the rich and the copper money of the poor. The people of Antioch, he tells us, found fault with the new coins. The burden of their complaint concerned the design. They did not like the emperor's bearded portrait – practical men were clean shaven – nor the pagan symbolism of the reverse design. Julian could do no good in their eyes.

There was no time in the eight months Julian spent in Antioch for any major public buildings to be erected. However he did offer a gift to the citizens, one that was typical of his interests and of their limitations. The library of Bishop George of Cappadocia, in which he had browsed as a youth at Macellum, and which he had ordered to be sent to him when its owner was lynched by his flock in Alexandria, at last reached him when he was in Antioch. He had it installed in the temple built by Hadrian two and a half centuries earlier in honour of his predecessor Trajan, evidently as a public library. A handful of teachers and their students may have been grateful for the gift. The mass of the citizens, rich and poor, greeted their sovereign's munificence with indifference. Or perhaps with positive hostility, since the books were burned by an angry mob shortly after Julian's death.

On 1 January 363 Julian inaugurated his fourth consulate. He had thrice held this ancient, prestigious and empty office in the reign of Constantius – in 356, 357 and 360 each time as junior colleague of the emperor. This time he chose as his colleague Flavius Sallustius, the Praetorian Prefect of Gaul, an upright pagan from Spain who was his senior representative in the west. This was a deliberate break with tradition. Neither Diocletian nor Constantine nor Constantius had ever shared the consulship with a private individual. Their only colleagues in office were their co-emperors. Julian was harking back to the second century, when an emperor would often honour one of his subjects by inviting him to be his colleague in the consulship. The gesture seems to have scarcely been noticed by Julian's contemporaries, who did not always share his sense of history.

When Julian first arrived in Antioch he had frequently been greeted with demonstrations of loyal support. The Antiochenes perhaps hoped for as much from him as he did from them. They found him strange, but intriguing, and a welcome change from the sanctimonious and remote Constantius. But by early 363 their interest had turned to indifference, and then to hostility. Lampoons against him appeared in public places. Scurrilous songs were sung about him. The Christians had naturally no sympathy for a ruler whose paganism was rapidly turning to aggressive anti-Christianity. Even non-Christians, dissatisfied with his failure to deal with rising prices and put off by his fanaticism and his air of contempt for the common man, grumbled against him. They mocked at his beard, at his chastity, at his preoccupation with books, at his obsession with sacrifices. Julian reacted by withdrawing more and more into the inner circle of his philosopher-friends, and making fewer and fewer public appearances. This only made matters worse. In the meantime his sense of isolation was increased by the death of several of his closest friends, including his uncle Julianus the *comes Orientis*. The lingering agony of his death – probably from cancer – was a source of jubilation to the Christians, who saw the hand of their God in it; for Julian had been an active supporter of his imperial nephew's religious policy.

By early 363 Julian's relations with the civic authorities at Antioch had become frigid and formal, despite the efforts of Libanius to bridge the gap. Julian was by temperament not interested in failure. Age had not yet taught him how to live with it. Antioch and its problems, which were an epitome of the difficulties facing the civil government of the empire, seemed to him less pressing than the task of teaching the Persians a lesson, and weakening if not destroying the great power to the east that disputed with Rome the control of the Fertile Crescent. The omens were good. Envoys had arrived from Egypt with the news that after a laborious and costly search, an Apis bull had been discovered, the harbinger of good fortune and victory. A swan had been captured in the marshes of the Orontes and kept in the gardens of the temple of Zeus. For it was as a swan that Zeus had come to Leda. As Julian was offering a sacrifice before the temple, at the very moment when the fire was first kindled at the altar, the swan took wing, circled the temple three times, and flew off towards the east. Those who were expert in such matters assured the emperor that Zeus himself was promising him victory over the Persians. Julian had no doubt other revelations of which we do not hear. He rejected the offer of a conference made by King Shapur, and pressed on the preparations for a major campaign.

Yet he was still a philosopher and a man of letters, and could not bear to leave the accusations of the citizens unanswered. Amid the hectic last minute preparations for battle he found time to compose his last work, the *Misopogon* or *Beard-Hater*, and posted up a copy of it at the Elephant Arch just outside the palace, for all to read and copy. It is an extraordinary exercise in public relations and a revelation of the complexity of Julian's mind. In form it is a satirical account of his relations with the people of Antioch, in which the satire is directed as much against the author himself as against his detractors. He professes to take at their face-value and admit all the accusations made against him, and by arguments based on exaggeration and paradox demonstrates their lack of foundation. He is a strange character, without any of the qualities that men seek in a ruler, he confesses, but he has been the victim of misunderstanding. Witty, wounding, utterly one-sided despite its veneer of impartiality, loaded with learned allusions and literary reminiscences the *Misapogon* must have been an enigma to most of those who took time to read it, standing beneath the triumphal arch crowned by its quadriga of elephants. And as most men distrust and dislike what they do not understand, it probably made more enemies than friends for its author. Perhaps Julian wrote it more for his own satisfaction than for its political effect. There is often a strange, dream-like quality about the pseudo-speeches of late antiquity that were never delivered nor meant to be delivered. A man may get deep satisfaction by writing down what he would never have the opportunity, or the courage, to say. It is a part of the technique of self-justification, and after eight months in Antioch Julian needed to justify himself to himself.

Within a couple of weeks of the publication of his *Misopogon* he had left the city to take command of his army in war.

9 Julian and the Christians

THE LEGISLATION of Constantine and his sons restricting or forbidding the performance of pagan rites – it is collected in the *Theodosian Code* 16.10.1–6 – did not mean the end of paganism. It is impossible to estimate the numbers of pagans and Christians in the empire at any particular time, and in any case the figures would be meaningless without more precise definition of terms. What can be done is to indicate regions, social classes and groupings, public occasions and situations in which Christian and various non-Christian practices were conspicuous. To go further and speak in terms of belief rather than practice can be at best tentative.

First the imperial household was firmly Christian. Indeed Constantine brought up his sons to be rather bigoted. Yet the Christian emperor continued to hold the ancient Roman office of *pontifex maximus*, and on occasion to take part in pagan ceremonies, provided they were of sufficient antiquity and prestige. The Roman senatorial aristocracy was still largely pagan. Their paganism had a traditionalist, antiquarian tone. But all of them were affected by the syncretistic monotheism of the age, with its emphasis on originally non-Roman cults, such as those of Mithras or of the *Magna Mater*. And some of their leaders were enthusiastic supporters of the Neoplatonist mystery-religion that had grown up among the educated classes of the east. Long after imperial legislation had forbidden public sacrifices, they continued to be performed by imperial officials in Rome. '*Cesset superstitio, sacrificiorum aboleatur insania*', thundered Constantius in an edict of 341 (*C.Th.* 16.10.2), and some years later he spelled out the details. Sacrifices were forbidden, those who performed them were to be condemned to death and their property forfeited to the State, and provincial governors who failed to carry out the provisions of the law were liable to the same penalties. Yet in 359, Tertullus, prefect of the city of Rome, offered sacrifice at the temple of Castor and Pollux at Ostia during a food shortage. He remained in office for the rest of Constantius' reign. The meetings of the Roman Senate were preceded by a symbolic sacrifice on the altar of Victory in the Senate House until it was removed by Constantius. The Lupercalia continued to be celebrated until 494. Constantinople, on the other hand, was a predominantly Christian city, founded as such by Constantine. There was no tradition of pagan ceremonies that could be perpetuated from antiquarian motives. The pagan cult sites of the old Megarian colony of Byzantium had been swallowed up by Constantine's new capital. The only temple Julian could find to visit was a small shrine of the Fortune of the city, hardly a true deity. Otherwise we hear nothing of established public pagan cult.

Throughout the empire peasants, who made up the bulk of the population, clung to their ancient rites and ceremonies. Christianity in the first three centuries of its existence, had been essentially an urban religion, spreading from city to city and leaping over the intervening countryside. In the fourth century the rural areas continued to be largely non-Christian. Even at the end of the century John Chrysostom urges the Christian landowners of Antioch to build churches and appoint priests to minister to their tenants, who are hardly touched by Christianity. And Augustine, writing around 400, complains bitterly of the open celebration of pagan rites, with singing and dancing, by the inhabitants of the little agricultural town of Calama (Guelma in Algeria). (*Letter* 91.) When the clergy protested, the church was repeatedly stoned and finally set on fire, and a Christian lynched. We hear of mass conversions in the countryside of Asia Minor under Justinian. This rural paganism gradually degenerated into peasant mummery, to be condemned by the Oecumenical Council of 680, but still going on in the twelfth century, or to be absorbed by the Church and christianized in the course of centuries, as happened with the Lupercalia at Rome, 'replaced' by the festival of the Purification of the Virgin by Pope Gelasius I in 494.

Particular cities varied very much in their religious profile. Alexandria about the middle of the fourth century seems to have been nearly equally divided between pagans and Christians, with the large Jewish community maintaining an uneasy neutrality. The great temple of Serapis was not destroyed until 385. Annual sacrifices were offered to the Nile (Mitteis-Wilcken, *Grundzüge und Chrestomathie der Papyruskunde* 1.134). At the same time the Christian population was well organized, and the first stages in the growth of the monastic movement were taking place. Both sides were fanatical, passionate, and ready to resort to violence. Antioch, the second city of the empire, was also divided, though we cannot really estimate the proportions of the two groups. Libanius gives the impression that his native city is almost wholly pagan, John Chrysostom that it is almost wholly Christian. But the one is writing in a literary tradition that ignores the existence of Christianity, the other is usually addressing a Christian congregation. At any rate there was much less tension between the two groups than at Alexandria. Sometimes two nearby cities offered very different pictures: Gaza in Palestine was predominantly pagan, its port of Maiuma only a mile or two away was largely Christian. Edessa in northern Syria was and had long been an almost wholly Christian city. Carrhae (Harran) only forty miles to the south-east was the centre of an astral religion stemming ultimately from Babylonia, which continued to be practised by virtually the whole population until centuries after the Arab conquest of Syria.

There were whole regions where one or the other religion predominated. Asia Minor was an area of early Christian missionary activity, and most of its cities at any rate were largely Christian by the fourth century. Peninsular and Aegean Greece and Macedonia were still largely pagan. It is not until the very end of the century that lamps with Christian motifs suddenly become common in the agora of Athens, though the city had long had a Christian community. Frontier provinces like Britain or Pannonia must still have been largely pagan. Mediterranean provinces were more likely to have strong and active Christian communities.

The Roman army was probably still more pagan than Christian, and certain cults, such as that of Mithras, were widely diffused among the soldiers. Much depended on the region of recruitment. Soldiers tended to carry with them the worship of the gods of their birthplace, and thereby to contribute notably to the dissemination and eventually the syncretism of cults.

Other professional groups were predominatly pagan. This is true particularly of the professional savants and men of letters of the Greek world, the rhetoricians and philosophers. It was in their circles that the curious fusion of antiquarian paganism, Neoplatonist philosophy, and the search for personal salvation took place, which gave rise to the Neoplatonist mystery cults. They were particularly linked in the fourth century with an emphasis on Hellenic rather than Roman traditions, a conscious failure to notice the Christian Roman empire of Constantine and his sons, a kind of spiritual resistance movement. Members of this group found themselves in a strange alliance with the pagan senators of Old Rome, with whom they shared a dislike for the Constantinian empire both because it was Christian and because it interfered in areas previously left to the initiative of the local upper classes. They also occasionally made common cause with the unenlightened pagan peasantry from whom they were separated by an immense social gap, and sometimes took over ceremonies and cults that were dying out in their original rural environment, practising them with an antiquarian fanaticism and interpreting them in allegorical fashion. Thus from the later fourth century we observe a revival of ancient Egyptian religious ritual taking place among the Greek or Hellenized populations of the cities, while the unhellenized indigenous peasants adopt a Christianity whose language of ritual and of intercourse is Coptic, not Greek. But in general these philosophical pagans were rather isolated. They were highly articulate professional communicators. But their message was one comprehensible only to their own kind. If they thought about the masses at all, it was in a vaguely paternalistic way. Individual salvation, not mass conversion, was their goal.

The imposition of Christianity from above, first as a tolerated religion, soon as a favoured religion, and later as the only religion that could be freely, publicly and legally practised, had created an appearance of Christianization that did not correspond with reality. In a period of mass conversion there is often little connection between formal affiliation and genuine belief. It was an age when men moved readily from one religion to another. Two generations of powerful State support had not made Christians out of the mass of the subjects of the empire. What they had done – and this was crucial – was to enable Christianity to make great progress among the upper classes who ran society at city level. Up to Constantine and Licinius' decree it had been mainly the artisan and mercantile classes in the cities who had been Christian. By Julian's accession the number of Christians among the landowning upper classes who dominated the city councils, preserved traditional culture, and had a network of contacts both with one another and with provincial and even palatine officials, had immensely grown. These men, the traditional leaders of their various communities, were beginning to move into the leadership of the Christian Church, bringing with them their habits, their values and their ability to manipulate the institutions of ancient society.

This was the situation when Julian came to power, and he at once made known his own adherence to pagan religion. What had been a secret before, if a fairly open secret, was now proclaimed to all. The head of the State was no longer committed to Christianity. Many Christians must have expected a full-scale persecution. Only a few ancients among them could remember such a thing. But the development of the cult of the martyrs had kept the concept of persecution alive in the popular consciousness, and probably even exaggerated its horrors. Similarly some of the more self-conscious urban pagans must have expected the immediate overthrow of the Christian Church. In some areas the tension must have been almost unbearable, as the two sections of the community eyed one another nervously, wondering whether it was better to wait to be attacked or to get in the first blow. In fact there was no persecution. All that emerged from the new pagan court were orders for the return of those exiled on religious grounds and for the restoration of temple property that had been illegally acquired by others. In the tension that then prevailed these edicts provided the occasion for disorders in some particularly sensitive areas. They were a great inconvenience to the Christian community and a source of joy to pagans, but they did not really change the balance of forces in the empire.

If Julian did not act with dramatic suddenness, it was not from in-difference. All our sources, including his own writings, make it clear that in the early months of his reign he was continually pondering the problem of religion, discussing it with his pagan friends, particularly the urbane and venerable Gaul Salutius Secundus, whom he had made Praetorian Prefect of the east, and from the middle of January with his old teacher Maximus of Ephesus, who had just arrived in Constantinople. Maximus was a fanatic, a devotee of clandestine ceremonies of theurgy, and probably something of a charlatan, though he may have deceived himself no less then he deceived others. It would be natural for his approach to the problem of the relation of religion and the State to be different from that of Salutius. Scholars have sometimes tried to distinguish between the two, seeing a 'moderate' period, when Salutius had the ear of the emperor, followed by a period of extremism, when Maximus exercised more in-fluence over him. There is very little support for this in the sources. And Julian's personality was a strong one, not easily dominated by this or that individual. There is progress from a more passive to a more active inter-vention by the emperor in religious matters. But it is more easily explained by the development of Julian's own thought and feeling than by the replacement of one *éminence grise* by another.

Julian's position as emperor and his power to carry out any policy, whether it concerned religion or permits to travel by the imperial post, depended on the continuing favour of the army and the military leaders, at first those who had accompanied him from Gaul, later those of the eastern armies too. He regularly addressed bodies of troops throughout his reign, and cultivated the support of the soldiers. Whether or not he retained the confidence of a group of Neoplatonist philosophers with a nostalgia for pagan religion was irrelevant. He respected them and he shared some of their ideals with a passion of which few of them were capable. But he did not appoint them to positions of any real power. The active, committed pagans whom he put in key posts are men who, like Salutius Secundus, had long and successful public careers behind them. Julian was a Greek philosopher, but he was also a Roman emperor, keenly aware of the realities of power.

Pitchforked in terrifying circumstances into the exercise of power over much of western Europe, without any of the training and experience that a prince of the imperial house might expect to have, he was preoccupied by the problems of leadership. What has to be done, and how does one get it done? How does one get it done, if possible, without bloodshed and violence, and without using the lever of fear? How does one get a society that has gone badly astray on to the right course? His handling of the problem of Constantius' counsellors and his series of administrative reforms bore witness to his sense of political realities.

What in fact was wrong with the Roman empire? Modern scholars, with centuries of hindsight, find it hard enough to explain what was happening in late antiquity. It would be too much to expect a man of the age, sharing its prejudices and its blindnesses, to come up with an answer. But clearly the empire of Constantine and his successors was not that of the Antonines. Men's wills seemed to have been sapped. Groups in society that had effortlessly performed their functions in the past were now shying away from the task. An obvious example is the city councils, whose failure to exercise leadership on a local level invited the intervention of an ever-growing bureaucracy. That bureaucracy in its turn, exposed to temptations that its predecessors had never known, became correspondingly more corrupt and cruel. The old, easy cooperation between a central ruling class and a local ruling class, each of whom had its own set of values and knew the limits of its power, had broken down. When one looked at the exercise of imperial power, it was seen to be both ineffectual and oppressive. The frontiers were constantly being penetrated by warlike peoples who left desolation behind them in what had been peaceful, well-ordered provinces. Emperors, instead of freely meeting their subjects and sharing the life-style of the most prosperous of them, had become remote, portentous beings, living fear-ridden lives behind a protective screen of eunuchs and courtiers, unable to know, let alone come to grips with, the problems of the empire. And in place of the easy-going traditional ways of relating man to man and man to god, there was now this extraordinary organization, the Christian Church. Its doctrines would have been laughable, were they not humiliating. So men of education and sincerity had thought for centuries; their arguments were still valid. The loose Christian doctrine of forgiveness after repentance removed any basis for morality. The flagrant discord between what Christians preached and what they practised led to a world of double-talk and hypocrisy. The Church had broken the ancient link between the spiritual and the secular and made men neglectful of their duties and of their responsibilities towards the society in which they lived. There would be a good deal of truth in this picture of general change since the heyday of the empire. Some distortion would be introduced by the false, idealized picture of the past that Julian shared with all his contemporaries. And the whole argument would be invalidated by the tacit assumption that change can only have been for the worse, an assumption that Julian sometimes makes openly, and that was shared by large sections of the pagan upper classes as well as by many of their Christian colleagues. In fact Julian proposed to make important innovations in the structure and functioning of Roman society. But his system of values obliged him to interpret his innovations as restoration of an imaginary past.

A historian today might look at the syndrome of symptoms that Julian found in the society of his time and seek an ultimate explanation in terms of economics, or demography, or climatic change, or challenge and response, or even birth-control or the use of lead water-pipes. A fourth-century man, pagan or Christian, was likely to find an explanation in terms of the relation of men in general or the Roman empire in particular with the higher power that he believed to govern the universe. Compared with the age of Cicero and Caesar, for instance, the fourth century was an age when religion was in the forefront of men's minds, when they were obsessed by their relations with the divine. To us this is part of the problem of late antiquity. To men of the time it prescribed the very terms in which the problem was posed. In a religious age Julian was a more than usually religious man. Whether this was an innate feature of his character, or whether it was the result of a youth in which he was prevented from forming emotional attachments with other human beings, was given no opportunity to turn his sharp intelligence to practical problems, and was often and for long periods afraid for his life, is for wiser heads to judge. At any rate Julian saw in Christianity the principal source of the corruption of the Roman State, and in the suppression or disarming of Christianity the essential precondition for its rebirth. For him Christianity meant the abandonment of that regard for reason and order that was the foundation of classical civilization. It was a return to barbarism. Scholars who see his struggle against Christianity as merely one among other administrative reforms fail to grasp the spirit of the fourth century, or to account for the extraordinary predominance of religious questions in Julian's own writings.

As well as being a visionary, Julian was a practical man. The spheres of government in which he had personal experience were defence and fiscal administration. When he found himself unexpectedly sole ruler he naturally continued what he had been doing in Gaul. His first few months of power were marked by a series of reforms of the taxation system, the imperial post, and other branches designed to stop abuses, reduce costs and redistribute burdens in a way favourable to the class of city landowners. This kind of tidy-up policy was continued in a series of enactments throughout the rest of his reign. It must be remembered too that only a fraction of Julian's legislation survived to be embodied in the Theodosian code seventy years later. In the same way he must have been thinking about the problem of the frontiers from the moment of his arrival in Constantinople. He had himself stabilized the important Rhine frontier and established a defensive system powerful enough to deter potential invaders. On a smaller scale his lieutenant Lupicinus had done the same for the less vital British frontier. The long Danube frontier from Bavaria to the Black Sea had been settled by Constantius in a series of campaigns from 351 to 359. There remained the crucial eastern frontier with Sassanian Persia. After nearly forty years of peace following on Diocletian's victory over King Narses in 297, there had been continuous Persian pressure since 335. Constantius had been unable to repeat Diocletian's triumph. Indeed his long concentration on the Danubian regions had enabled King Shapur II to strengthen his positions in Armenia and Mesopotamia. In 359 he had taken the key Roman fortress of Amida (Diyar-bakir), protecting one of the routes into Asia Minor, and in the next year Singara (Sinjar) in Mesopotamia. The Persians had not seized the opportunity of Julian's accession to make peace. Though they had not exploited their advantage in 361, their threat was poised over the eastern provinces, and in particular over Syria. The restoration of stable city life in this rich and populous region required the stabilization of the frontier. Julian did not set out for Syria until early summer 363. But the logistic planning of his Persian campaign must have begun soon after his arrival in Constantinople.

In the early months of Julian's reign the problem of religion had to take second place. But it was not forgotten. His speeches or treatises on the Mother of the Gods and on the Cynics show him feeling his way towards a systematic theology of Neoplatonist religion. Salutius' little handbook, which must have been written with Julian's encouragement, given the relation between the two men, is another pointer in the same direction. One of the weaknesses of traditional religion was its lack of any coherent doctrine under which different cults and practices could be subsumed. In earlier times it would have been impossible to formulate such a doctrine, nor would it have occurred to many to try. The flowing together and reinterpretation of traditional cults that took place in the late second and third centuries had led to a kind of non-exclusive monotheism, in which the existence of a single supreme god was not inconsistent with the worship of a variety of subordinate deities. The metaphysical interpretation of the relation between supreme and subordinate deities furnished by the Neoplatonists from Iamblichus onwards made possible the formulation of a kind of pagan credo, which could be accepted by practitioners of almost any cult, new or old. Only exclusive monotheists such as Jews or Christians, or thorough-going dualists like the Manichaeans, would find it unacceptable.

Julian never reached the point of formulating an explicit theological doctrine, but he was clearly moving in that direction. And in so doing it is hard to believe that he was not influenced by Christian example. One of the strengths of Christianity was evidently the sense of solidarity among its adherents, which depended at any rate in part on the possession of a common faith. The very diffuseness of paganism, even the syncretistic paganism of the fourth century, precluded this sense of solidarity among the mass of its followers. Only those initiated into secret cults, which gave to their followers knowledge not available to the common man, possessed the sense of togetherness that marked the Christians. As we shall see, this was not the only sphere in which Julian has been suspected of borrowing from his Christian enemies, though he naturally never acknowledges the debt. He may very well have been unconscious of it.

Julian at first hoped that if the Christian Church lost its special advantages granted it by Constantine, it would rapidly lose ground. No longer protected by its association with the State and the prohibition of most other public religious ceremonies, its doctrines and practices would be exposed to the rational criticism of enlightened opinion, and their lack of foundation revealed. Patience was not Julian's strong point, and he did not give enlightened opinion very long to do its work. More than that, he made an extraordinary error of judgement for a religious man, and one that is revealing of a weak point in his own character. Apodeictic argument plays very little part in religious conversion, though it may strengthen and support allegiance originally given on quite other grounds. Emotion is always important in conversion, and it often depends on a sense of sin and of the need for salvation pre-existing below the level of consciousness. Julian's failure to recognize this feature of his own experience suggesst that he found difficulty in facing and coping with the irrational elements in human behaviour. They had to be represented on the intellectual level by rationally valid arguments. His apparent lack of any need for sexual relations points in the same direction. He could not admit and give full play to a trait so clamantly irrational in his own psychological make-up.

It may be that the peculiar circumstances in which he had passed his childhood, deprived of close and continuing contact with any one person, had impaired his emotional make-up. His mother he had never known, and his father had been killed, perhaps before his eyes, when he was still a young child. He had been suddenly removed from the care of his tutor in his early teens. He had learned the crucial importance of distrusting first impressions. Yet he does not give the impression of a neurotic. He was at his ease in society, communicated with almost too great facility, and had no fear of making decisions. That he kept his mother's jewels and trinkets for many years and that he named after her a city that he founded – Basilinopolis near Nicaea – is evidence of a certain sense of loss, but hardly of a warped personality.

Be that as it may, Julian evidently expected more from a regime of free competition between Christianity and paganism than he got. There were some instances of apostasy, but no general swing away from Christianity. And even those committed pagans on whose support he counted were not always willing to be associated with his efforts. Some refused his invitation to join his court; others, like Eustathius of Cappadocia, who had undertaken a diplomatic mission to Persia for Constantius, came, but soon asked to be allowed to return to their city and their pupils. Preoccupied as he was with preparations for war with Persia and with the elimination of administrative abuses, Julian had still found time to ponder the problem of Christianity in Roman society. His next step was an unexpected one. On 17 June 362, when he had either already reached Antioch or was on his way there, an edict was published, of which this is the text, or at any rate the section of the text that has survived:

> Schoolmasters and teachers should excel in morality in the first place, and next in eloquence. But since I cannot be present myself in each city, I order that whoever wishes to teach should not rush hastily or uncircumspectly into this profession, but should be approved by the judgement of the council and obtain a decree of the curials, by common agreement and consent of the best men. For this decree will be referred to me to deal with, so that they may take up their posts in the city schools with my approval as a kind of higher commendation [*C.Th.*13.3.5].

There was nothing new in the imperial government concerning itself with teachers in schools. Indeed it had to, since in many cases it allowed them various immunities from taxation and the performance of civic duties. So the numbers of those enjoying such privileges was limited, the approval of city councils was required for the appointment of teachers, and so on. There is a whole body of legislation dealing with these matters.

What is unusual at first sight in Julian's edict is first, the emphasis on the moral qualities required of the teacher, and second, the obligation for city councils to submit nominations to the emperor for approval. The first of these merely spells out what everyone had always assumed, though they may not always have acted upon it. The second could be merely another example of Julian's tendency to centralize decisions. Yet this edict aroused the fury of the leaders of the Christian Church, and enlightened pagans like the historian Ammianus Marcellinus condemned it as 'inhumane and worthy to be buried in eternal silence' (22.10.7). The Christian historical tradition, hostile to Julian, always counts this law as the principal among his crimes. So there was evidently more to it than today meets the eye.

When the law was first promulgated, and especially when copies of it were received in the offices of the various provincial governors, the schools would be on holiday. Speculation must have been widespread on the way in which the law was to be applied. Was it to be a matter of formal confirmation of the decisions of city councils, or was the central government going to investigate the morals of teachers independently? What moral principles were to be applied? Was the law to apply only to teachers seeking a new appointment or was it to be retrospective in its effect? Was it to apply only to teachers appointed by and paid by municipal authorities or to private teachers as well? What kind of teachers was it to apply to? Teachers of literature, of rhetoric, of medicine, of law, of philosophy? The law was doubtless less obscure to contemporaries that it is to us, but there was plenty of room for uncertainty, and more apprehension on the part of the Christian communities.

In the course of the summer, perhaps only a short time after the issue of the edict, Julian published a rescript or official circular setting out at length the considerations that had moved him and the way in which he expected the law to be applied. It may have been in the form of a letter to some official who had asked for guidance. In fact it was an amplification of the original edict, and like the edict would be sent to all provincial governors and probably to city councils. What survives is a Greek version – the government would communicate in Greek with the cities of the east – in which there are many gaps, due perhaps to the squeamishness of Christian copyists. Julian begins by reminding his readers that true culture does not consist in a command of elegant language, but in a healthy disposition of the rational mind and in true beliefs on good and evil, beauty and ugliness. So any man who thinks one thing and teaches another is not only uncultured but also dishonest. Minor discrepancies of this kind are regrettable but tolerable. But in important matters a difference between belief and teaching indicates a fundamental defect of character, and implies deliberate deception of one's pupils. All teachers of any subject must be men of integrity, without contradictions of this kind between their public professions and their private beliefs. But this was especially crucial for grammarians and rhetoricians, who taught literature to the young and expounded classical authors. For they desire not merely to teach words, but to form the character, and claim that their subject is the philosophy of practical life. Whether their claim is true or not, they are the more deserving of commendation if they are not guilty of contradiction. Now for the classical authors the gods were the beginning of all culture, as their invocations of Hermes or the Muses shows. It is absurd for those who expound such authors to treat with dishonour the gods whom the writers honour.

But I do not on this account call on them to change their beliefs. I give them rather the choice either not to teach what they do not believe, or if they do teach, to do so honestly, and not to praise the ancients while condemning their religious beliefs. Since they live by their writings, it would be an admission that they will do anything for a few drachmae. Hitherto there were many reasons for not going to the temples, and secrecy about one's beliefs was excusable. But now that the gods have granted us freedom it seems to me absurd for men to teach what they disapprove. If they are real interpreters of the ancient classics, let them first imitate the ancients' piety towards the gods. If they think the classics wrong in this respect, then let them go and teach Matthew and Luke in the Church. . . .

This law is laid down for all teachers alike. But no pupil is to be excluded from attending school. 'For it is unreasonable to exclude from the noblest path those too young to know where they are going through fear of leading them against their will to their heritage. Yet it would have been right to heal these people against their will, as one does with madmen. But they deserve pardon. Fools are to be taught, not punished. . . .'

The rescript made it unequivocally clear that the edict was directed against Christian teachers, that its effect was to be retrospective, and that it was to apply to all teachers of grammar and rhetoric, and not only to those paid from public funds. For a Christian teacher there was no problem in expounding grammar and prosody, in analysing figures of speech and thought, in explaining allusions, and in discussing the meaning and etymology of poetic words. These formed the bulk of the task of the grammarian as set out by Dionysius the Thracian in his 'Techne grammatike'. The conflict between faith and teaching might arise in connection with the last – and for Dionysius the most important – of the grammarian's tasks, 'krinein poiemata' (to judge poems). This 'judgement' or 'evaluation' of works of literature was for the ancient world not so much a matter of aesthetics as of ethics. The tradition that the poet was a teacher and that literature, to be good, must be edifying, still dominated educational theory and practice. What sort of moral lesson was the Christian to draw from Achilles or Orestes, Oedipus or Medea? The obvious answer for the Christian teacher to make was that, like Julian himself, he interpreted the classics allegorically. The material was already at hand, amassed and systematized first by the Stoics and later by the Neoplatonists. But it is clear that Julian is not prepared to allow the Christians the same escape-route from the horns of a dilemma that he had used himself in expounding the meaning of the myth of Attis and Cybele. He has already made his mind up. The Christian teacher is presented with the choice of giving up his Christianity or giving up his job. It should be noted that any ban on

Christian pupils is expressly excluded in the rescript. The story that Julian forbade Christian children to attend pagan schools is first found in the ecclesiastical historians Socrates (*History of the Church* 3.12.7) and Theodoret (*History of the Church* 3.8.1), both writing some eighty years after the event. Julian's contemporary Gregory of Nazianzus, who bitterly criticizes the law from a Christian point of view, does not make this confusion. It is therefore probably the result of misunderstanding or malice on the part of intermediate sources rather than a charge made against Julian by contemporaries. This point is of some importance, as will be seen.

Either in the rescript itself, or more probably in separate letters, Julian exempted certain teachers from the provisions of the law. One of these was Prohairesios, a Christian of Armenian origin who taught in Athens and was one of the most celebrated rhetoricians of his age. Julian knew him personally and had perhaps attended his lectures. Shortly after his arrival in Constantinople he had invited Prohairesios to write the history of his conflict with Constantius. Prohairesios apparently pleaded that his teaching duties left him no time for such a task. He was probably wary of being beholden to Julian. To his credit he refused to avail himself of the special dispensation, but gave up his official teaching post in Athens. The only other teacher known by name who gave up his post under the provisions of Julian's edict was the Roman rhetorician Marius Victorinus, whose conversion to Christianity had made such an impression in cultured Italian society only a few years before. But it is clear that many teachers all over the empire were forced to abandon their profession. The law was enforced.

As a countermeasure against growing Christian influence among the upper classes of the cities it was well conceived. Familiarity with classical literature and ability to express oneself not merely in classicizing literary language, but in terms of a classical framework of reference and allusion was essential for any youth who wished to pursue a career in the law or in the higher civil service, or to take an active part in the public affairs of his city or province. It was also a mark of social distinction, the sign of belonging to a class. The man who had not a classical literary education lacked prestige and influence in his local community. He was excluded from the network of correspondence and recommendation that we find exemplified in the letters of St Basil as well as in those of Libanius. He could not exercise individual or collective leadership. Christian parents belonging to this class would either have to deny their sons the education traditionally associated with their station and so make them into 'outsiders', or to expose them during some of the most formative years of their life to the influence of a teacher concerned to combat Christianity. For now that the issue had been brought into the open it would be very difficult for a teacher to maintain a position of professional neutrality. If he did not draw anti-Christian lessons from the texts he studied with his class, he would lay himself open to suspicion as a crypto-Christian, and risk summary dismissal. The choice before parents was a real one. There was nothing unusual at the time in Christian youths studying under pagan teachers. Most of the great fourth-century Church fathers had done so. Had it been inconceivable or even unlikely that after the issue of the edict a Christian father should send his son to a pagan teacher, we may be sure that Gregory of Nazianzus would have made the point and accused Julian of preventing Christian children from going to school. Christian children could still go to school, and no doubt most of them continued to do so, but they would do so henceforth in an atmosphere of open conflict between the Christianity they learned at home and the paganism of the school.

Many parents no doubt kept their sons at home rather than expose them to this danger. It was for such parents that a father and son, both called Apollinarios, natives of Berytus, where the father was a teacher of grammar, tried to offer a third choice. They reasoned that what mattered in literature for the teacher was the form, not the content. If Christian material could be presented in traditional literary form, then the Christian teacher could educate his pupils in a way socially acceptable without laying himself open to the charge of dishonesty. So they set to and translated as much as they could of the Bible into the forms of classical Greek literature. The historical books of the Old Testament were transformed into an epic poem in hexameter verse, divided into twenty-four books. Other parts of the Bible became Euripidean tragedies, Pindaric odes, and comedies in the manner of Menander. The gospels and epistles were presented in the guise of Platonic dialogues. All that survives of this bizarre enterprise is a paraphrase of the *Psalms* in Homeric hexameters, and there is some doubt concerning its authorship. It is unlikely that these works were ever much used as school texts. The need for them did not last long. And as a church historian of the fifth century remarks, men preferred antiquity. Quite apart from the literary quality of the work of the Apollinarioi, which we can scarcely judge, their basic premise was false. Classical culture was not just a matter of grammatical forms and literary genres. It comprised both factual knowledge – such as mythology and history – and a whole structure of values and attitudes. The time was to come, two centuries later, when it was possible to write a textbook of grammar based on the Psalms. But by then society had changed, and the thread of tradition had worn thinner. Yet the Psalms never replaced Homer as the textbook of literary Greek during the Middle Ages; they merely offered an alternative to Homer, chosen only by a minority.

Julian's law on the school was a well-thought-out attempt to weaken the attraction of Christianity for the educated upper classes of society, to emphasize its anti-intellectual element, and to oust it from the positions of prestige and influence that it had attained in the generation and a half since Constantine. What might have happened had Julian lived to old age and maintained his edict in force is an unhistorical, albeit fascinating, question. Any attempts at intuitive answers had better be left until the whole story of Julian's life has been told. It is fair to point out here, however, that in the opinion of a hostile, but well-informed and intelligent observer, Julian was too late. Gregory of Nazianzus charges him with trying to make literature and Greek culture a pagan monopoly (*Oration* 4.102). But by the 60s of the fourth century this was clearly impossible. A whole generation of Christian men of letters had grown up. The rules of rhetoric were observed in the pulpit as much as in the theatre or the law-court. Literary Greek had become the language of the Church hierarchy, in which it conducted its voluminous correspondence and transacted the business of its councils and synods. Dogmatic arguments were set out in the terms of Neoplatonist philosophy and with a good deal of the spirit of that philosophy. It was no longer plausible to represent the Christian communities of the empire as ignorant and anti-rational, and to make of traditional culture a reserved area for pagans. Nevertheless Julian's edict caused great alarm and ill-feeling among the Christian communities, far more than the isolated cases of lynching that provided the church with a few more martyrs.

As a supplement to the edict on the schools, the emperor decided to set out systematically for the literate Greek world the arguments against Christianity. He worked at intervals on his treatise *Against the Galileans,* which seems to have been made public some time early in 363. The position of its author and the religious tension of the time guaranteed it a wide readership when it first appeared. Nearly eighty years later, when the influence of paganism had dwindled almost to nothing, Cyril, patriarch of Alexandria, saw fit to refute Julian's book in a long polemical work. But the unreality of the problem in the Middle Ages and the piety of scribes caused Julian's treatise to be lost. We can reconstruct it in part from the numerous passages quoted in full or summarized in Cyril's refutation, but we must bear in mind that Cyril is a hostile witness.

Others had written refutations of Christianity before, notably the Platonist Celsus and the Neoplatonist Porphyry, the pupil and successor of Plotinus. Julian compiles from the work of his predecessors, and adds arguments drawn from other sources, notably some used by the dualist Gnostics and dealing with the events in the Garden of Eden. In the surviving portions much is made of discrepancies between the Old and New Testaments and between the different Evangelists. The Christians are rebuked not only for having abandoned Judaism, but also for having introduced practices without warrant in the New Testament, such as the cult of martyrs. The account of the creation in Plato's *Timaeus* is set against that of *Genesis*. Pagan saviour-gods, particularly Herakles and Asklepios, are compared with Jesus. They brought salvation and help to mankind throughout the known world, while Jesus was active only in a few insignificant villages of Judea. The persecution by the Christians of those whom they treat as heretics is contrasted with their professions of universal love.

Julian was deadly serious. But his refutation of Christianity is a disappointing book, and not only because of hostile selection of passages by Cyril. Julian simply did not succeed in dominating his material. He is repetitive and woolly, unable to distinguish between the fundamental and the trivial. Throughout his life he tried hard to be a great thinker and a great writer, although nature had not fitted him to be either. The heady atmosphere of post-Iamblichan Neoplatonism, with its tendency to confuse teaching and initiation, blunted rather than sharpened his intellect. As a writer he had the good taste to reject the tinselly adornments of much contemporary rhetoric, but his talent was for satire and lampoon rather than for sustained argument. And he was always in a hurry. *Against the Galileans*, though perhaps long pondered, was written in a few months, in moments of freedom from civil administration and military preparation. Julian may have wanted it to be his greatest work. But he failed.

Julian was concerned in the last resort not so much with the discouragement of Christianity as with the encouragement of pagan cults. The crucial issue was sacrifice. Julian never missed an opportunity of participating in public sacrifice, often as an officiant. He delighted in large-scale sacrifices, sometimes offering a hundred oxen at a time. Citizens saw their emperor's hands and clothes dripping with the blood of slaughtered beasts. Some of those who had no religious objections to sacrifice found Julian's conduct undignified. Men said that if he returned victorious over Persia there would soon be a shortage of cattle. But Julian himself took his sacrificial activities with deadly seriousness. Spectators were forbidden to applaud or cheer when he appeared at a sacrifice. Acclamations on such occasions were for the gods alone.

Knowing from his youthful reading of the Old Testament that the Jews had offered animal sacrifices in the past he enquired why they did not resume this form of worship now that it was permitted and encouraged. He was told that it was not lawful to sacrifice to Yahweh elsewhere than in the Temple in Jerusalem, which had been destroyed by Vespasian and Titus three hundred years earlier. At once he gave permission for the temple to be rebuilt and offered to contribute to the cost from imperial funds. This decision he announced in an open letter to the Jewish communities in the empire, who raised money rapidly, and the work began. Julian's close friend Alypius, an Antiochene pagan, who had been *vicarius* of the British provinces when Julian was in Gaul, was put in charge of the work, with the rank of *comes*. With the aid of many Jewish volunteers, including women, the site was cleared. Those who had built houses there were probably squatters with no good title. By early in 363 work was begun on the new building. But an earthquake took place, as a result of which there was a fire in a building store, and the work was suspended. Julian was already in the field against the Persians. It is likely that the Hillelite Rabbinate was lukewarm towards a proposal that would have handed over most of their power to a High Priest. After Julian's death the reconstruction of the Temple was abandoned. Julian was certainly anxious to encourage the resumption of sacrifice. And Yahweh was in his eyes an ethnic god, responsible for the fortunes of a single people. There was room for such deities in the Neoplatonist hierarchy. But the importance that he attached to the Temple project and the rank of the official appointed to supervise it suggest that he saw in it an anti-Christian move. It was not so much a matter of favouring the Jews because they had been harshly treated by the Christians as of demonstrating by a concrete example the falsity of the Bible. Several passages in the Gospels (*Matthew* 24.2; *Mark* 13.2; *Luke* 19.44; 21.6) were usually interpreted as prophecies that the Temple would never be rebuilt.

The revival of public sacrifices, the renewed consultation of oracles and the like produced a feeling of confidence among many pagan intellectuals. Libanius, who had been unwilling to join Julian in Constantinople, welcomed him when he came to Antioch and soon became one of the personalities of the court. The rhetorician Himerius came to Antioch from Athens. There was a feeling of renewal in the air. Writing to a pagan friend in 362 Libanius asks, 'What more could one seek now that the sacred heavens have been opened to mankind?' (*Ep.* 697.3). In another letter written about the same time he expresses his joy at hearing that a friend had restored a shrine of Artemis and prays that he may hand on the cult to his children (*Ep.* 710). But Julian himself was dissatisfied, and complains of the lack of enthusiasm of his subjects for the old religion and of the poverty of the sacrifices offered. Too much depended on individual initiative or the lack of it. Julian looked back nostalgically on the past when religious ceremonies had been part of the life of cities. And he was well aware of the strength that its hierarchical organization had given to the Christian Church. He longed to give to paganism the same kind of organizational structure and to integrate it in the life of the communities of the empire.

What he would have done had he lived we cannot tell. But in the short time between his arrival in Antioch in summer 362 and his departure for the eastern front in spring 363 he took a number of steps in the direction of overcoming the fragmentation of pagan religion. First he emphasized the role of the priest. Most pagan priesthoods were not full-time professions; a man officiated at a sacrifice, and then returned to everyday life; the distinction between clergy and laity in general did not exist. A priest was not because of his position a leader in his community. Julian did all he could to elevate the position of the priest in society. He was to be assiduous in his duties, officiating at fixed hours on fixed days, and not merely to perform occasional sacrifices. He was to set an example of conduct to his fellow-citizens. As well as performing ritual acts he was to preach to those assembled at the temple, interpreting the myths to them, urging them to improve their conduct, and explaining the destiny of the soul after death, and the rewards and punishments that awaited it. He was not to engage in degrading occupations – indeed he is usually assumed not to engage in any other occupation at all. He was to avoid low or frivolous company. He was not to go to the theatre – where he would in the fourth century have witnessed not classical tragedies but the scurrilous farce of the *mimus* or the enervating ballet of the *pantomimus*. He was to read only edifying books, preferably works of philosophy, and avoid all vulgar, trivial or scabrous literature. In other words he was to behave as a Christian priest was expected to. The conclusion is inescapable that Julian models his pagan *hiereus* on the Christian clergy. Traditionally certain priests might have to avoid ritual impurity and submit to all kinds of curious limitations on their freedom of action, like those surrounding the Flamen Dialis at Rome. But there is little precedent in pagan tradition for the social and moral responsibilities that Julian places on his priests.

At the same time he tried to establish a hierarchical relationship among pagan priests. The priests of the various official cults were to be subordinate in disciplinary matters to the archpriest of their province, the archpriests in turn to Julian as *pontifex maximus*. There was some precedent for control by archpriests of cults in their province. But the ordered hierarchy that Julian seeks to establish is clearly an imitation of that of the Christian Church. It is significant that in a letter to an archpriest he describes his surveillance of subordinate priests by a verb (*episkopein*) cognate to the word for a Christian bishop (*episkopos*). The discipline exercised by the archpriests was in principle to extend to laymen too; Julian reprimands a provincial governor and excludes him from attendance at sacrifices for three months because he has illegally punished a priest. The new pagan church was to establish orphanages, hospitals, homes for vagrants and so on, so that, as Julian puts it 'we may take care of the unfortunate among our enemies, and not they of us'. The reference to Christian charitable organizations is clear, and there is little doubt that Julian was animated in part by the desire to imitate and outdo the Christians. But he was also consciously harking back to a pagan tradition of philanthropy, one particularly emphasized by the Stoics, for whom the brotherhood of man was a basic principle of conduct. What the Stoics and the Christians had in common was that they gave succour to the needy because of their need, whereas the highly developed charitable organizations of the ancient city provided food, baths, medical care, amusement, education, and so on to citizens in virtue of their citizenship. Julian's attempt to revive Stoic traditions and to copy a Christian model was a tacit admission that the cities of the empire could no longer play their old role of distributing the revenues from their territory to their members, and that the old solidarity of citizens against outsiders had been replaced by new loyalties and new common interests. Just as Constantine had contributed liberally from State funds to Christian caritative work, so Julian wished to subsidize his new pagan hospitals and homes for vagrants from the resources of the central government.

Julian's reorganization of paganism to enable it to compete effectively with Christianity remained largely a pious wish. Realization of the scheme was postponed until the eastern frontier had been stabilized. But the spirit that animated it can best be grasped in one of the many open letters on the subject that the emperor wrote in late 362 or early 363. In these documents, which are veritable pagan encyclicals, he lays down the principles that are to guide priests in the performance of their functions and outlines the position that he wishes them to occupy in society. Here is his letter to Arsacius, archpriest of Galatia:

If Hellenism [=paganism] is not making the progress it should, the fault is with us who practise it. The work of the gods is splendid and great and beyond our prayers and hopes (may Adrastea be propitious to these words of mine). For not long ago no one would have ventured even to pray for a transformation so great and so important. What then? Do we think this is enough? Do we not see that what has most contributed to the success of atheism [=Christianity] is its charity towards strangers, the care it takes of the tombs of the dead, and its feigned gravity of life? Each of these virtues, I believe, ought to be genuinely practised by us. And it is not enough for you to be such a man, every one of the other priests throughout Galatia should be the same. Appeal to them or persuade them to be serious, or remove them from their priestly offices, if instead of worshipping the gods with their wives and families and servants they permit their slaves or their sons or their Galilean spouses to show irreverence to the gods and to prefer atheism to religion. Next, instruct your priests not to frequent the theatre nor to drink in taverns nor to supervise any craft or trade which is shameful or of ill fame. Honour those who obey you, expel the disobedient.

Establish numerous hospices in every city, so that strangers may benefit from our charity, not only those of our own number, but any one else who is in need. I have already taken measures to provide you with financial resources. I have ordered thirty thousand bushels of wheat to be given you every year for the whole of Galatia and sixty thousand pints of wine. I order that one-fifth of this be spent on the poor employed in the service of priests, and that the rest be distributed to strangers and beggars who approach us. For it is disgraceful that not a single Jew is a mendicant, and that the impious Galileans maintain our poor in addition to their own, and that our needy are seen to lack assistance from us. Teach friends of Hellenism to contribute their part to such public services, and Hellenic villages to offer the first fruits of their harvests to the gods. Accustom Hellenes to acts of good will of this kind, and teach them that this has long been our task. Homer, for instance, represents Eumaeus as saying: 'Stranger, it is not lawful for me, even if a more wretched man than you should come, to treat a guest with contempt. For from Zeus come all strangers and beggars. I have little to give, but I give it from my heart.' Do not let us permit others to continue our good work, while we dishonour our cause by indifference, or rather betray our worship of the gods. If I hear of you doing this, I shall be filled with joy.

Visit governors in their homes rarely; correspond with them in writing as a general rule. Let no priest go to meet them when they enter the city, but only when they visit the temples of the gods, and that without leaving the forecourt. Let no soldier precede them within the temple, but let anyone who likes follow them. For as soon as they set foot in the sacred enclosure they become private citizens. It is you, as you know, who are in charge within the temple, since this is what divine law demands. Those who obey it are really devout, those who cling to their power are arrogant and vain [Julian, *Letter* 84].

Another project put forward by Julian at this time, though probably never realized, was for the establishment of pagan 'monasteries' and 'convents', where men and women who felt the call of religion could devote themselves to the study of philosophy and the worship of the gods, free from material cares. The model is here purely Christian, and the project owes virtually nothing to the tradition of philosophical communities like that of the Pythagoreans 900 years earlier.

As the autumn of 362 wore on Julian grew more and more dissatisfied with the slow progress of the pagan revival and lukewarm welcome that his proposals found, even among those whom he regarded as his friends. Among the cult sites that he had restored was the temple of Apollo at Daphne, a suburb of Antioch to which the citizens resorted for sophisticated amusement rather than worship.

Julian himself describes the neglect of the ancient ceremonies.

In the tenth month there is a festival established by your forefathers in honour of Apollo, and it was your duty to be zealous in your visits to Daphne. As for me, I hurried there from the Temple of Zeus Kasios, thinking that there if anywhere I should be delighted by your affluence and public spirit. And I pictured to myself, like a man seeing visions in a dream, what the procession would be like, the animals for sacrifice, the libations, the hymns in honour of the god, the incense, the youth of your city gathered about the sacred precinct, their souls enveloped in reverence for the god, their bodies dressed in white garments. But when I entered the precinct, I found neither incense, nor barley-cake, nor sacrificial victim. For a moment I was amazed, and supposed that I was still outside the precinct and that you were awaiting a signal from me, out of respect for my position as high priest. But when I enquired what sacrifice the city was going to offer to celebrate the annual festival of the god, the priest replied: 'I have brought with me from my own house a goose as an offering for the god, but so far the city has made no preparations' (Julian, *Beard-Hater* 361D–362B).

Julian at once addressed himself to the city council complaining that Antioch had done less than a poverty-stricken backwood village to honour the god, that the members of the council thought nothing of spending vast sums on dinner parties and orgies, but could not find the price of a single chicken for Apollo on his annual feast day, that they allowed their wives to hand over the family property to the Galileans, who then won the goodwill of the poor by their charitable enterprises. There is an undertone of menace in this scarifying denunciation.

When he enquired why Apollo was not producing oracles as he had in time past, he was told that it was because the sacred enclosure had been polluted by dead bodies and must be purified. Now in fact the remains of St Babylas, a bishop of Antioch who had been martyred under the emperor Decius (249–251), had been buried in a church built just in front of the temple of Apollo by no less a person than Julian's brother Gallus, who had remained a devout and rather bigoted Christian. Julian at once gave orders that the remains of the saint be removed elsewhere. When the day for the removal came the Christians of Antioch gathered at Daphne and accompanied the reliquary on its journey to one of the churches of the city. Feeling was tense. The crowd, led by the clergy, sang psalms, repeating antiphonally after each verse: 'Confused are all they who worship graven images and who put their trust in idols.' (*Psalm* 97.7.) No doubt some of them accompanied their words with threatening gestures. It was a direct insult to the emperor and his gods, and Julian lost control of himself. He ordered his friend Salutius, the Praetorian Prefect of the east, to have the ringleaders arrested. Salutius was a convinced pagan, but he did not wish to exacerbate a delicate situation. However he had to make some arrests. One of the arrested Christians, a young man named Theodorus, showed extraordinary steadfastness under torture, and the rumour spread that an angel had stood by his side as he was being flogged. Salutius returned to Julian and advised him to proceed no further in the matter. Julian, calmer now, followed his advice and released all the prisoners. A few days later, on 22 October 362, the temple of Apollo at Daphne caught fire and was burned to the ground, along with the cult statue made seven hundred years earlier by the Athenian sculptor Bryaxis. Everyone suspected the Christians, and they may well have been guilty. Another possibility put forward at the time was that votive lamps burning round the statue of a Cynic philosopher Asclepiades may have started the fire. But investigations produced no clear answer. The emperor was discomfited, and the Christians triumphant. Julian promptly rationalized his feelings by discovering that an earlier divine communication vouchsafed to him signified that the gods had abandoned the temple before the fire occurred. He also closed the octagonal Great Church of Antioch, which Constantine had built, and confiscated the golden liturgical vessels. There was little doubt in his mind who was responsible for the fire.

The fire at Daphne marks a turning point in Julian's attitude towards his Christian subjects. In his *Caesars*, a curious satirical survey of his predecessors written for the feast of the Saturnalia in mid-December 362, Constantine goes off in the arms of two personifications, Effeminacy and Debauchery, together with whom he finds Jesus wandering up and down, proclaiming to all: 'Let every seducer, every murderer, everyone under a curse, every scoundrel, come to me confidently. For I will wash him with this water, and make him immediately pure, and if he ever again commits the same errors, he has only to beat his breast and strike his head and I will make him pure again.' This is a collective libel, which implies guilt by association. It is based ultimately on such passages as I *Corinthians* 6.9–11. In the atmosphere of increased tension that ensued, there were further incidents of mistreatment of Christians, which Julian failed to deal with, as well as deliberate attacks on pagan-cult sites by gangs of Christians, some of whom were probably hoping to achieve martyrdom. Occasionally their hopes were fulfilled. The Christian Church records the names of a number of martyrs put to death under Julian. Many of these are mentioned only in late sources, and the circumstances of their martyrdom are often highly improbable. They can be dismissed as the result of error or misplaced zeal. There is however a core of well-attested martyrdoms that have withstood the criticism of sceptical historians. These include not only two officers involved in an attempt on the emperor's life – who are hardly respectable witnesses for the faith –

but also a priest and a nun in Antioch, a priest at Ancyra, another at Heliopolis in Lebanon, the man who destroyed the temple of Fortune at Caesarea, and a few others. They do not amount to evidence for any policy of active persecution.

The emperor began to deal with cities in accordance with their religious affiliations. Thus Constantia, formerly Maiuma, the port of Gaza and a Christian stronghold, lost its city rights and was attached to Gaza. This could be represented as part of the policy of restoring the *status quo ante*, since Constantia had been detached from pagan Gaza by Constantine. The same excuse could not be offered for the demotion of Caesarea, the capital of Cappadocia, which lost its city rights and reverted to its former name of Mazaka. The citizens were predominantly Christian and had long ago closed most of their temples. When the sole remaining temple, that of Fortune, was destroyed by the Christians, Julian ordered an investigation, reproached the pagan minority with being unwilling to fight for their rights, fined the city 300 pounds of gold, enrolled all the clergy in the provincial civil service, and demoted the city – which had the effect of making the citizens pay more taxes. When the inhabitants of Nisibis in Mesopotamia complained that they were unduly exposed to Persian attack, the emperor replied that they would be given no military protection at all until they abandoned their Christianity. On the other hand the citizens of Cyzicus were given everything they asked for because of their zeal for the old religion, and in addition their bishop was banished from the city together with various non-citizen Christians. The facts of each of these cases may not be exactly as they are recounted by the ecclesiastical historians. But the impression that Julian was abandoning his earlier policy of toleration of Christianity is hard to resist. In October 362 Athanasius, the Bishop of Alexandria, who had returned to the city under the provisions of Julian's law for the return of exiles, was once more banished. It was alleged by Julian that the earlier law only gave him the right to return to his city, not to take up his bishopric again. The true reason was probably the resistance to the emperor's religious policy led by this uncompromisingly combative prelate, whose return to Alexandria had not divided the Christians, as Julian probably hoped it would. This action made Julian hated by the turbulent Christians of the city.

In Antioch itself there was much to frustrate Julian. Some of his closest collaborators in the campaign to revive the old religion were no longer with him. His uncle Julianus, the *comes Orientis*, died early in 363. The Christians said his death was a punishment for having taken part in the seizure of

Church property of Antioch a little earlier. The persuasiveness of this interpretation was strengthened by the death about the same time of Felix, the Count of the Sacred Largesses, who had been involved in the same confiscation. Felix had been converted to Neoplatonist paganism by Julian and become one of his most trusted advisers. At the same time hostility to the emperor was growing among the population of Antioch. The Christians were naturally opposed to him. Few of the pagans shared his enthusiasm or were interested in making proselytes. And his firm control of profiteering angered the commercial classes. It was whispered behind his back, and sometimes declared before his face in the anonymous safety of the crowd, that he was a boor, a narrow-minded pleasure-killer, unfit for human society. Others alleged that his endless sacrifices were excuses for debauchery with women of ill-fame. 'Chi and Kappa have done us no harm', said the citizens, and it needed no great perspicacity to discern beneath these initials Christ and Constantius. His personal appearance was ridiculed, in particular his beard, the mark of the philosopher in a world of clean-shaven practical men. Men called him the butcher because of his insistence on himself slaughtering sacrificial animals.

All of this was probably trivial. But Julian had learnt to enjoy public approval in his days as Caesar in Gaul, and he could not do without it. In particular he had hoped for more understanding in Antioch, one of the great centres of Hellenic culture. Had he perhaps forgotten that it was also the seat of one of the oldest Christian communities in the Roman world? He felt misunderstood and hurt, and gave way more and more often to petty displays of bad temper. He threatened to leave Antioch and establish the court in another city, probably Tarsus. And before he left at the beginning of March 363 to take the field, there had been a complete rupture of relations between the emperor and the citizens. He refused to receive a deputation from the council, and it took the intervention of Libanius to patch up some semblance of concord, in spite of Julian's warning that his patience was exhausted.

There is something curiously childish in all this, though if one reflects on the matter it is probably no more childish than some of the public positions taken up by statesmen at other times. A less sensitive man than Julian would simply have ignored the grumbling and the malicious witticisms of the Antiochenes. A man more sure of the rightness of his own conduct would have soldiered on, however much he might be hurt by his lack of popularity. A more practically minded man might have decided that the restoration of the old religion was not worth so much trouble and concentrated upon other and less controversial goals. But Julian, for all the intellectual stance that he took up, was unable to examine his own goals objectively. He had had too many divine signs, heard too many voices, received too many messages from the beyond. He could only criticize the means adopted to further his ends. He seems in the months after the fire in the temple of Daphne to have come to the conclusion that his original policy of toleration, and his new policy of active encouragement of paganism and discouragement of Christianity were alike inadequate. He had misunderstood the signs given by the gods. For a man who depends as much as Julian did on the approval of transcendent beings, this is a very unhappy situation, and it explains much of Julian's tetchiness in his last months at Antioch. It is probably a factor accounting for his increased obsession with ritual purification. In the first days of his independent reign he had written to Maximus. 'The gods bid me observe purity in everything as far as I can, and I zealously obey their command.' His unbroken chastity since the death of his wife was probably in part an avoidance of pollution. In Antioch we find him introducing offerings from sacrificial altars into the water supply and sprinkling with holy water the goods offered for sale in the market.

On 12 February 363 he issued an edict forbidding funeral processions to take place by day, and accompanied it by a rescript explaining that he wished to avoid dead bodies passing before the open doors of temples and polluting them by their effluences, and the light of the divine sun being offended by spectacles fit only for the gods of the underworld. It may well be that Julian felt that some impurity in himself was blocking his communication with the transcendent world. Instead of exteriorizing his own difficulties of character, he was interiorizing objective problems of the outside world. He seems to have come to the conclusion in the end that what the gods wanted was a much more positive anti-Christian policy. Before he left for the Persian front he announced that much more severe measures – which he forbore to define – would be taken against the Christians on his return. There had in fact already been some discrimination against Christians in the public service, discrimination which points to the growing polarization of upper-class Roman society round the religious question and the abandonment by Julian of his claim to be the leader of all his subjects.

The Church historians, writing long after the event, relate that Julian excluded Christians from the imperial guard, from provincial governorships and the staff of governors, and from the army because their principles forbade them to take human life. No date is given for this ban. It is impossible that Julian can have made rejection of Christianity a condition of service in the Roman army. He depended too much on army support. And many of the officers and soldiers were Christians. Gregory of Nazianzus, in his bitter attack on Julian, makes no mention of a ban on Christian soldiers. The confusion is probably due to misunderstanding of a Greek term which can mean both military and civil service (*strateia*) and to general ill-will against Julian. The exclusion from the units of the imperial guard and from the provincial government was probably dated shortly before Julian's departure for the eastern frontier, when he had decided not merely to encourage paganism but to force Christians out of key positions. We do not know of any individual who was actually expelled from his post under this law, and it seems likely that it was never systematically put into effect. A letter of Julian to Atarbius, governor of Syria Euphratensis, written by the emperor's own hand, gives guidance on the application of the new measure. It reads: 'By the gods, I do not wish the Galileans to be put to death or beaten illegally, or to be maltreated in any way. But I declare that those who revere the gods should be given absolute preference over them. For practically everything has been turned upside down thanks to the folly of the Galileans, and it is the favour of the gods that preserves us all. So we must honour the gods and those men and cities which revere them.' (Julian, *Letter* 37.) In other words when more than one candidate presented himself for a post in the governor's service, preference was always to be given to the pagan. This was how things stood when Julian set out from Antioch for the eastern front on 5 March 363.

10 Persian War and Death

SINCE SYRIA HAD BECOME a Roman province in the second century BC, Rome and Persia had had a common frontier. Its general line ran from the Caucasus through the high plateau of Armenia, down to the confluence of the Euphrates and the Khabur, then across the desert to the head of the Gulf of Akaba. On the northern, mountainous sector of this frontier the two great powers were often separated by an Armenian buffer state, which in its turn might fall under the influence of one or other of them, or be divided between them. Its importance was strategic: it commanded the routes between Asia Minor and the Iranian plateau. In Julian's time the northern section of the frontier formed a great s-bend, running south-west from about modern Batum to join the Euphrates at its westernmost bend, near Divriği, following the river for about a hundred miles, then making a great sweep eastward, south of Lake Van, to the neighbourhood of Hakkari, from which point it again ran south-westwards to join the Euphrates again just south of Circesium. In the southern section Rome and Persia were always in direct contact. Much of the southern frontier, however, ran through thinly populated desert. Here each power tried to establish its own influence among the largely nomadic Arab tribes, with the result that two loose Arab confederations usually confronted one another in the desert zone, both of them often seeking to play off the great powers against each other.

Between the mountains and the desert lay the Fertile Crescent, perhaps the oldest region of civilization in the world, stretching from Palestine and the Phoenician coast through Antioch to Edessa and Nisibis and finally turning south to Babylonia. It was relatively densely populated, with a great number of cities, and depended, except at its western extremity, on an elaborate system of irrigation built up over millennia. It was a centre of industrial production, whose textiles, metal work, glass ware and other goods were exported all over the Roman and Persian worlds, and far beyond their frontiers, even to distant China. Much of the long-distance trade between east and west was handled by its merchants. And it had a unity of culture and life-style that long antedated the arrival of Roman or Persian power. The cities of Roman Syria conducted their official business in Greek. But the peasantry spoke Aramaic, and so in fact did many of the citizens. From the gates of Antioch, the capital of the Roman east, to those of Ctesiphon (near present-day Baghdad), the capital of the Persian empire in the fourth century, stretched a uniform belt of Aramaic speakers, whose attachment to either empire might not be very heartfelt. There was a great deal of movement to and fro across the frontier. This zone was of crucial importance for the economy of both empires.

Neither empire could hope to destroy the other militarily. Their centres of power were too distant, in the Mediterranean basin and the high plateau of Iran respectively. Yet for century after century Roman and Persian armies fought one another in the bleak hills of Armenia and on the parched plains of Mesopotamia. The best outcome that could be hoped for was a minor rectification of the frontier. In a sense it was one of the stupidest wars in history. Yet it had its rationale. Neither power could afford, for economic as much as for strategic reasons, to let the other dominate the disputed zones of Armenia and Mesopotamia. What they fought for was prestige, to show the Armenians and above all the Aramaic peoples which of them was 'top nation'. There are parallels in later history for two great powers fighting a long and bloody war to impress those upon whose territory it was waged.

In the days of the high Roman empire Rome had usually been the dominating power, sometimes pushing its frontier downwards into southern Babylonia, as under Trajan. Persia had been ruled by the weak Parthian dynasty, which could not count on the undivided support of the Iranian nobility. Since the middle of the third century a new dynasty had taken over in Persia, the Sassanians, who emphasized Iranian traditions and represented themselves as the heirs of Darius and Xerxes. Rome, on the other hand, had been racked by civil wars and struggles for power. It had been an age when Persian influence was predominant in the disputed regions. Diocletian's restoration of order within the Roman empire was followed by a successful war against Persia. King Narses was decisively defeated in 297, and a treaty concluded that introduced forty years of peace. In Armenia the westernmost portion became a Roman province, and the rest of the country an independent state in which neither Roman nor Persian influence was to predominate. Further south a stable frontier was fixed corresponding roughly to that before Trajan's victories, and dividing the Fertile Crescent into two almost equal halves.

At the end of Constantine's reign the new Persian King Shapur II (309–379) decided to reopen hostilities. In 335 he seized control of neutral Armenia and initiated a long series of indecisive engagements between the great powers. From 338 to 350 Constantius was involved in almost continuous operations in Mesopotamia. Their inconclusiveness was largely due to his inability to concentrate the main weight of the Roman armies in the east. The constant threats along the Rhine and the Danube meant that enormous forces had to be maintained and supplied in those regions. The revolt of Magnentius in January 350 forced Constantius to move the bulk of his army westwards to deal with the usurper. In late summer 350 he left Syria and remained in the west until autumn 359. The Persians were slow to exploit the change in the balance of power in the east. Shapur had his own problems in other regions of his vast empire, which were so open to attack by the nomads of the steppe lands. Finally, however, he mounted a major operation and in 359, after a long siege, he took the key Roman fortress of Amida (Diyarbakir), guarding the approaches to Asia Minor. A little later he improved the Persian position in Mesopotamia, taking Bezabde (Cizre) on the west bank of the Tigris and Singara (Sinjar) in the low hills between the Euphrates and the Tigris. But in the meantime he had lost his control of Armenia. Once again thousands had died for a few miles of desert. But the war was fought for men's minds rather than for territory, and at this level Persia had scored a minor but yet significant victory.

Such was the situation when Julian became sole emperor at the end of 361. The problem had for him two aspects. On the one hand he wished to stabilize the eastern frontier, as he had that of the Rhine, so that city life might flourish undisturbed, without fear of raids or permanent occupation by the enemy. This would imply the expulsion of the Persians from the regions that they had recently taken from Rome, the restoration of the frontier as it was after Diocletian's victories, the neutralization of Armenia, and the conclusion of a realistic peace treaty likely to be observed by both sides. This was a perfectly feasible aim, though it would not be easy to accomplish. On the other hand a war against Persia had for a man of

Julian's upbringing and interests seductive overtones. It was difficult for him not to see himself as a second Marcus Aurelius in whose reign there had been a significant adjustment of the frontier in Rome's favour. Behind Marcus Aurelius loomed the challenging figure of Trajan, who had carried Roman arms to the Persian Gulf and earned the title of 'Parthicus'. And since Julian was more Greek than Roman, or rather represented a Rome that had absorbed and assimilated Greek traditions, he could not help seeing himself sometimes as a new Alexander. Alexander had not merely defeated, but destroyed, the Persian empire of his time. And Alexander was a pupil of Aristotle, whose doctrines in Neoplatonist eyes were indistinguishable from those of Plato, thus he was in a sense a Platonic philosopher-king, just as Julian imagined himself. This was a preoccupation that Julian shared with most of his contemporaries. The ghost of Alexander haunted late antiquity. A romantic version of his life story was beginning to spread over the Roman world and beyond, into Persia itself. Mothers tied coins of Alexander round their children's necks to ward off evil spirits. Many a young man must have dreamed of repeating or even surpassing Alexander's astonishing exploits. Few were in a position to do anything about it.

A Church historian of the following century relates that Maximus of Ephesus had convinced Julian that he was a reincarnation of Alexander. How seriously Julian took Maximus' pronouncements is hard to determine. He certainly believed, as did all good Platonists of late antiquity, in the migration of souls from one body to another. Even if at the level of rational thought he dismissed Maximus' assurance, yet it may have answered some of his deepest emotional needs, and so been retained and accepted at a level of understanding no less important for being largely subconscious. Be that as it may, the realities of war against the Persians were certainly liable to be distorted in Julian's mind by historical parallels of strong emotional appeal but doubtful practical relevance.

Julian must have decided in early spring 362 to take up the war in the east where Constantius had left it. When he left Constantinople for Antioch in May 362 the logistic preparations for a major war were already under way. Perhaps he never hesitated, but from the day when he learned of the death of Constantius he began to arrange for the continuation of a war that he regarded as quite inevitable. There is no clue in his surviving writings, no suggestion that he ever considered a different kind of solution on the eastern frontier to that offered by war. He was probably inclined towards war in the east by a further consideration. As has been seen, the basis of his power was essentially military. He could count on the support of the Gaulish army, which he had many times led to victory. The eastern army had proclaimed its loyalty to him, and he had made concessions to its leaders at the trials held at Chalcedon. But it had not fought under his command, its soldiers had long been without the intoxication of victory and its material concomitant, booty. Their morale was low, their loyalty suspect. They might be persuaded to support a rival candidate for the imperial throne. The sooner Julian led them in a victorious campaign the better, both for him and for them.

The preparation for his campaign must have been Julian's principal task during the nine months that he spent in Antioch. We hear little about it from the emperor or from anyone else. The logistics of war did not fire the imagination of rhetoricians or historians. But the accumulation of supplies of food, fodder and munitions, their distribution to forward depots without giving too much away to the enemy, the bringing of units up to strength, the training of the soldiers from Gaul to fit them for the very different conditions of warfare in the east, the diplomatic correspondence with satellites and allies in the mountains of Armenia and in the deserts of southern Syria and Mesopotamia, these were all tasks calling for much expenditure of time. And Julian had learnt in Gaul the importance of attention to detail. Nothing was too trivial for the attention of a commander-in-chief. The provisions made for the army's needs probably contributed to the rise in food prices and the economic crisis at Antioch, though, as has been seen, they were not the sole cause of the crisis. The resultant political hostility towards Julian poisoned the last period of his stay in the capital of the Roman east, and he must have been glad enough when the time came to take the field. Perhaps a victory would change the situation. This is a common illusion among those men of action who have a contemplative side to their character.

Julian was an experienced commander, but his experience had been all of one kind – warfare against tribal peoples, brave and resourceful, but politically fragmented and technologically backward. He had repeatedly exploited the superior mobility and greater striking power of his army by making a deep thrust into hostile territory and taking the enemy in a pincer movement, either between a mobile striking force and the fixed frontier defences or between two columns of a striking force. Such operations, carried out with the resolution and dash typical of Julian, had regularly brought success against the Germans, who needed only to be defeated in a single battle. A war against the Sassanid Persian empire was a very different matter. Julian seems to have seriously underestimated the training and logistic ability of the Persian empire and the great resources of the Persian hinterland. Surprisingly, too, he does not seem to have realized the implications of the great distances involved. The change of scale involved a qualitative change in the methods of warfare called for. It was not enough to take the model of a raid into Germany and merely increase all the parameters. On the Rhine frontier the army was never far from its bases, and in any case could usually live off the land. In the east it would have to march for many days through hostile territory in which not only might there be nothing for men or horses to eat, but even the problem of water supply might be very serious.

There was also a failure to define objectives clearly. The primary aim of the campaign was to recover Roman territory and to defeat such Persian forces as were encountered. Ephraim *h. in Iulianum* 2.16 speaks of a letter in which the emperor explained that he intended to humiliate Persia and to recover Singara. Such had been the aim of Diocletian and Constantius. And it was within the capacity of the Roman army. But Julian had also in mind to capture the Persian capital of Ctesiphon and to replace King Shapur by his brother prince Hormizd, who had long been a refugee in Roman territory. This was a very different kind of operation, calling for much greater resources, such as would be needed for the siege of a large and very strongly defended city. We can only judge Julian's intentions from his actions; he left no record of his war aims. But it does appear, as will be seen in the course of the narrative, that he had not thought out clearly the relative priority of the two objectives and the successive choices that would have to be made in the course of the campaign. There are many traces in the historical record of opposition to his plan in military circles. Pressure was put on the soothsayers whom Julian regularly consulted to find unfavourable omens. The Sybilline books were consulted in Rome and their not very encouraging message relayed to the emperor; on no account should he quit Roman territory. There was a conspiracy to assassinate him, which was hushed up. But two officers of the imperial guard, Juventinus and Maximinus, were executed. As it happened, both of them were Christians. Finally Sallustius, the Praetorian Prefect of Gaul, sent Julian a letter dissuading him from the campaign in the strongest of terms. He was, said this elder statesman who was Julian's colleague in the consulate in 363, on the brink of irreparable disaster. When Julian received Sallustius' letter he was already on the march into Persia.

Julian brushed aside all this advice. Criticism in his eyes could only be a sign of hostility. He pursued his purpose unwaveringly, like Hercules among the Pygmies, in the words of the historian Ammianus, who was with him at the time. At this point in Julian's life the stubbornness that had always marked him seems to become almost pathological. He had so often been right in the past when others had been wrong. He had come to trust his own judgement too much. His self-assurance was strengthened by his ever growing conviction that the gods had marked him out for a great destiny – to restore the lost glories of the Roman empire. Many of his own immediate entourage, like Maximus of Ephesus, encouraged his sense of mission from motives that were not always disinterested, and played down the advice of experienced military men who did not share their own philosophical and religious views.

There was probably another factor behind the hardening of Julian's attitude. His far from negligible efforts to tidy up the administration of the empire, to put efficiency before long-standing administrative custom and justice before privilege had not won him much open popular support. His equally great efforts to discourage a pernicious religion which, in his eyes, had sapped the moral fibre of the Roman people, and to set them once again upon the true path had brought him only hostility and hatred. The problems of ruling a great empire were proving difficult. There were no quick solutions. There was even a smell of failure in the air of Antioch in winter 362–3. Julian was a young man in a hurry. He looked with nostalgia to the days when he returned victorious from a campaign against the Franks or the Alamanni to be greeted by the sincere adulation of the civil population. The time had come to take the field again. This was something that he knew how to do, and that brought immediate results. When he returned victorious, with the ancient and glorious title of Parthicus added to his name, everything would be all right. The problems would disappear, and he would bask once again in the public approval that had become so necessary to him. Hence his impatience to be on his way, and his unwillingness to listen to those who took the long view and counselled caution.

Julian was still a good commander. His troops in general idolized him. And the detailed preparations for the war were carried out with his usual meticulous thoroughness. But he was in a very dangerous state of mind, impeccable in detail, of inspiring physical courage, but capable of making gross errors of judgement in the larger strategic decisions. He was not a second Alexander.

Perhaps his first mistake was to reject proposals for negotiation made by Shapur in winter 362–3. The Persian king was evidently alarmed by the news of large-scale military preparations on the Roman side and was perhaps prepared to buy peace. All of Julian's entourage, says Libanius who belonged to it, pressed the emperor to accept. He would be able to negotiate from a position of strength. But Julian curtly rejected the Persian overtures, replying that there was no need to send envoys, as Shapur would soon see him arrive himself. A diplomatic victory, which in the nature of the case could not be complete, would not have satisfied Julian's longing for personal glory. It would not have offered the elusive 'final solution' to the eastern question that so attracted him. So the military preparations went ahead.

Messengers went back and forward between Antioch and the various client-kingdoms and protectorates on the eastern frontier. Most offers of military assistance were politely turned down. The contingents furnished by the King of Iberia (in present-day Georgia) and by the tribal and cantonal chiefs of Kurdistan would have been more nuisance than they were worth. Armenia, however, was an important ally. Its king, Arsaces, had been put on the throne by Constantius when he recovered the country from Persian control, and had been married to Olympias, daughter of Flavius Ablabius, a self-made man of Cretan birth who had risen through his friendship with Constantine to the Praetorian Prefecture from 329 to 337 and to the consulate in 331. Arsaces was instructed to mobilize his army in the spring of 363 and to await further orders from Julian.

Meanwhile the numerous units of the Roman field army in Syria were ordered to leave their winter quarters and to rendezvous at Hierapolis (Membidj), some sixty miles north-east of Aleppo and fifteen miles west of the Euphrates. For those units that were quartered for the winter east of the river, this meant a withdrawal further from the frontier. Hierapolis itself was a major military base with rich supplies of food, fodder and arms. The concentration of the army there was a clear sign to the Persians that hostilities were about to begin. But it gave no indication of the direction to be taken. It could as easily be the prelude to a march north-eastwards to recapture Amida as to an advance south-eastwards into Persian Mesopotamia. Shapur must have mobilized his forces at the same time. But he had to keep them back in rear areas, probably largely in Assyria, until he saw which way the Romans were going to move. It was no part of Persian strategy to let the King's army be caught in a pincer movement or forced to fight a pitched battle in circumstances of the enemy's choosing. Indeed it was a Persian principle to avoid general engagements altogether, except in peculiarly favourable circumstances. So Shapur waited, and Julian had the initiative for the time being.

On 5 March 363 the emperor left Antioch for the east. The first day's march along the Aleppo road, stretches of which can still be seen, had the character of a procession. Julian and his bodyguard were accompanied by the city council and the leading citizens of Antioch, the provincial governor and the *comes Orientis* with their staffs, and a throng of civilians. The atmosphere was tense. The councillors and citizens accompanied their good wishes with the hope that Julian would be more easy going when he returned victorious. The emperor replied that he would never see Antioch again, as he had arranged to establish his headquarters at Tarsus when he came back. The first night was spent at Litarbae (Al-Terib), about thirty-five miles from Antioch. From there on he travelled with only his bodyguard and his entourage of friends – among whom were Maximus and Priscus the philosophers and Oreibasios his doctor – and his spirits rose as he left Antioch and its problems behind him. At Beroea (Aleppo) he visited the ancient acropolis, addressed the city council briefly, and sacrificed a white bull. By 9 March he reached Hierapolis. His arrival was marred by the collapse of a colonnade by the city gate, which cost the lives of fifty soldiers. Julian does not seen to have been dismayed. In a long letter written to Libanius a day or two after his arrival he recounts the events of his journey and describes the places through which he passed. The letter radiates confidence. Julian was once again in a situation with which he knew how to deal.

Within a day or two the whole army was on the move. A bridge of boats prepared in advance was thrown across the Euphrates, and by 12 or 13 March the whole force was encamped around Batnae (Seruj), about forty miles beyond the river. There another unfortunate accident occurred, when an immense pile of straw collapsed and crushed fifty grooms who were taking fodder from the bottom of it. The story underlines the scale of the logistic preparations involved. At Batnae too Julian was met by a delegation from Edessa, where Constantius had regularly made his forward headquarters. It was a predominantly Christian city, which is probably why Julian avoided it. Carrying on his forced march, the emperor and his army reached Carrhae (Harran) the next day. It was an ominous name in Roman history, since it was there that the Triumvir Crassus and his army had been annihilated by the Parthians 416 years earlier. But it was also a firmly pagan city, whose citizens continued to practise their ancient astral religion of Babylonian origin in spite of the proximity of Christian Edessa. In fact they went on practising it long after the Arab conquest in the seventh century. It must have been a curious, inward-turned community, consciously detached from the world in which it lived. Julian spent several days there. Naturally he offered sacrifices to the local gods. There were unconfirmed reports, too, that he handed over to his maternal kinsman Procopius an imperial purple cloak, with instructions to take over power if he heard that Julian had been killed in Persia. But this may well be a rumour spread by Procopius later, when he set himself up as rival emperor to Valens. In 363 Procopius was about thirty-seven years of age, and had had a successful but undistinguished career as a civil servant. Since Julian's accession he had held the high rank of *comes*. He was now given command, along with the general Sebastianus, of a force of 30,000 that was detached from the main army at Carrhae.

For two roads led from Carrhae into Persia. One went due east, through Nisibis (Nusaybin), across the Tigris, and into Media. As far as the Tigris, this is the route followed by the Baghdad railway. The other runs south to the Euphrates, the line of which it follows to the region of southern Mesopotamia in which four great cities have succeeded one another – Babylon, Seleucia, Ctesiphon and Baghdad. From Carrhae onwards, Julian's intentions would be revealed to the Persians by his movements. Perhaps this consideration brought on the bad dreams from which he suffered, and which delayed the departure from Carrhae for a few days. When the army did move on, every care was taken to give away as little as possible to the enemy, whose reconnaissance patrols were operating in the area. The force of 30,000 under Procopius and Sebastianus was large enough to be mistaken for the main force, at any rate for a time. Its orders were to move up to the Tigris, but not to cross it until a junction had been made with King Arsaces' Armenian army. Then they were to march through Kurdistan and Media and eventually join Julian's main force in Mesopotamia. Thus their role was first to protect the left flank and rear of the army against an attack that could cut it off from its bases, second to tie up as many Persian units as possible in the north, and third to form the left claw of a pincer movement in which hopefully Shapur's army would get caught. Sebastianus was an experienced officer, who had been commander-in-chief in Egypt. He was the effective military commander. Procopius was attached to him for diplomatic purposes, and in particular to deal with the King of Armenia. A joint command by two men of such different experience was almost a guarantee of failure. And in fact this very considerable force played no significant role in the events that followed.

Julian and the main body of the army were to take the other route, to the Euphrates and into Mesopotamia. But in order to deceive the Persians, whose patrols were out in force and who had many adherents among the Aramaic speakers of this frontier region, he set off at first on the northern road, as if he were following Procopius and Sebastianus to the Tigris. Dummy supply dumps had been established along the route to add verisimilitude to the deception. Only after dark did he wheel his column sharp right and take the road across the desert to the Euphrates bend. By 26 March, after four days march, he reached Callinicum (Raqqa) at the confluence of the Belias (Balikh) and the Euphrates. Callinicum was a substantial place, and the main centre through which trade was routed between the Roman empire and Persia and the lands beyond. The day after the army's arrival was the festival of Cybele, the Mother of the Gods, of whose secret cult Julian was an initiate. He celebrated the rites according to ancient Roman prescription, washing the image of the goddess in the waters of the Euphrates.

From Callinicum onwards the road led along the high left bank of the Euphrates. It was about five days' march to Circesium on the frontier, the biblical Carchemish. During this march the sheikhs of the pastoral Arab tribes under Roman protection joined the army and paid formal homage to the emperor. They no doubt received gifts of money and instructions to protect the desert flank of the army and to keep their pro-Persian kinsmen occupied. Their value as allies was not great, and was all the less for their being largely Christian. But to pass through their territory without recognizing them as a political entity would have been dangerous. On 1 April Circesium (Beseire) was reached, at the confluence of the Abora (Khabur) and Euphrates. Here the forward line of frontier defences began. The actual line of the frontier between Rome and Persia at this time lay somewhere between Circesium and Dura to the south.

In the meantime military engineers had been preparing a fleet of boats on the upper Euphrates. Some were built of wood from the mountains of Armenia. Others were rafts floated by inflated skins, such as are still used for the downstream journey on the Euphrates. They not only served to transport men and horses; some were equipped with catapults and other siege engines, others formed pontoons for temporary bridges; and there were fifty regular warships, equipped for naval engagements. This fleet

sailed down the Euphrates and made junction with the land army a little
north of Circesium, as Julian was receiving the Arab sheikhs. It was
commanded by the tribune Constantianus, an uncle of the future emperor
Valentinian and so probably himself a Pannonian, and a *comes* named
Lucillianus of whom nothing else is known. The total number of vessels is
variously estimated at 1100 or 1250. Many of these would have been small
river boats or rafts, but in total they represented a considerable transport
capacity. The Euphrates begins to rise in March and high water is reached
by the end of May. Then the river begins to fall rapidly, and reaches low
water by October. There would be plenty of water for the fleet until
mid-summer or later.

From Circesium onwards the fleet accompanied the army, greatly
simplifying the supply problem. The emperor himself travelled part of
the way in an official barge. A bridge of boats across the Abora had been
already prepared. It was while the army was crossing this river that Julian
received the letter from the Praetorian Prefect Sallustius in Gaul beseech-
ing him to call off his Persian expedition. It was too late, even had Julian
wished to withdraw. Before crossing the frontier, at a place called Zaitha,
some twenty miles down the Euphrates from Circesium, Julian assembled
his troops and addressed them. The occasion was a moving one. For the
first time for nearly seventy years a Roman army was about to operate on
Persian soil. Apart from a few cavalry patrols observed near Carrhae there
had been no contact with the enemy. Yet Julian knew that their every
move was being watched and reported to the Persians. This might be the
last opportunity to form up his men and address them. Ammianus
Marcellinus, the historian, was present. Many years later he includes his
own version of the speech in his history, of which this is a summary:

> This is not, as some evil-minded men suggest, the first time that the
> Romans have invaded Persia. To say nothing of Lucullus, Pompey, and
> Antony's lieutenant Ventidius, the emperors Trajan, Lucius Verus and
> Septimius Severus returned victorious from Persia, as would the younger
> Gordian, had he not been assassinated. Angered by the fate of captured
> cities and defeated armies, I am resolved to make our territory safe and
> strong. Should I be killed in battle, it will be as a willing sacrifice for my
> country. We must destroy Persia as our ancestors destroyed Carthage, or
> Veii. From you I ask for steadfast discipline. When it is all over, I shall
> be accountable to you for all that I have done [Ammianus Marcellinus
> 23.5.16–23].

It is a curious speech, if Ammianus has recalled it right. There was clearly some alarm among the troops at the idea of fighting on Persian soil. This Julian tries to calm by recalling Roman history. The unresolved conflict in his war aims comes out clearly. He wishes to make the eastern provinces safe. This could be accomplished by a limited victory followed by a treaty, which is what Diocletian – who is not mentioned among the historical precedents – had done. At the same time he speaks of destroying Persia as Carthage had been destroyed – or as Alexander had destroyed the empire of the Achaemenids. A soldier with a feeling for history might well have asked himself on hearing this speech whether he was to march to the Tigris or to Sogdiana. Finally the promise of accountability harks back to the Roman principle of centuries before, when an Augustus or a Marcus Aurelius might give a detailed account of his stewardship to the Senate and the people. This is not the language of the autocratic dominate of Diocletian and his successors, nor is it that of the Christian Roman empire from Theodosius to Heraclius. In so far as it is not a mere populist phrase – and the eve of battle is perhaps not the moment for a well thought-out political *prise de position* – it betokens a blindness to the differences between the early empire and the fourth century that Julian had shown on earlier occasions.

On 6 April the army crossed the Persian frontier. From now on it no longer moved in column of route, but in battle formation, with advance, flank and rear guards, and gaps between the units of the main infantry force. As they marched along the left bank of the Euphrates they saw on the other bank the deserted city of Dura-Europos, the excavation of which by the Princeton University expedition has revealed so many details of the everyday life of the eastern provinces of the early Roman empire. They had been marching for four days along the river bank before they encountered the first Persian defended position, the ancient city of Anatha (Ana) on an island in the Euphrates. It is today the northernmost point where the date-palm is cultivated in Iraq. Its garrison surrendered after a parley with Prince Hormizd and the fortress was burned. The garrison commander entered the Roman service and later became commander-in-chief in Egypt. Among the inhabitants of the city was a former Roman soldier who had served under Maximian almost seventy years earlier, and had got left behind in Persia. Now nearly a hundred years old and patriarchal head of a vast family, the veteran was overjoyed and assured his fellow-countrymen that he had always known that he would find a grave in Roman soil.

Marching on down the river bank the army took what it needed from the narrow belt of cultivation that lined the river, and set fire to the rest. There was virtually no direct contact with the enemy, but everyone knew that they were close at hand. A soldier who foolishly crossed the river was seized by Persian soldiers who sprang up from nowhere, and killed before the eyes of his companions, who could do little to help him across the 300-yard wide river. A few defended posts either surrendered or – in the case of one fort on an island in the river – undertook to remain neutral and to surrender later to whichever side won the war. Any towns the army passed were burned, and all of the inhabitants who had not fled were killed. Julian had shown in Germany that he was not squeamish about barbarian lives where Roman power had to be asserted. And he was anxious to leave nothing behind him which could be of use to the enemy. Where was the enemy? There was no sign of organized opposition, and no indication at all of what King Shapur and his field army were up to. Yet there were sudden reminders of Shapur's watchful attention. As the army, for the time being on the right bank of the Euphrates, was resting by the smoking ruins of the little town of Ozogardana (perhaps Sari al-Hadd near Hit), and Prince Hormizd was about to set out with a reconnaissance party he was nearly captured by a force of pro-Persian Arabs under their king, accompanied by no less a person than the Surena, the hereditary commander of the Persian King's army. Only the unfordability of the river at this point saved Hormizd from being forcibly reunited with his brother. The Persian party, in gleaming armour, was driven off by Roman troops.

The army was now entering a region of irrigation and intensive cultivation, and the terrain was criss-crossed with canals, some of which joined the Euphrates and the Tigris. The greatest of these, the Naar-Malcha (the 'King's River' in Aramaic), was navigable, and joined the Tigris close by Ctesiphon. The army and fleet followed this route. At what point they left the Euphrates is not clear from the accounts of contemporaries, who may themselves have been puzzled to distinguish between river and canal in this strange landscape. It is impossible today to trace the course of the fourth-century Naar-Malcha. The irrigation system has undergone too drastic modifications in the course of centuries. Some of the canals were defended by the Persians, and a crossing had to be forced under enemy fire. But all such engagements were on on a small scale. Finally by 27 or 28 April the army reached the first large defended city, Porisabora (al-Ambar), the largest city of Persian Mesopotamia after Ctesiphon itself, and about forty miles from the Tigris. It was almost surrounded by canals and river branches. At first the Romans tried to persuade the garrison to surrender, but to no avail, so a regular siege was begun. The walls were well defended by trained soldiers, who used their heavy leather shields and strips of thick felt to ward off Roman missiles. Again and again the defenders asked to speak with Prince Hormizd, but when he approached the walls they merely showered him with insults and abuse. Perhaps they hoped to shoot him if he came close enough. By the next day heavier siege-engines had been brought up, and early in the morning a breach was made in the walls. The garrison at once withdrew to the citadel, which had its own defensive walls built of kiln-baked bricks, and occupied a high prominence over-hanging the Euphrates. The fighting went on all day, and powerful retroflected bows of the Persians took a heavy toll. They shot a heavier arrow and with greater velocity than the Roman bow. On the next day, under Julian's personal direction, a Roman detachment approached the gates with their shields interlocked over their heads – the famous Roman *testudo* – and tried to force them, but was finally driven back. At last the fighting was becoming difficult. On the following day the Romans moved up a great tower on wheels, equipped with catapults and rams. Bringing it close to the citadel walls must have involved a good deal of demolition in the lower city, whose narrow streets would certainly not permit the passage of the 'helepolis', as Ammianus calls it. But walls of sun-dried brick are easily knocked down. As the defenders of the citadel saw the great engine slowly approaching, and realized that it would overtop their walls, they decided to surrender, and lined the walls, their arms outstretched in gestures of supplication. At first the garrison commander talked from the top of the walls to Prince Hormizd. Satisfied with the assurances that he obtained, he was let down on a rope and taken before Julian. It was agreed that none of those in the citadel would be harmed if they laid down their arms, the gates were opened, and those within came out, to the number of 2500, civilians and military alike. They were removed, and the city and its citadel set on fire.

On the next day, 30 April, three squadrons of Roman cavalry patrolling near the burnt-out city were suddenly attacked by a similar Persian force under the personal command of the Surena, a few men were killed, and a standard captured. Julian was bitterly angry at this symbolic defeat – and probably also at the fact that the Persian high command knew what the Romans were doing, while he remained in complete ignorance of the whereabouts of King Shapur and his army. He took command himself of a cavalry force that sent the Surena and his party packing. Then he cashiered the two surviving officers of the Roman patrol, and, following what he believed to be ancient Roman practice, discharged and put to death ten of the soldiers under their command. The punishment seems to have been unusually severe. Only treason and mutiny were automatically punished by death in the late Roman army. Was Julian trying to restore what he believed to be ancient standards of discipline? Or was he beginning to lose his nerve? It is hard to say. But morale was certainly beginning to fall in the Roman army, though they had suffered virtually no losses up to now. On the very day on which he ordered this exemplary punishment he harangued his assembled troops once again, congratulating them on their victory at Porisabora, urging them to continue in the same spirit, and promising each man a hundred pieces of silver as additional pay. It is difficult to judge the value of this donative. It is the equivalent of eight and a half *solidi* at the official rate of exchange between silver and gold. When he was proclaimed Augustus at Paris he offered five *solidi* and a pound of silver, making the equivalent of just under eleven *solidi*. That offer was apparently well received. But this time the soldiers were roused to uproar. Julian replied, according to Ammianus, by reading them a lecture on the poverty of the Roman State, the result of the policy of his predecessors, and on his abstemiousness. Apparently this explanation restored the men's loyalty and calm. But it cannot have removed their uneasiness, which probably stemmed from their feeling of remoteness, as they marched day after day through desert sands or irrigated fields in this strange land, and from the uncertainty of their objective.

The next few days took them through an irrigated area that had been flooded by the Persians. This was easy enough to do as the Euphrates was by now in full flood. Bridges and pontoons had to be used, and progress was slow. And the Persian archers were always liable to open up on the Romans from a concealed position, and then to vanish before they could be flushed out by infantry. The soldiers had plenty to eat from the millions of date-palms that grew in the region, but they were tired and edgy. When they found a Jewish town whose inhabitants had fled, they set fire to it, apparently without waiting for orders. The Jewish population in this region was considerable, and many communities traced back their origins to the Babylonian exile. In general their relations with the Sassanid empire were good. It was in this milieu that the Babylonian *Talmud* was compiled a little later. Unfortunately it is completely silent on Julian's invasion of 363, although it clearly caused great hardship to the Jewish communities of Babylonia.

By now the army had probably left the Euphrates and was following the line of one of the great canals connecting the Euphrates and the Tigris. On about 8 May they reached the city of Maiozamalcha (perhaps the Mahoze of the *Talmud*). It would have been dangerous to go on leaving so powerful a defended position in their rear. So siege operations had to be set on foot. During a preliminary reconnaissance of the walls Julian was nearly killed by a small group of Persian soldiers who made an unexpected sortie from a postern gate. He ran through one of them with his sword, and his companions dispatched another; the rest then ran off. Before beginning the siege the camp was moved to a safer site, well protected by waterways. The Romans were clearly very nervous of the Persian cavalry, as well they might be now that they were within a day or so's march from Ctesiphon. In fact a cavalry force under the Surena did attack the pack animals but was driven off before it could do any serious damage. The inhabitants of two small 'islands' in this water-logged landscape tried to get away to Ctesiphon along the waterways, but most were killed or captured by the Romans who lined the banks and sped back and forth across the canals in boats.

The city of Maiozamalcha stood on a rocky eminence, difficult to approach. Its walls were formidable and its garrison numerous. Calls to surrender were contemptuously rejected. So the attack began. It soon became clear that there was little hope of taking the city by direct assault. Siege-engines were brought up, and work begun on raising embankments and driving mines under the walls. In the meantime Victor, a Sarmatian officer who had served under Constantius in the east and had been in command of the rearguard during the advance from the frontier, reconnoitred the roads as far as Ctesiphon and reported that there was no significant body of Persian troops between Maiozamalcha and the capital. This news fired the enthusiasm of the soldiers and they pressed on their attacks at various points along the walls. But the heavily armoured Persian defenders were immune to their missiles. The rough ground made it difficult for the Romans to approach under cover of their shields in *testudo* formation. Their artillery hurled showers of arrows and stones, but to no avail. Losses were heavy, and the heat of the day began to tell on the Roman soldiers. Southern Mesopotamia in summer is one of the hottest regions on the surface of the earth, the temperature often rising to forty degrees centigrade. As evening came on the wearied troops withdrew.

The next day was passed in the same fashion. Julian began to become anxious. He had probably hoped to be out of Mesopotamia before the great heat of summer. And every day passed in reducing Maiozamalcha gave more time for King Shapur to bring up his field army, whose whereabouts was still uncertain. However, by evening Dagalaifus who was in charge of the mining operations reported that one of the mines was nearly through. Julian decided not to wait until the next day. The wearied soldiers mounted yet another general attack on the walls to distract the defenders' attention and to drown out the noise of the tunnellers. As dusk was falling the miners broke through the surface and found themselves in a room where a woman was grinding corn. As she was opening her mouth to scream the first of them killed her with a single blow. They went on to dispatch the other occupants of the house without attracting attention and crept up on the guard at the nearby gate. The Persian soldiers, pleased with the day's events, were singing in the guard house and did not hear their approach. Within a minute they were all killed, the gates were open, and the Romans poured in. As they ran through the streets of the city they killed every living being they encountered, and set fire to buildings. Many of the inhabitants succeeded in getting up on to the walls. But these offered no safety, and many of them hurled themselves in despair down from the battlements. The height was such that few escaped serious injury. The Roman soldiers below went round putting the maimed wretches out of their misery. Nabdates, the garrison commander, and eighty of his men were taken alive and brought before Julian, who ordered their lives to be spared.

The city yielded much booty, which was divided among the soldiers the next day. The young Persian women, renowned for their beauty, were among the choicest items. Julian took nothing but a deaf and dumb boy adept at sign language, who aroused his pity. There was a last alarm as the army was about to leave, when it was learned that a body of Persian soldiers was still hiding in an underground pit near the walls, waiting to fall on the rear of the Romans. They were smoked out and killed to a man. It had been a hard and costly battle for the Romans. Its outcome for the citizens of Maiozamalcha was succinctly put by Ammianus: 'Thus a great and populous city was destroyed by the strength of Roman arms, and reduced to dust and ruins.'

It was about the middle of May when the army set off from the ruined city on the road to Ctesiphon. Progress was slow because of the need to bridge canals. A Persian detachment under a son of King Shapur had occupied some fortifications and tried to hold up the Roman advance guard, but was soon put to flight. At the end of the first day's march the

Romans had reached the Persian king's zoological garden, the inmates of which their cavalry butchered. Another day's march brought them to the vicinity of Seleuceia, where they camped for two days. The heat was already proving exhausting, and the plentiful water and abundant supplies of this region of intensive cultivation made it an attractive place to rest and recover. While his troops rested Julian went on to reconnoitre as close as he could to Ctesiphon. Though there was no sign of King Shapur's army, Persian resistance was resourceful and effective. Julian's party lost its baggage train when Persian soldiers made a sortie from a small town and were joined by others who sprang out of hiding among the dense cultivation. Julian himself barely escaped with his life when he was recognized by the defenders of a fort, close to which he was riding. His armour-bearer was wounded and he himself had to be extricated from danger behind the locked shields of his bodyguard. Honour demanded that the fort be taken. So siege operations were begun. But during the night the defenders made an unsuspected sortie, were joined by other Persians who had been hiding in the undergrowth nearby, and inflicted heavy casualties on the besiegers, who nearly broke and ran. Julian was furious. He was not used to tactical defeat. The survivors of the units concerned were punished. Julian took personal command of the attack on the fort, which in due course yielded to superior numbers. But several days – and who knows how many lives – had been lost in reducing an isolated post that could probably have been made ineffective by merely surrounding it out of missile range. And every day lost by the Romans was a day gained for Shapur.

After these operations the army again needed a period of rest, this time behind the walls of a fully defended camp. After a couple of days they went on to remove a barrage placed by the Persians in the main canal, and at last their fleet was able to sail into the Tigris. The problem now was to get the army across to the left bank of the Tigris to attack Ctesiphon. The walls of the Persian capital could be clearly seen arising from among the palm trees on the other side of the river. But the bank was protected by a large Persian army, and not by an advance guard with orders to fall back if attacked. The gleam of their armour could be seen by the Roman soldiers on the right bank of the river. And mingled with the neighing of their horses came a new and more ominous sound, the trumpeting of their elephants. Whatever the real value of elephants may be in warfare, they were certainly an effective psychological weapon against the Romans. An experienced officer like Ammianus was evidently mortally afraid of them.

Still more would they inspire terror in the soldiers of the Rhine army, who had never seen them before. And their unaccustomed scent made the horses nervous.

Julian was for a quick solution. He advised an immediate opposed landing on the opposite bank. His generals and advisers tried to dissuade him. We do not know what their plan was. But presumably it involved marching up the Tigris, crossing at a less well defended spot, and marching downstream on the left bank. But Julian had made up his mind. Victor was sent across with five ships filled with soldiers. He failed to get up the steep escarpment under the hail of Persian missiles. Julian, unwilling to recognize defeat, gave the order for the rest of the army to cross over before a bridgehead had been seized. The sheer numbers of vessels and men more than absorbed the Persians' fire-power, and the Romans got up the bank and dug in on the Persian side. Once again Julian had been right while the experts had been wrong. He had gone against all the rules of strategy by reinforcing defeat, and he had got away with it. His self-confidence, if it had been shaken by recent events, was now restored. And the walls of Ctesiphon were only a mile or so away.

Between the Romans and Ctesiphon, however, stood the Persian army. Not King Shapur's field army, but still a formidable force, under the command of the Surena. At close quarters now, the Roman soldiers – many of them youths from the forests and marshes of the lower Rhine – could see the gleaming plate-mail of the Persian cavalry, and the heavy leather accoutrements of their horses, the long curved shields of the infantrymen, protecting them from head to foot as they advanced in close order, and behind them the ponderous bulk of the elephants, 'like walking hills' in the words of an observer. The Romans could not afford to waste time, and the day after their successful crossing they attacked. It was 29 May. A hail of javelins and arrows gave cover to the Roman infantry as it advanced towards the Persian lines. But soon there was no room for missiles, as the two armies locked in close combat. Julian was everywhere, encouraging and inspiriting his men, and in constant risk of his life. Then the Persian line began to break, and soon they were in headlong flight towards the nearby city walls, with the Romans in hot pursuit. Some of them might have made their way into the city itself, says Ammianus, had not Victor given them the signal to halt. The danger was evident of allowing a battle-weary army whose order has been broken to get too close to a fortified city from which fresh Persian troops might issue. And the Persians were famous for their tactic of fleeing and suddenly turning round to fight.

A great victory had been won. 2500 Persians had been killed against only seventy Roman losses. The common soldier had learned that he could meet the Persian in the field and beat him, elephants and all. Rejoicing was great in the Roman camp as decorations were distributed, and Julian, excited by the acclamations of the men he had led to victory, was sure that the gods were on his side. The next day his assurance was shaken. Of ten bulls that were brought for sacrifice nine collapsed and died before reaching the altar, while the tenth broke loose and escaped. And when it was recaptured and sacrificed, its liver showed ominous signs. The sceptical historian may hazard the guess that someone had poisoned the sacrificial animals for reasons of his own. To Julian and many of those who surrounded him the message was that their enterprise was unpleasing to the gods.

The council of war met under the shadow of these events. It had to decide whether to besiege Ctesiphon or not, and if not, what to do. On the first point opinion was divided, but the majority were against a siege. The city was well defended, and the besiegers would risk being caught between King Shapur's army and the city walls. What Julian's view was is not recorded. But he accepted the advice of the majority. There was to be no siege of Ctesiphon – and therefore presumably no attempt to oust King Shapur and put his pro-Roman brother on the Persian throne. One may well ask why in that case Julian had come to Ctesiphon at all. Would it not have been more effective to lay waste Persian territory nearer the Roman frontier, where lines of communication would have been shorter and less vulnerable? This would have had no less deterrent effect. Several answers are possible to this question. Julian – and possibly his generals – may simply not have realized the size and impregnability of Ctesiphon until they got there. This is unlikely. There was plenty of traffic to and fro in times of peace. Or Julian may have been in secret communication with a group inside the city, and hoped that it would be betrayed to him. It is important to remember that behind the overt war of arms there was a secret war of spies and agents. Though their technology may have been primitive, their exploitation of human weakness was sophisticated. Pirisabora had been surrendered without any serious resistance. We learn from a throw-away remark of a contemporary historian that Nabdates, the defender of Maiozamalcha, had been in contact with the Romans and had promised to surrender the city to them. This may explain both why his life was spared when he was captured and why a few days later he was burned to death by the Romans. Prince Hormizd doubtless had his adherents in Ctesiphon. Did a plot to surrender the city misfire? Or was there never any plot, but was Julian led to believe by Persian agents that there was? As will be seen, there do seem to have been Persian agents at Julian's headquarters at the time of the council of war, or shortly afterwards, whose task was to lead the Romans into a trap. These hypotheses cannot now be tested. What can be done is not to rule them out as implausible or absurd. But perhaps the most likely explanation is the one suggested earlier in this chapter, that Julian had not made clear even to himself the objectives of his campaign and had not thought through all the possible contingencies. He must have expected to have encountered the main Persian army before reaching the capital. If he defeated it, Ctesiphon might well fall of its own accord. And in any case there would be plenty of time for siege operations. As things turned out the Romans reached Ctesiphon while King Shapur's army was still intact somewhere behind them. Had this contingency been omitted in the original calculations? Was there no plan to meet it?

Be that as it may, Ctesiphon was to be abandoned. What next? Most of the members of the council of war seem to have been in favour of withdrawing as quickly as possible from Persia. This would mean marching back up the Euphrates to Circesium, a distance of more than 300 miles, in the heat of the Mesopotamian summer, without the fleet, which could not sail upstream. It would be a long march, but it could be done, especially if they kept the river between themselves and Shapur. And every day would bring them nearer to safety. But it would bring no glory, said Julian; Persia was all but theirs; why let it go through cowardice or love of ease? He insisted that the army march further into the interior. Did he hope to force Shapur to fight a battle? Or was it his intention to outmanoeuvre him and get behind him? One factor in his decision seems to have been the arrival at his camp of two Persian noblemen, whose noses had been cut off. They explained that they were victims of the tyranny of King Shapur, that they had escaped from Ctesiphon, and that they were anxious to help the Romans against their former master. What exactly they promised to do for the Romans is not clear from the accounts of contemporaries. They may have said that they knew of a route to join the other Roman army south of Armenia, and this is the most probable hypothesis. But they could have offered to lead Julian into Persia proper while giving the slip to Shapur's army.

At any rate the boats were collected together and set on fire. The skin rafts can never sail upstream. And the wooden vessels could make only very slow headway against the rivers in flood. If the army was not proposing to remain by the Euphrates the fleet was useless. But it must not be allowed to fall into the hands of the enemy. Its destruction would free 20,000 men for more active military duties. The sight of the rising smoke alarmed the soldiers, who only then realized that there was to be no immediate return. Someone at headquarters became suspicious of the Persian deserters' story, and put them to the torture. They admitted that the story they had told the Romans was false, and that they had been disfigured out of loyalty to King Shapur. Orders were at once given to stop the burning of the fleet. But it was too late. Only a few boats were retained for crossing any rivers upon which they might come.

The decision to march into the interior was not abandoned, so it cannot have depended entirely on the false information supplied by the Persian agents. But the accounts of contemporaries give the impression from now on that the army did not really know where it was going, or why. If Julian hoped to make a junction with Procopius and Arsaces, then either he was grossly misinformed of their situation, or he had no conception of the distance to be marched up the Tigris under the full heat of the summer sun. Neither hypothesis seems likely. So perhaps it was not Procopius he was looking for, but Shapur, and he still entertained the hope of forcing him to a battle. We cannot tell. And it is likely that Julian did not know exactly where either Procopius or Shapur was in the vast empty landscape.

The first day's march was through fertile cultivated land on the left bank of the Tigris. But from then on the Persians began burning the crops and even the grass in front of them, holding up their advance as well as facing them with starvation. The Persians continually attacked with missiles from long range, and from time to time made cavalry raids on the Roman column. Some thought that King Shapur's army had arrived. They could not avoid Persian harassment by crossing to the other bank of the river because of the loss of the fleet. Everywhere they looked the Roman soldiers thought they saw the flashing of Persian armour, and morale rapidly sank.

Another council of war was held. The soldiers clamoured to go back the way they had come. Julian and his generals were at one in rejecting this proposal. They had scorched the earth themselves, and there would be nothing for men or horses to eat. And the Euphrates, now in full flood, had burst its banks in many places, turning the land into a quagmire. But no positive suggestion emerged. Victims were sacrificed and their entrails examined to determine whether to try to get back through Mesopotamia or to march along the foot of the Zagros mountains, plundering as they went. The signs indicated that neither course would meet with success. Finally it was decided, *faute de mieux*, to advance northward along the foot-hills. The army would at any rate get closer to the safety of Armenia; and it was likely that they would be able to link up with the force under Procopius and Arsaces. The manner in which this decision was reached suggests that Julian no longer felt himself in control of the situation, but was floundering in fits of alternate indecision and obstinacy. Whatever it was that actually happened outside the walls of Ctesiphon, its effect upon the emperor was shattering.

On 16 June the army set out again, marching up the left bank of the Tigris, and under constant light attack by the Persians. As the day wore on a great cloud of dust became visible to the north. Some said it was caused by a herd of wild asses, which are common in Mesopotamia. Others translating their hopes into thoughts, declared that it was the army of Procopius and Arsaces coming to meet them and save them. Others suspected that King Shapur had at last come upon them. Since no one knew what was happening, it was decided to pitch camp for the night, though few slept. The first rays of the morning sun fell upon rank after rank of glittering armour. It was indeed the King's army.

Shapur had apparently been taken in by the feint attack towards Armenia made by Procopius, and had waited in the north until it became clear that this was not the main Roman thrust. Or perhaps he merely wished to avoid a regular battle with a major Roman army, and preferred to wear down his enemy by attrition, and to let the Mesopotamian summer do its work. Now at last he had come down from the hills and was facing Julian. To the left of the Romans was the river Tigris, which they could not cross. To their right was the desert, stretching to the Zagros mountains. It would have been suicide for the army to try to turn the Persian flank on that side. In front of them, across a small stream, was Shapur and his army. Confident that they would beat the Persians in a regular infantry engagement, the troops wanted to attack at once. But Julian had learnt caution, and feared a Persian trap. However skirmishing soon began between forward units, and went on until the Persians withdrew from their position. It was a Roman victory. The only disquieting feature was that the Persians had not bothered to fight. As the Romans moved forward after the battle to a place called Barsaphthai, they were constantly harried by Arabs in the Persian allegiance. But these mounted troops were careful to keep out of reach of the Roman infantry, whom they evidently feared.

The next day's march took them to a large estate on irrigated land where they were able to rest and refresh themselves for two days.

When they set out again on their march it was already 20 June. The main Persian force was nowhere to be seen. But suddenly a large body of cavalry appeared over the low hills and fell on the rear of the Roman column. The Roman cavalry spread out, riding up the wadis and threatening to cut off the Persian retreat, and the enemy soon fell back. But they had inflicted many casualties. And the uncertainty of the situation was telling on the Romans. Units began to accuse each other of cowardice. One cavalry corps was publicly disgraced and ordered to march on foot with the baggage and the prisoners. Four light infantry officers were reduced to the ranks. The heat, the flies, the knowledge that Shapur was shadowing them just over the hills, all made the uncertainty of their objective more difficult to bear. Everyone was tired, nervy and suspicious. The rate of march was slow, as the grass, and such crops as there were, was always burning in front of them. Supplies were once again very low. On 21 June the army advanced less than ten miles, to a place called Maranga, about thirty miles south of Samarra, and encamped there.

As day broke the next day the sentries descried an immense Persian force approaching them. The appearance of the armour-clad Persian soldiers, their faces concealed by visors, was unnerving. The sight and sound of the elephants that followed them was even more alarming. Julian knew that he must on no account let himself be outflanked. If the Persian archers once got behind his line, disaster was likely. He also knew that though the Persians were better equipped and trained in the use of missile weapons they could not stand up to Roman infantry in close combat. So he disposed his army in wide crescent formation, and approached the enemy at the double, so as to reduce the time during which they were open to attack by the Persian archers. The battle was long and bloody, and in the end the Persians fell back, leaving many dead on the field. Another Roman victory. But it did not solve the problem of supplies, and it did not prevent Persian mounted troops and their Arab allies from continually harassing the Roman army and wearing down its strength.

The next three days, 23, 24 and 25 June the army remained in camp at Maranga. The dead had to be buried and the wounded cared for. Food reserves were very low. The regular ration for a Roman soldier at this time comprised biscuit or bread, pork or mutton, and wine or vinegar. Perhaps the element of biscuit and vinegar was increased for a campaign so far from base. They are more easily transported, and Julian in a letter written at the beginning of the campaign (*Letter* 98) speaks of loading river boats with biscuit and vinegar for the army. But now there was nothing but wheat porridge for emperor and soldiers alike, and not much of that. Julian slept little. One night as he was reading in his tent he thought he saw the spirit of the Roman people, its head and its horn of plenty alike veiled, pass out through the curtains of his tent. On the same night he saw a falling star. The conviction grew in his mind that the gods were displeased with him and were abandoning him. Before dawn he summoned the Etruscan haruspices who accompanied him and practised their ancient art of divination. They warned him that he must on no account join battle, quoting chapter and verse from the sacred books for their assertion. But Julian, usually so obsessed with divination, brushed aside their objections. At all costs he wanted to get out of the trap he was in. For he knew that the Persians could now attack his army at times and places o their own choosing, and that he had completely lost the initiative. The haruspices begged him at least to put off his departure by a few hours. But this would have meant going on marching through the hottest part of the day. As soon as it was light on 26 June the army set off, not far from the river bank in the direction of Samarra. They were under continuous attack from the surrounding hills, and had to march in battle formation. Julian was marching with the advance guard when news reached him that the rear of the column was being heavily attacked. The emperor rode back to see what he could do, not stopping to put on the heavy breastplate that his armour-bearer carried. On the way he learned that his left flank was being attacked by a substantial cavalry force supported by elephants, and was falling back. Riding up to the battle area he rallied the retreating soldiers. His presence and his example steadied the ranks, and the Persians began to fall back. Julian rushed forward, signalling to his men to follow him. His bodyguard had got broken up and separated from him. But some of its members saw him riding out into a confused mêlée of fleeing Persians and called on him to come back. He probably did not hear them. All of a sudden a cavalry spear grazed his arm and pierced his side. He tried instinctively to pull it out, but only succeeded in cutting his hand, and a few seconds later collapsed and fell from his horse. His bodyguard had by now rallied round, and took him back for medical treatment. The army halted and pitched camp. Oreibasios attended to his imperial patient. Soon Julian felt well enough to call for arms. But it was an empty gesture. He was too weak to walk, let alone to fight. He asked the the name of the place, and was told that it was called Phrygia. An oracle had once told him that he would meet his fate in Phrygia. Julian had always supposed that the province of Phrygia in Asia Minor was meant. Now he realized the true meaning of the oracle and fell silent. As he lay dying, another indecisive battle was raging, with heavy losses on both sides. We are told that Julian made a formal death-bed speech. He may well have done so. It was what the situation called for, and Julian was responsive to such demands. Gibbon even suggested that he may have prepared and rehearsed it in advance. The speech given by Ammianus cannot, for a variety of reasons, represent what the dying emperor actually said. Though a staff officer on the Persian expedition Ammianus was certainly not present at Julian's death bed, nor was Magnus of Carrhae, whose account he probably uses to supplement his own recollections. Perhaps the only element of truth in Ammianus' version is Julian's refusal to designate a successor. There was certainly no mention of his kinsman Procopius, which casts doubt on the story that Julian gave Procopius an imperial cloak and told him to take over the direction of the empire should he himself not return.

Maximus and Priscus, who were in Julian's suite, gathered round the dying emperor's bedside to offer him the consolations of philosophy. Perhaps they engaged in a Socratic dialogue on the nobility of the soul, as Ammianus recounts. More probably their talk had the disconnectedness of failing strength and dimming lucidity. Suddenly the wound in Julian's side, which Oreibasios had staunched, burst open and he began to bleed profusely. Gasping for breath, he asked for a draught of cold water. When he had swallowed it he lay quietly, and died in a few minutes without uttering another word. He was in his thirty-second year of age and his second year as sole ruler of the Roman empire.

This is not the place to conduct an exhaustive enquiry into the manner of Julian's death. His successor Jovian was the only person who might have launched a successful enquiry, and he did not do so. All that will be done here is to set forth what contemporary or near contemporary sources say, to see if any conclusions can be drawn from these, and to outline the growth of the legend of Julian's death that prevailed in the Middle Ages. First the contemporary witnesses. The monk Ephraim, writing in Nisibis in the year of Julian's death, sees in it the vengeance of Heaven, but does not suggest that the instrument of that vengeance was other than a Persian. Gregory of Nazianzus, writing in 363 or 364, says he has consulted participants in the campaign. Some said that Julian was killed by a Persian as he rode forward rashly into a mêlée. Others said that his assailant was a Roman, angry at a remark of Julian's that it would be a pity to bring so many men back to Roman territory. Libanius gives two accounts of Julian's death, and the date at which each was written is not entirely clear. In what was probably the earlier version, the *Monody on Julian* (*Or.* 17) written in 363 or 364, he merely says that Julian was killed by a cavalry spear, and apparently assumes that his assailant was a Persian. In the later account, the *Epitaphios* (*Oration* 18), he argues that the assailant cannot have been a Persian, since no one came forward to claim the reward offered by Shapur. He suggests that the assailant was a Christian, probably an Arab of the desert. The expression he uses here ('*Taienos tis*') makes it likely that he had picked up the story from a Syriac speaker, for in Syriac the Bedouin are called 'Tayyayē'. Magnus of Carrhae, who took part in the expedition, apparently gave an open verdict, if the sixth-century chronicler Malalas copied him correctly. Ammianus Marcellinus, who was present at the battle, but did not write his description of it until about 390, by which time he had certainly had occasion to read other accounts, expressly declares that the hand that threw the spear was unknown. His emphasis suggests that he is rejecting the accounts of others who claimed to know who threw it. Eutropius, Festus and Aurelius Victor all merely report that Julian was killed by an enemy. This is the sum of the contemporary evidence. What it suggests is that no one knew who threw the fatal spear. In the confusion when a battle is turning into a rout and pursuit, friend and foe are inextricably mingled and the situation changes with bewildering rapidity. In the few seconds after the emperor was wounded and fell from his mount, all the attention of his bodyguard would have been concentrated on getting him out of the battle area. The argument that the assailant cannot have been a Persian because no one claimed the reward is valueless. The assailant could have been killed in the next few minutes of battle. Or he may not have known that the man whom he struck with his spear was Julian. He was not wearing his breastplate, and so probably had nothing to mark him out as emperor. The Persians did not know at first that Julian was dead. If this verdict of *non liquet* seems disappointing I can only claim that the confused circumstances scarcely permitted anything else, and observe that twenty volumes of detailed evidence have not yet assured all of President Kennedy's contemporaries on the precise manner of his death.

It was natural that men should feel that this was no ordinary death, even if they were not sure whose hand propelled the spear. Ephraim, we have seen, speaks of divine vengeance. A certain Kallistos, a member of Julian's bodyguard, wrote a hexameter poem on the death of his master. We do not know when. In this work, which is lost, Julian's death is attributed to a demon. Libanius too speaks of demons at work. This would be the view of those who approved of Julian. For those who disapproved of him, and this includes all the Christian leaders of the time, the supernatural authors of his death would be not demons but angels or saints. The Church historian Sozomenus, writing some eighty years later tells the story of a traveller sleeping in a lonely church, who saw in a dream an assembly of saints and prophets, two of whose number went off to kill Julian and returned later to report that their mission had been successfully accomplished. A similar story is found in the Armenian historian Faustus of Buzanda, who probably wrote before the end of the fourth century. *The Life of St Basil* wrongly attributed to Amphilochius of Iconium says that it was St Basil who had the prophetic vision. The names of the two saints who are charged with getting rid of Julian vary from one account to another. N. H. Baynes has argued that the story must have originated in Arian circles in Antioch. This may well be so, but is not proven. In all these stories we see the development in concrete detail of the idea expressed by Ephraim that Julian's death was an act of divine vengeance. On this basis was constructed the medieval legend of Julian, which will be discussed in Chapter 11. The charge that Julian's assailant was a Roman, which in the context means a Christian, will have arisen in pagan circles. Libanius knows of it in 365, but cannot vouch for it. For what it is worth, Ammianus writing in *c.* 390 makes the Persians a day or two after Julian's death taunt the Romans with having killed their emperor. Even if the story is true it proves nothing. The Persian soldiers were not on oath, and anything that would annoy the Romans and weaken their morale was good enough.

On the next morning the army leaders met to discuss the succession. They had no doubt that imperial power in the fourth century was based on control of the army and that they could not avoid a choice even if they wanted. So, in an armed camp east of the Tigris, ringed by Persian soldiers who watched the army's every move, picked off stragglers, and from time to time attacked, the business of choosing the new ruler of the Roman empire was begun. The generals called in the legionary commanders and the commanders of cavalry regiments, in order to sound out the army's opinion. The old division between the army from Gaul and that which had fought in the east under Constantius became evident again, now that

Julian was dead. Arintheus and Victor supported one candidate from their own party. Nevitta and Dagalaifus another from theirs. A compromise candidate was found in Julian's old friend Salutius Secundus, now Praetorian Prefect of the east and present with the army. He was a civilian respected by both military groups, and apparently also by the population at large. Himself a pagan, he had no sense of mission and had disapproved of Julian's strong measures to suppress Christianity. But he was an old man, and pleaded ill health and age. While these deliberations went on a faction among the officers declared in favour of Jovian, the commander of the imperial guard, and son of Varronianus, who had long held the same office under Constantius. Having no other candidate to propose, the council of senior officers accepted him. According to one source Jovian protested that as a Christian he would be unable to lead a largely pagan army. 'We are all Christians here', replied the generals, and Jovian was reassured. He was hastily dressed in Julian's purple cloak and paraded along the ranks of the army as it was already setting out on the march.

Jovian's exploits are no part of the present story. So a brief résumé must suffice. He led the army up the east bank of the Tigris, under continuous Persian attack but without any regular battle. Roman losses were heavy. In the first four days of July the army succeeded in forcing a crossing of the Tigris, more in spite of Jovian's leadership than because of it. Supplies were very short, and the Romans were close to starvation. However King Shapur, who still feared the outcome of a pitched battle with the Roman legions, decided to settle for what he could. The Surena and other Persian dignitaries arrived in the Roman camp with peace proposals. Negotiations at once began, and soon a thirty years' peace treaty had been signed, on terms highly disadvantageous to the Romans. Five frontier provinces on the left bank of the Tigris, which Maximian and Diocletian had conquered, were handed back to Persia, as well as the key fortress of Nisibis (Nusaybin) and Singara (Sinjar). An undertaking was given not to protect King Arsaces of Armenia against the Persians. Arsaces was in fact shortly afterwards arrested by Shapur and blinded. This was the price that Jovian had to pay to extricate his army from its predicament. He was also anxious to get back to Roman territory quickly, before Procopius could have himself proclaimed emperor.

The Roman army marched through Hatra to Nisibis in conditions of the greatest hardship. Only by killing and eating their camels and pack mules did they succeed in staying alive until Cassianus, the army commander in Roman Mesopotamia met them with fresh supplies. When they reached Nisibis, Jovian refused to enter, but camped outside the city, for it would be undignified for a Roman emperor to set foot in a city that he had ceded to a foreign power. On the next day a high Persian officer arrived, and in full sight of the Roman army encamped before the gates, entered the city and raised the Persian flag on the ramparts of the citadel.

The army still had Julian's embalmed body with it. As it lay in state outside Nisibis the old monk Ephraim came out from the gates and looked at it. He was a poet and his thoughts and feelings are preserved in the Syriac hymn that he wrote shortly after the event:

I went, my brothers, and approached   the corpse of the unclean one,
I stood over him   and mocked his heathendom
and I said, 'Is this the one   who raised himself
against the living name   and forgot that he is dust?
God has let him return to dust   that he may learn that he is dust.'

Ephraim goes on to reflect on Julian's death and its lessons, on the burning of the ships, on the lance that killed him. He concludes that Julian 'chose death' and removed his armour so as to be hit. He is not thinking in terms of suicide, rather that Julian was made the instrument of his own punishment – *quem deus vult perdere prius dementat*.

Procopius joined Jovian and his army at Nisibis. As a kinsman of Julian he was given the task of escorting his remains to Tarsus, the city where he had intended to establish his court when he returned victorious. He was buried just outside the city walls, by the road that leads to passes over the Taurus, facing the tomb of the emperor Maximinus Daia. When Jovian passed through Tarsus in the autumn of 363 he embellished the tomb. Perhaps it was he who had a Greek couplet carved on the tombstone:

'Ιουλιανὸς μετὰ Τίγριν ἀγάρροον ἐνθάδε κεῖται
ἀμφότερον βασιλεύς τ'ἀγαθὸς κρατερός τ' αἰχμητής.

(Here lies Julian after the strong-flowing Tigris,
both a good king and a brave soldier)

Another version of his epitaph reads:

Κύδνῳ ἐπ' ἀργυρόεντι ἀπ' Εὐφρήταο ῥοάων
Πέρσιδος ἐκ γάιης ἀτελευτήτῳ ἐπὶ ἔργῳ
κινήσας στρατιὴν τόδ' 'Ιουλιανὸς λάχε σῆμα,
ἀμφότερον βασιλεύς τ'ἀγαθὸς κρατερός τ' αἰχμητής.

(By the silvery Kydnos, coming from the streams of
the Euphrates and the land of Persia, after launching
his army on a task it did not complete, Julian found
this tomb, alike a good king and a brave warrior)

His grave was by Tarsus. His friend Libanius, writing a few years later,
declares that he deserved to be buried in the Academy at Athens, near the
tomb of Plato, so that he might share in the grave-offerings made to his
master by generations of students (*Oration* 18.306). The historian
Ammianus Marcellinus, who had served under Julian's command, writes:
'It is not the Cydnus, pleasant and limpid stream though it be, that should
look on his mortal remains: but the Tiber, which divides the Eternal City
and passes close by the monuments of the ancient gods, should flow beside
his tomb and make everlasting the fame of his noble deeds.' In these two
judgements we see graphically exemplified the two aspects of Julian's
character, as Greek philosopher and as Roman emperor. He failed as both.
Yet his memory has lasted through the ages, and the enigma of his personality has stimulated the intellect and the imagination of fifty generations.

11 Epilogue

WHEN ATHANASIUS, the Bishop of Alexandria – whom Julian had brought back from the exile to which he had been driven by his fellow-Christians – heard of the emperor's anti-Christian measures, he observed that it was only a little cloud that would soon pass. And so it was that Julian did not leave a world irreversibly changed by his life in it. The contrast with his hero Alexander is striking, both died at the same age, but Alexander's conquests transformed the Near East. Most of Julian's measures were put into reverse or forgotten, and the Christian Roman empire that Constantine had founded continued its course.

The shock of the Roman defeat in Persia frightened people for a time, and there was some half-hearted persecution of pagans thought to have been closely associated with Julian. Libanius and his friends in Antioch had to lie low for some months. There was an atmosphere of repression that discouraged Julian's friends from writing or even recounting anything about him. Gregory of Nazianzus, the future archbishop of Constantinople who had known Julian as a student in Athens, launched a violent and sometimes scurrilous posthumous attack upon him. Nerves were tense, and in the aftermath of his death prominent pagans in Antioch went in fear of their lives. But few, if any, lost them. And there was little interference with Julian's former partisans elsewhere in the empire.

Maximus remained in favour under Jovian, was arrested under Valentinian and Valens on charges of misconduct in Julian's reign, was set free through the intervention of powerful friends, resumed his career as a lecturer, and years later was put to death for involvement in a plot to discover by magic the future of the emperor Valens. Priscus was arrested but allowed to return to Greece, where he was still alive and active as a teacher thirty years later. Oreibasios was condemned to exile and his property was confiscated, but he was soon restored to favour because of his medical skill, and went on to marry a rich wife in Constantinople, and beget four children. Seleucus, a zealous pagan member of Julian's court, had to pay a heavy fine. Aristophanes the governor of Macedonia and one or two others had to give up their public offices. But otherwise there was little persecution of Julian's associates.

After a few months the sense of danger faded away, and Julian's friends began to collect his writings and to compose accounts of his life. These were hardly published, in the sense of being readily available in the book market. Rather they were circulated among those pagan and often backward-looking groups in whose eyes the Constantinian empire was a ghastly mistake. Julian's own writings, or some of them, have survived. The works of those of his friends who kept the memory green have perished, with the exception of two long commemorative orations by Libanius, both of which were probably delivered to a select audience of pagan friends at Antioch, and preserved only through the interest that students of rhetoric had in all that Libanius ever wrote. Before long legend began to colour reality, and Julian became for the tiny but tenacious group of pagan intellectuals an ideal philosopher-king. Eunapius, writing at the end of the fourth century, sees him as a model emperor. Zosimus, a pagan lawyer who compiled a history of the late empire round the year AD 500, adopts an almost hagiographical tone in recounting his life and exploits. The philosophical school of Athens, which could trace back a tenuous connection with Plato's Academy, seems to have begun a new era with Julian's accession. The biographer of Proclus, who died as head of the school in 485, dates his death as in the hundred and twenty-fourth year after the accession of Julian. Some even went so far as to establish a cult of the dead Julian – not as deified emperor, but as martyred leader, still watching over his followers. Even the Church historians of the fifth century made use of pagan accounts favourable to Julian among their sources. John Malalas, writing his pious world-chronicle in Antioch in the sixth century could consult contemporary accounts of Julian's last campaign composed by his admirers. Even John Zonaras, an ecclesiastical lawyer in twelfth-century Constantinople, shows in his history of the world traces of the romantic life of Julian composed in pagan circles after his death. So much for the pagan Julian-legend, which was probably always confined to a limited circle of intellectuals.

The Christians too soon turned history into legend. And their legend dominated the Middle Ages and still colours our thinking about Julian today. Later in this chapter we shall return to this topic. In the meantime we must try to make our own evaluation of Julian's achievements, without paying attention to the body of legends that grew up round his name.

Measured by the rigorous standards of the historian, Julian achieved singularly little. Some of his laws were still there to be recorded by the Theodosian Code in 434. A very few were still in force a century later when Justinian's legal commissioners compiled the Justinianic Code. But they had been absorbed into the ongoing development of Roman law, and they mostly concerned matters of secondary importance. He left no great buildings or public works to perpetuate his name, and no cities were named after him – though one city did bear the name of his mother. The great processes of social change that he had sought to resist – such as the decline of the city councils and of the class from which they were drawn – went on uninterrupted by his brief reign. And his great purpose of breaking the link established by Constantine between the Christian Church and the Roman State, and of regaining the upper classes of society to a renovated and intellectually respectable paganism, was an irredeemable failure. But Julian died in battle at the age of thirty-two. There was nothing inevitable about that. Perhaps his impact on the history of the empire would have been very different had he been granted the normal span of life.

If Julian had lived as long as his uncle Constantine, it would have been he and not the stupid and impulsive Valens who would have had to deal with the first great episode in the age of migration, when the Visigoths, driven on by the Huns in their rear, came to the Danube frontier clamouring for land to settle on. Valens and his advisers by their vacillation and corruption so mishandled the situation that within three years the Visigoths had annihilated a Roman army in battle, killed the emperor, and were in control of the Balkans. A generation later they were to sack Rome. Julian's record in Gaul suggests that he might have dealt much more realistically and successfully with this crisis. And though the movement of peoples would still have gone on, its impact on the Roman empire and the Mediterranean world might have been delayed or modified.

If he had lived to the biblical age of three score and ten he would still have been at the head of affairs at the end of the century. As things turned out, the Roman empire was by then divided, never to become reunited. Would Julian with his curious combination of Roman political sense and Greek culture have maintained its unity, and so prevented the fragmentation of the western empire into barbarian kingdoms? This is not the kind of question that the historian is willing to answer. But it is legitimate to ask it. Finally if Julian had lived as long as Anastasius or Justinian he would still have been on the throne in the second decade of the fifth century, at a time when Alaric had already captured Rome and Augustine had begun to work on his *City of God*. Would either of these events have taken place had Julian, rich in experience and in the prestige of age, been there to formulate policy and guide its execution?

These excursions into what science fiction writers call an 'alternative universe' can neither prove nor disprove anything. They can merely suggest that to evaluate Julian's programme by the results it had achieved at his early death may well do its author less than justice. He realized that the political viability of a vast Mediterranean empire depended on the loyalty and prosperity of its cities, that this loyalty and prosperity were being threatened by ever increasing and apparently capricious intervention by the central government, that the balance between local initiative and authoritarian rule had swung too far towards authority. The proper sphere for the exercise of authority, in his eyes, was the vigorous defence of the imperial frontiers. This alone could create the conditions in which city life and the complex economic exchange between city and country could develop and prosper. Effective defence was possible only if the empire remained united. Divided rule sooner or later led to civil war, in which the soldiers were employed in killing those whom they should defend. These were not perhaps very profound insights, but they were a good enough basis for practical action.

As for Christianity, it was clearly far too late to eradicate a religion that appealed to many different classes, that was superbly organized, and that flourished on martyrdom. But it was not unrealistic, given time, to hope to dissolve the marriage between the Christian Church and the Roman empire. Christianity could have survived as a mass religion, without becoming as it did the sole permitted religion. This would have greatly reduced its appeal to the upper classes of Roman society, who were for the most part quite recent converts.

Julian clearly misunderstood the dimensions of the problem posed by Christianity. His law on Christian teachers shows a shrewd sense of the weak point in the Christian allegiance of the upper classes. His encouragement of pagan charitable institutions reveals his understanding of the social role of the Church in a world in which the old, civic system of social security was breaking down. What survives of his anti-Christian polemic is evidence of his sharp awareness of the growing gap between Christian preaching and Christian practice, now that the Church had become rich and powerful. Yet for all his own deep religiosity he never seems to have grasped the force of Christianity's appeal to the common man, and the sense of assurance, false though it may have been, that Christians drew from their religion in a society of rapid change. In fact he probably never understood the common man at all. Utterly isolated in the formative period of his youth, he was unable to trust anyone, caught in a Kafkaesque world of unpredictable dangers; then suddenly thrown into situations demanding rapid decision and unquestioned exercise of authority, Julian was too much of an outsider to enter easily into the minds of those less harshly tried by fortune. And he had, perhaps as a result of his early agonies, a sense of personal salvation and personal mission, which most of his Christian contemporaries almost certainly lacked. He was an all-or-nothing man in a situation where compromise might have brought success.

There was an even deeper weakness in his attitude to Christianity as a political and social phenomenon. He regarded it as a debilitating force, weakening men's resolution and blurring its once sharp outlines. If the Roman empire was in a crisis, the cause was to be sought in the prevalence of the new religion. So the first task for a ruler who wished to restore the power and effectiveness of the empire and to ensure the viability of its society was to reduce the influence of the Christians as rapidly and decisively as possible. Yet most historians today see the growth and spread of Christianity as one of the effects or symptoms of social and political change in the Roman empire, not as its cause. Julian fruitlessly devoted his energy and his talents to combating a phantom. The irrationality and irritability that he occasionally displayed in the last months of his reign are easily understandable as the effects of a frustration that we can perhaps see to have been inevitable. To men of the time things were not so clear.

So far from dissolving the bonds of Roman society, Christianity became one of the principal elements of its strength. The sense of unity, of common purpose, and of divine protection that the east Roman world enjoyed was one of the factors that enabled it to survive through the Middle Ages, withstanding the onslaught of the Moslem Arabs, the Avars, the Slavs, the Bulgars, only to fall in 1204 to the rapacity of its fellow-Christians. But this outcome could hardly have been discerned by Julian and his contemporaries, in whose generation the synthesis of Christian and classical culture was only beginning. They could not know that the soldiers of a Christian Roman empire would guard its frontiers successfully for eight centuries, while its scribes and scholars copied and explained the texts of Hellenic literature and thought, including Julian's own writings, which were prized as models of literary style.

In a sense all historical figures are tragic for us, since we know what was for them unknowable – the future. Julian has an added dimension of tragedy, in the contrast between his outstanding personal qualities, and the total failure of all that he tried to do. He survived a youth that would have turned most men to cynics if not to psychopaths. He retained a capacity to pursue with fervour aims that rose above mere personal gratification, and to devote to them an intelligence, a courage and an application that far surpassed most of his contemporaries. More than any other ruler of the late empire he had a clear idea of the kind of society that he wished to see. His character possessed a nobility that makes him shine out like a beacon among the time-servers and trimmers who so often surrounded him. Yet he failed. And his failure was in part due to the very sincerity and candour with which he pursued his purposes. Lack of worldly experience combined with eagerness for the best marked him as a predestined victim for the dilettantes and charlatans who deluded themselves that they were preserving the traditions of a glorious past. They often took themselves only half seriously. Julian credited them with a seriousness as great as his own. And so he gradually found himself entrapped in an anti-Christian position that had little relevance to the problems of the Roman world. His bounding springs of energy were more and more devoted to the wrong tasks. And his lucid but uncritical intelligence found itself operating in a world where delusion and reality became ever harder to distinguish. Had he been a stupid or an ignorant or a lazy man he might have muddled through, as so many of his predecessors and successors did. It was his very excellence that made him so vulnerable. Yet his fate moved men's hearts and minds, and in spite of his failure he was not forgotten.

The romantic pagan view of Julian has already been alluded to. The hostile Christian picture depends above all on Gregory of Nazianzus, who in two blistering attacks, branded the dead emperor as an instrument of the devil. Gregory was not trying to evaluate Julian with the eye of an historian. His sole concern was theologically partisan – Julian was the enemy of the Christian Church, so any human virtues that he may have possessed were irrelevant. By careful selection of topics, slanted presentation, caricature and exaggeration he depicts Julian as wholly evil, and exults in his premature death. The wide dissemination that the Church gave to Gregory's two orations on Julian soon made his stark, black-and-white characterization the dominant one in the Greek east.

In the Latin west, where the impact of Julian's anti-Christian measures had been less felt, and where perhaps there was greater appreciation of his military skill and his Roman understanding of power, more balanced judgements prevailed. Ammianus Marcellinus, the soldier from Antioch who in his retirement settled in Rome to write the history of his own times in Latin, had served under Julian and knew him personally. He was a pagan, but without animosity towards the Christians. His observations, which display sympathy for Julian combined with sharp criticism of certain of his measures, have been quoted from time to time in this book. His final judgement on Julian is too long to quote here (Ammianus Marcellinus 25.4.1–27). 'He was a man', begins Ammianus, 'worthy to be counted among the heroic spirits, and marked alike by the distinction of his achievements and his natural dignity.' He goes on to enumerate the positive features of his character, using as his framework a scheme of the principal virtues drawn up by teachers of rhetoric, but ultimately derived from Plato. Then he turns to Julian's shortcomings: he was inclined to flippancy, but trained himself to avoid it; he talked too much; he was too much addicted to divination and other superstitious practices; he sought popularity and was over fond of praise; though most of his legislation was salutary, his ban on Christian teachers and his forcible recruitment to city councils of persons no longer liable to serve were to be condemned. After a description of Julian's personal appearance, which has already been quoted (pp. 65–6), he goes on to deal with the charge that he was a war-monger. He was nothing of the kind, he declares, as it was Constantius who first provoked military reaction from the Persians, and was responsible for much loss of life and destruction. Julian merely tried to repeat in the east what he had done in the west – to establish a firm basis for lasting peace.

At the end of the century the Christian poet Prudentius, a Spaniard who had had a distinguished career as a public servant, while he condemns Julian's religious attitude, has an eye for his greatness and for the tragedy of his life.

> Principibus tamen e cunctis non defuit unus
> me puero, ut memini, ductor fortissimus armis,
> conditor et legum, celeberrimus ore manuque,
> consultor patriae, sed non consultor

habendae relligionis, amans ter centum milia divum.
perfidus ille Deo, quamvis non perfidus orbi,
augustum caput ante pedes curvare Minervae
fictilis et soleas Iunonis lambere, plantis
Herculis advolvi, genua incerare Dianae,
quin et Apollineo frontem submittere gypso
aut Pollucis equum suffire ardentibus extis.

(Yet of all the emperors one there was in my boyhood, I remember, a brave leader in arms, a lawgiver, famous for speech and action, one who cared for his country's weal, but not for maintaining true religion, for he loved myriad gods. False to God, however true to the world, he would bend the head of majesty before Minerva's feet, would lick a clay Juno's sandals, grovel at the feet of Hercules, wax the knees of Diana, and bow before a plaster Apollo or smoke Pollux's horse with the burning of entrails.)

Even Augustine in the early fifth century recognizes the conflict within Julian's character. Mentioning him incidentally in his *City of God*, he has this to say of him: 'He had unusual talents, which were led astray through his ambition for power by a sacrilegious and detestable inquisitiveness. He abandoned himself to its empty prophecies when, sure of victory, he burned the ships carrying the necessary supplies. Then he rashly pressed on with immoderate ventures, was killed in consequence of his imprudence, and left his army destitute in enemy territory' (*City of God* 5.21). Imprudence, inquisitiveness and ambition for power are human errors that often accompany excellence. Augustine's Julian is not diabolical.

But the devil was what the Christian masses wanted. He made Julian easy to understand. A legendary version of his life and death soon grew up, probably in Syria. The *Church History* of Sozomenus, written in the mid-fifth century, tells of a sophist on his way to join Julian in Persia, who had a dream in a wayside chapel. He saw an assembly of saints and prophets discussing the sufferings of the faithful under Julian. Two of their number went off to deal with the situation. A little later they returned and announced that Julian had been killed. A similar story is told by the Armenian historian Faustus of Buzanda, who may be earlier than Sozomen. Soon popular imagination supplied names and details missing in the earlier version. We find the fuller story already in outline in the popular chronicle of John Malalas (sixth century) and in the *Easter Chronicle* (mid-seventh century). A more detailed version appears in a romantic *Life of St Basil* falsely attributed to his austere friend Amphilochius of Iconium: it was probably composed in the sixth century. The kernel of the story is a dream of Basil's, in which he sees St Mercurius dispatched by the Virgin to kill the 'serpent' Julian. When Basil awakens, he finds the sword and spear preserved among the relics of St Mercurius wet with fresh blood. Shortly afterwards news arrives that the emperor has been slain by an unknown hand in Mesopotamia. More elaborate, novelistic versions of this story survive in Syriac. In one Julian is a monster who tears out children's hearts and plucks living foetuses from the womb for magical purposes. St Mercurius prophesies his death to the future emperor Jovian and in the middle of the last battle with the Persians a heavenly voice is heard proclaiming that Julian's end is come. In another Syriac version the young Julian unlawfully seizes the property of his aunt, Constantine's sister, and through this sin falls into the clutches of a demon. The demon promises him dominion over the world in return for obedience. Julian accepts and becomes emperor. The familiar story of St Mercurius concludes the account.

One of these versions, close to the pseudo-Amphilochius *Life of St Basil,* was translated into Latin by a Roman sub-deacon, in the ninth century. In it Libanius is introduced as a supporter of Julian who is converted and adopts the religious life under Basil. This version rapidly spread in the west and is retold by many medieval writers, such as Vincent of Beauvais in the thirteenth century in his influential *Mirror of History.*

In the meantime spurious accounts of alleged martyrdoms under Julian had sprung up all over the Christian world as a means of shedding lustre on undistinguished local churches. One such account is set in Rome – which Julian never visited; – and is connected with the cult of two legendary martyrs John and Paul. The great church of St John and Paul, south of the Colosseum, has long been dedicated to these pseudo-martyrs. But excavations at the end of last century suggest that it was originally the site of the cult of quite different, and very possibly authentic, martyrs. The story of the martyrdom of John and Paul is an adaptation of that of Saints Juventinus and Maximinus. The story of Julian and the two Roman martyrs is followed by Jacobus of Voragine in his much read *Golden Legend* in the thirteenth century, as well as by the tenth-century German nun Hrotsvitha of Gandersheim in one of the curious Latin dramas in imitation of Terence that she wrote for performance by her fellow-nuns. In it John and Paul give away the property of a daughter of Constantine, whose

Christian husband has been exiled to Egypt and put to death. Julian tries to tempt them by offering them lucrative palace appointments if they abjure their religion. They stand their ground and are finally put to death for refusing to sacrifice to Jupiter.

These legends dominated the view of Julian in the western Middle Ages. They are reflected in the twelfth-century German *Regensburg Chronicle*, which tells an elaborate story in which the young Julian is haled before the Pope for embezzling the property of his pious foster-mother. He swears he is innocent, and the woman is eventually reduced to taking in washing for a living. In the Tiber she finds a statue of Mercury. The demon in the statue makes Julian return the stolen property, and later offers to make him emperor if Julian will do his will. He accepts, succeeds Constantine, and begins to persecute the Christians, including two rich dukes John and Paul, whom he puts to death. Then he goes on a campaign to Greece where he encounters and persecutes the abbot Basil, and puts to death a young officer called Mercurius, who refuses to forswear Christianity. In a dream Basil sees Mercurius rise from the grave, take his spear and shield, and ride off to avenge himself on Julian. The emperor is stabbed by the ghostly horseman, and his body miraculously conveyed to Constantinople where it is to remain uncorrupted till the day of judgement. Meanwhile Basil goes to Mercurius' tomb and finds his shield and spear there, stained with fresh blood. It would be difficult to disentangle the elements of folk-tale, history and fiction that make up this farrago.

The Renaissance and the Reformation brought with them new insights into Julian's role in history. His abandonment of Christianity, so incomprehensible to medieval man, for whom the Church provided a total environment, appeared in a very different light to a generation that saw the Church divided and its different groups engaged in savage polemics and even resorting to arms against one another. The new, secular attitude of the humanists towards human character and achievement took Julian out of theology and returned him to history. And the political experience of princes and city-states, and the new analysis of political power to which that experience led, caused men to approach Julian's performance as a statesman without being hypnotized by horror of his apostasy.

In 1489 Lorenzo de Medici wrote a play on Julian for the feasts of Saints John and Paul that would have been inconceivable a century earlier. The plot is still substantially that of the medieval legend, as the occasion demanded. John and Paul are put to death for refusing to renounce Christianity, and St Mercurius rises from the grave in answer to Basil's prayer and kills the emperor, who rejects an astrologer's warning of his imminent death. The emperor is no longer the medieval monster, but a renaissance hero, resourceful, ambitious, intelligent and articulate. His life is a human tragedy, not a theological example.

In Germany Hans Sachs, in several of his ballads, retells the medieval story. But his Julian is cast in the image of a burgher of Nürnberg, wily and astute rather than utterly evil. In one ballad Hans Sachs combines the Julian legend with the folk-tale of the king whose clothes were stolen in the bath and who was recognized by none of his former courtiers nor even by his wife. This free handling of the traditional story is further evidence of the secular, and untheological view that the sixteenth century was beginning to take of the legendary Apostate. He could even be made the hero of a moralizing tale.

He could also be a tragic hero. In the great age of European drama plays on Julian were written in England (by an anonymous author in 1596), in Italy (by Melchior Zoppio in 1612), in Spain (by Juan Crisóstomo Velez de Guevara in the seventeenth century), in Germany (by Johannes Herbin, a Lutheran pastor from Silesia in 1668), and in Switzerland (by an anonymous author of Lucerne in 1624). Of these only Herbin's play appears to have been printed. Meanwhile the Jesuits of southern Germany took Julian as the hero of several of the plays that they wrote in the seventeenth century for performance in their colleges. These lengthy and spectacular dramas – there had to be a part for everyone – combined uneasily the medieval legend of Saints John and Paul with the account of Julian's life given by his contemporary Ammianus Marcellinus.

The same century saw the publication and critical study of the sources that were to enable later scholars to make a clean break both with the diabolical Julian of the Middle Ages and with the tragic Julian of the Renaissance. Godefroy's learned commentary on the Theodosian Code, published in six volumes between 1626 and 1652, put Julian's surviving legislation in its place in the history of the fourth century. The erudite French Jansenist Jean François le Nain de Tillemont in his *Histoire des empereurs* (1690ff.) examined, compared and criticized in immense detail the contemporary sources for the life of Julian. His purpose was apologetic. Julian was still for him the Apostate, who had abandoned the faith. Yet Tillemont's integrity and precision and his unrivalled command of his material provided for the first time a sound basis for an evaluation of Julian as a phenomenon of history rather than of theology. Editions of Ammianus Marcellinus equipped with scholarly commentaries, in which innumerable points in his account of Julian were cleared up once and for all, were published by the Frenchman Henri de Valois in 1636 and by the Dutchman Jacob Gronovius in 1693. The voluminous works of Julian's friend Libanius were published between 1606 and 1627 by Frédéric Morel in an edition that for the first time offered a more or less intelligible text. As for Julian himself, forty-eight of his letters had appeared in print as early as 1499, as models of Greek prose style. And some of his other works were printed in rather unsatisfactory editions in the course of the sixteenth century. But it was in the seventeenth century that there appeared for the first time two complete editions of his surviving works in a reliable text and equipped with scholarly commentaries. The first, by the French savant Denis Petau, was published in Paris in 1630. The second, by the German Ezechiel Spanheim, appeared in Leipzig in 1696.

The works of the *érudits* of the seventeenth century provided the foundation for the Age of Reason in the eighteenth. Already in 1699 Gottfried Arnold in his *Impartial History of the Church and Heresies* gave a balanced and moderate account of Julian, rejecting the legendary material and basing himself firmly on the authentic sources. Montesquieu in his *Grandeur et décadence des Romains* (1734) and *De l'esprit des lois* (1748) bestowed on him the highest praise as a statesman and legislator. In 1735 Philippe René de la Blèterie published the first full-length biography of Julian, the tone of which is uniformly favourable. Henry Fielding in his *Journey from this World to the Next* found Julian not in Hell, but in Elysium. In 1782 there appeared the second volume of Edward Gibbon's *Decline and Fall of the Roman Empire*, in which three memorable chapters were devoted to Julian. While seeing in Julian a philosophic monarch who sought in a decadent age to restore the glory of the Roman Empire, Gibbon often expresses regret that he should have allowed himself to be degraded by the superstitions of the society in which he lived. He wrote:

> The generality of princes, if they were stripped of their purple, and cast naked into the world, would immediately sink to the lowest rank of society, without a hope of emerging from obscurity. But the personal merit of Julian was in some measure independent of his fortune. Whatever had been his choice of life, by the force of intrepid courage, lively wit, and intense application, he would have obtained, or at least he would have deserved, the highest honours of his profession; and Julian might have raised himself to the rank of minister, of general, of the state in which he was born a private citizen. If the jealous caprice of

power had disappointed his expectations, if he had prudently declined the paths of greatness, the employment of the same talents in studious solitude would have placed beyond the reach of Kings his present happiness and his immortal fame. . . . The theological system of Julian appears to have contained the sublime and important principles of natural religion. But as the faith which is not founded on revelation must remain destitute of any firm assurance, the disciple of Plato imprudently relapsed into the habits of vulgar superstition. . . . The genius and power of Julian were unequal to the enterprise of restoring a religion which was destitute of theological principles, of moral precepts, and of ecclesiastical discipline; which rapidly hastened to decay and dissolution, and was not susceptible of any solid or consistent re-formation. In the exercise of his uncommon talents he often descended below the majesty of his rank. Alexander was transformed into Diogenes; the philosopher was degraded into a priest.

The men of the eighteenth century tended to see Julian in their own image, as the incarnation of dispassionate reason and the foe of obsolete superstition. Gibbon was honest enough and learned enough to perceive the difficulties of this interpretation. Others often lacked one or other of these qualities. Thus Diderot made of Julian *'l'honneur de l'éclectisme'*. And Voltaire, who was constantly using him as an example, was embarrassed by his evident religiosity, which he tried to explain away or to ignore as unimportant. In a passage that finally appeared in his article 'Julian' in the *Dictionnaire philosophique* he writes:

Ce qui est très-singulier et très-vrai, c'est que si vous faites abstraction de son malheureux changement, si vous ne suivez cet empereur ni dans les églises chrétiennes, ni aux temples idolâtres; si vous le suivez dans sa maison, dans les camps, dans les batailles, dans ses moeurs, dans sa conduite, dans ses écrits; vous le trouvez partout égal à Marc-Aurèle. Ainsi cet homme, qu'on a peint abominable, est peut-être le premier des hommes, ou du moins le second.

Friedrich Schiller long intended to make Julian the hero of a tragedy. But the difficulty of the task grew on him, and in the end the drama was never written. Indeed the Romantic Age as a whole found Julian curiously difficult to swallow. Perhaps the virtual absence of a love interest in his life is part of the explanation. And as a compulsive writer and talker he was not given to those silences that the spirit of the age associated with profundity. He tended to be treated as a figure of defeat. August Neander, in a scholarly study of his life first published in 1812 and several times revised, the emperor was seen as a deeply serious seeker after truth who was misunderstood by almost all those round him. It was to Neander's book that most nineteenth-century writers turned for information on Julian. Disillusioned intellectuals tended to identify themselves with Julian, the rebel and outsider, who was greater than the enemies who defeated him. Thus Alfred de Vigny in his *Daphné*, a kind of moral biography in dialogue form begun about 1837, made of Julian a man of deep insight struggling with insoluble moral problems. Henrik Ibsen's two-part tragedy *Emperor and Galilean* (1873) was both bad history and bad theatre, and has seldom been staged. But it was the result of years of struggle by its author to depict the struggle between two irreconcilable principles of life – idealism and immediate enjoyment of life – valid for every age. Julian's synthesis of the two, failure though it was, represented Ibsen's solution for the moral disease of capitalist society that he so often diagnosed and described.

The Russian mystic Dmitri Merezhkovsky in his novel *Julian the Apostate* (1894) imagines a struggle in Julian's nature for a synthesis between senses and soul, between pagan and Christian religiosity. The true hero of Merezhkovsky's novel is perhaps the philosopher Maximus, who knows that the gods of Hellas do not exist, but goes on worshipping them in expectation of the coming of an unknown saviour. The novel, turgid in expression and confused in plot, is symptomatic of the state of mind of a section of the Russian intelligentsia at the close of the nineteenth century. It adds nothing to our understanding of Julian. It is noteworthy that both Ibsen and Merezhkovsky saw fit to provide Julian with a *femme fatale*. For Ibsen it was the shadowy Helena, who is turned into an ideal woman. For Merezhkovsky it is a pagan sculptress who is converted to Christianity and refuses to marry the emperor.

Meanwhile at the other end of Europe Kleon Rhangavís, son of a more famous father, published in Athens in 1877 a gigantic tragedy (1500 lines of prose and nearly 9000 of verse), *Julian the Apostate*. His Julian is a humanist, disillusioned with the sterile tyranny of religion. Once again romantic love is introduced. Julian as a student in Athens meets a Christian girl and later as emperor wishes to marry her. To save herself from such a marriage the girl drowns herself in the Bosphorus. Her father, driven mad by the death of his daughter, is used by Christian conspirators to murder Julian in Persia. The play was far too long to be staged, and even to read it demanded an unusual effort, since it was written in the most uncompromisingly classical Greek. Yet because of its implied criticism of the Orthodox Church it was fiercely attacked and had to be withdrawn from the bookshops.

In France, where Julian's association with Paris gave him a special interest, Étienne Jouy published a tragedy, *Julien dans les Gaules,* in 1823. Its theme is romantic love rather than religion or politics. Sainte-Beuve and Renan in the middle of the century both saw Julian as a bizarre and muddled mixture of fanaticism and self-conceit, in spite of his manifest intelligence. Anatole France in *L'empereur Julien* (1892) made of him a unique tolerant fanatic, a man who through his own bitter experience had learnt respect for human life and human thought.

Along with these major works the nineteenth century saw a multiplicity of plays, poems and novels on Julian, which have now been forgotten by all but specialists. Germany was particularly fertile, and German writers often used Julian for tendentious ends. Wilhelm Molitor's play *Julian the Apostate* (1866), though following the sources closely, presents a strongly Catholic picture of Julian, with medieval echoes. An even more demonic Julian appears in Adam Trabert's *The Emperor Julian the Apostate* (1894). Felix Dahn's three-volume novel *Julian the Apostate,* once acclaimed as a minor masterpiece, makes Julian an enthusiastic young commander filled with a sense of his mission to revitalize the Roman empire but misled into a wrong approach by unscrupulous advisers. The only man to tell him the truth is Serapio, a Hellenized German, who is built up by the author from a single mention in Ammianus Marcellinus. France, Italy, Holland, Poland and Denmark also produced their crop of imaginative reconstructions of Julian, usually in dramatic form, and rarely enjoying more than a fleeting success.

Julian has not been one of the heroes of the twentieth century, in spite of his evident appeal to the psychologist, and few works of imaginative literature have been written round his life and personality. The most notable exception is Nikos Kazantzakis' tragedy *Julian the Apostate* (1945), in which the emperor is depicted as an existentialist hero committed to a struggle which he knows will be in vain. It was first staged in Paris in 1948. Scholarly study of Julian and his age has flourished, however, as part of the increased and deepened interest in the late Roman empire and the transition from antiquity to the Middle Ages. Innumerable articles in learned periodicals have illuminated – or occasionally obfuscated – details

of his life, his legislation, his military strategy, his religious attitude and
his literary purposes. Full-length studies addressed in part to the general
reader have not been lacking. J. Geffcken's *Kaiser Julianus* (1914) is a sober
account by a scholar sensitive to the changes in the world of thought and
feeling that marked the end of antiquity. The Belgian scholar Joseph Bidez
in his *La vie de l'empereur Julien* (1930) wrote with a sureness of touch, a
clarity and a grasp of the problems that have made his book authoritative
ever since. The only subsequent study of Julian that can challenge that of
Bidez is by the Italian historian Roberto Andreotti, *Il regno dell'Imperatore
Giuliano* (1936).

The curiously irresolute judgement of the first half of the present
century is best summed up in the words with which the French historian
André Piganiol concluded his chapter on the reign of Julian in his volume
on the Christian empire from 325 to 395:

> So this hero led his army to a disaster which weighed heavily on the
> future of the empire. This friend of liberty was destined to rule as a
> sun-King in the manner of the Incas. This philosopher, misunderstand-
> ing the pagan moralists of Rome, linked the cause of paganism with the
> most foolish elucubrations. His true greatness is on the moral plane.
> The nobility and even the restlessness of his character, the criticism
> which he made of himself, his unending dialogue with the gods demand
> our respect. He possessed, says Ammianus, the four cardinal virtues,
> temperance, prudence, justice and courage. More than most of the
> theologians of his time to whom that honourable title has been granted
> he would deserve to be considered a saint.

Peter Brown, in his *World of Late Antiquity* (1971) gives not so much a
different verdict as a different kind of verdict, typical of the new concerns
of the second half of our century:

> Julian spoke up for the 'community of the Hellenes''. He represented
> the depressed gentry of the ancient Greek towns of Asia Minor – 'honest
> men' who had watched with growing anger the blasphemies, the
> indecent affluence, the deep intellectual confusion of the court society
> of Constantine and Constantius II . . . He reminded the upper classes of
> landmarks that had been washed away by the social fluidity of the early
> fourth century. . . . It was not that Julian was unrealistic. He saw, with
> a clarity bred of hatred, one blatant feature of his age – Christianity
> rising like a damp stain up the wall of his beloved Hellenic culture.

What he did not see was that this same Christianity was able to pass the classical culture of an élite to the average citizen of the Roman world [pp. 91–93).

It is hardly surprising that Julian has once again attracted the attention of a creative writer. Gore Vidal's *Julian* was published in 1962. It is a book that reflects the interests of the mid-twentieth century. The narrative technique – a diary kept by Julian, punctuated by comments made twenty years later by Libanius and by the philosopher Priscus, who was present at the emperor's death – permits a combination of self-revelation and objective assessment peculiarly acceptable to a generation familiar with the literature of the psycho-analysist's couch. Julian is credited with a number of sexual adventures for which neither he himself nor his friends nor his enemies provide any evidence, and there are a few descriptive passages that in the early sixties may still have verged upon the pornographic. Julian is less surely and clearly delineated in his relation to political power or to God than he is in relation to his fellow men or to his own inner life. Yet it is a powerful and compelling novel, with a strong appeal to all who feel a little lost in the world that they inhabit. One can readily identify with Vidal's Julian.

The real mass arts of the second half of this century, television and the cinema, do not seem to have discovered Julian yet. Perhaps he is too intellectual and not visual enough, too much a man of words and too little a man of action. Yet he is still, after sixteen centuries, a symbol that helps men to understand themselves. His obsession with communication, his consciousness of being an outsider with a mission to heal a sick society, the tragic and brutal finality of his unnecessary death, all make him potently attractive to many in our age. American students have spontaneously compared him with President John Kennedy. If Julian's soul survives in some refulgent Neoplatonist heaven he must surely be pleased with the immortality of his memory here on earth.

Note on Sources

Contemporary and near-contemporary sources for the life and reign of Julian are numerous. First and foremost come the writings of Julian himself – his letters, his panegyrics on members of the imperial family, his pagan religious treatises, his satires, the fragments of his anti-Christian polemic. These are most readily accessible in English translation in W. C. Wright, *The Works of the Emperor Julian*, 3 vols (London: Loeb Classical Library, 1913–24).

The most detailed narrative history of the period is that of Ammianus Marcellinus, an Antiochene Greek who served as an army officer and after retirement wrote the history of his own time in Latin. Ammianus was an eye-witness of many of the events of Julian's career, which is recounted in Books 15–25 of his *History*. There is an English translation in J. C. Rolfe, *Ammianus Marcellinus*, 3 vols (Loeb Classical Library, 1935–52). Eutropius wrote a compendium of Roman history about 369, the concluding chapters of which treat the reign of Julian. There is an English translation by J. S. Watson (London, 1848). Eunapius of Sardis, an ardent pagan who lived towards the end of the fourth century, gave in his *History* a highly favourable account of the reign of Julian based in part on the memoirs of Oreibasios, Julian's doctor and friend. The original is now lost, but it was the principal source used by the pagan historian Zosimus about AD 500, who recounts the reign of Julian in Book III of his *New History*. There is an English translation by J. Buchanan and H. T. Davis (San Antonio, 1967). Eunapius also has something to say about Julian in his 'Life of Maximus', which forms part of his *Lives of the Philosophers* – English translation by W. C. Wright (Loeb Classical Library, 1922).

The address to Julian by the consul Claudius Mamertinus at Constantinople in January 362 is preserved in the collection of Latin panegyrics most recently edited by R. A. B. Mynors (Oxford, 1964). I know of no English translation, but there is a French translation by E. Galletier in *Panégyriques Latins*, vol. 3 (Paris, 1955). Libanius, teacher of rhetoric at Antioch and the leading Greek man of letters of his age, knew Julian and devotes several of his speeches to him. Orations 12 and 13 were delivered in early 363, while Julian was still alive; Orations 15, 16 and 17 were composed and circulated, though probably never publicly delivered, in 365, and Orations 18 and 24 belong to 379. The Greek text of all of these was published by R. Foerster, *Libanii opera*, vols 1–4 (Leipzig, 1903–8). They are available in English translation in A. F. Norman, *Libanius, Selected Works*, I (Loeb Classical Library, 1969).

The two attacks made upon Julian by Gregory of Nazianzus, the future archbishop of Constantinople, shortly after the emperor's death, are published in English translation by C. W. King, *Julian the Emperor* (London, 1888). Three ecclesiastical historians writing in Greek towards the middle of the fifth century – Socrates, Sozomenus and Theodoret – devote considerable space to Julian's religious policy, of which they naturally give a partisan account. Socrates' *Church History* is translated by A. C. Zenos (London, 1891), that of Sozomenus by C. D. Hartranft (London, 1891), and that of Theodoret by B. Jackson (London, 1892). The Latin *Church History* of Jerome's friend Rufinus of Aquileia is translated by W. H. Fremantle (London, 1892). Later Byzantine Chronicles, particularly those of John Malalas (sixth century) and John Zonaras (twelfth century) provide information on Julian not furnished by contemporary sources; but its reliability is uncertain. Malalas is translated by M. Spinka and G. Downey (Chicago, 1940).

Many fragments of Julian's laws, usually torn from their context, but reliably dated, are preserved in the Theodosian Code (compiled at the order of Theodosius II in 432) and in Justinian's Code (compiled in 534). The former is translated by Clyde Pharr, *The Theodosian Code and Novels and the Sirmondian Constitutions* (Princeton, 1952).

The Syriac poems on Julian of the monk Ephraim are published with German translation in *Ephraem des Syrers Hymnen de Paradiso und Contra Julianum* (Corpus Scriptorum Orientalium 79) (Louvain, 1957).

Suggestions for Further Reading

The literature on Julian is immense, but much of it is out of date in its approach to the period and its use of sources. This is true of virtually all nineteenth-century work, which is summed up in P. Allard's three-volume *Julien l'Apostat* (Paris, 1900). J. Geffcken, *Kaiser Julianus* (Munich, 1914), is a penetrating and scholarly study by a historian with a deep understanding of late antiquity. By far the best general introduction is still J. Bidez, *La vie de l'empereur Julien* (Paris, 1930). R. Andreotti, *Il regno dell'imperatore Giuliano* (Rome, 1936), supplements and corrects Bidez on many matters of detail. None of these works is available in English translation. Alice Gardner, *Julian, Philosopher and Emperor* (London, 1890), is outdated and W. D. Simpson, *Julian the Apostate* (Aberdeen, 1930), is of little value. Anna Morduch, *The Death and Life of Julian* (London, 1960) is a work of imaginative fiction rather than a biography.

Surviving portraits of Julian are reproduced and critically examined by Raissa Calza, *Iconografia romana imperiale da Carausio a Giuliano* (Rome, 1972). On coin-portraits see also J. P. C. Kent, 'An introduction to the coinage of Julian the Apostate', *Numismatic Chronicle*, 6th Series, 19 (1959), 109–17.

R. C. Blockley 'Constantius Gallus and Julian as Caesars of Constantius II', *Latomus*, 21 (1972), 433–68 and R. T. Ridley, 'Notes on Julian's Persian expedition', *Historia*, 22 (1973) 317–30 are valuable discussions of particular episodes of Julian's life.

General histories of the period are numerous. Among the best are A. Piganiol, *L'empire chrétien, 325–395* (Paris, 1949), E. Stein, *Histoire du*

Bas-Empire, vol. 1 (Paris, 1959) and J. Vogt, *The Decline of Rome* (London, 1967). A. H. M. Jones, *The Later Roman Empire 284–602. A Social, Economic and Administrative Survey* (Oxford, 1964), 3 vols and maps, is, as its title implies, much more than a narrative history. The earlier, narrative, section deals briefly and clearly with the political history of Julian's reign, and the later chapters on the various institutions of the later empire constantly return to aspects of his age.

Julian's policies and the problems which he faced cannot be understood without some acquaintance with the work of Constantine. All of the books listed in section 4 deal at some length with the reign of Constantine. A. H. M. Jones, *Constantine and the Conversion of Europe* (London, 1948) and R. MacMullen, *Constantine* (London, 1970) are good short introductions.

N. H. Baynes, *Constantine and the Christian Church* (Oxford, 1929), gives a balanced introduction to the complex and changing relations of church and state in the period. H. Chadwick, *The Early Church* (Harmondsworth, 1967), treats this topic from the point of view of a non-sectarian church historian. A. D. Nock, *Conversion: The Old and the New in Religion from Alexander the Great to Augustine of Hippo* (2nd edition, London, 1952), examines the implications in the ancient world of adherence to a new religion. Most of the relevant documents are translated by P. R. Coleman-Norton, *Roman State and Christian Church*, 3 vols (London, 1966). A detailed examination of most of the new problems posed by the existence of a Christian Roman empire will be found in J. Gaudemet, *L'église dans l'empire romain, IVe–Ve siècles* (Paris, 1958).

The relation of the new religion to the inherited Graeco-Roman culture is discussed in two recent books, which are both scholarly and highly readable. They are E. R. Dodds, *Pagan and Christian in an Age of Anxiety* (Cambridge, 1965) and A. D. Momigliano (ed.), *The Conflict between Paganism and Christianity in the Fourth Century* (Oxford, 1963). Another, somewhat older, study is M. L. W. Laistner, *Christianity and Pagan Culture in the Later Roman Empire* (Cornell, 1951).

The Neoplatonist philosophy is the subject of an extensive literature, much of which is not easy reading. Two excellent introductions are A. Armstrong (ed.), *The Cambridge History of Later Greek and Early Medieval*

Philosophy (Cambridge, 1967) and R. T. Wallis, *Neoplatonism* (London, 1972).

The overriding question of the economic, social and political changes which took place in Mediterranean society at the end of antiquity and the beginning of the Middle Ages has preoccupied historians since the Renaissance. It was essentially the problem to which Edward Gibbon addressed himself in *The Decline and Fall of the Roman Empire*. Although he does not ask some of the questions which historians ask today, and did not have access to the evidence of archaeology, papyrology and other auxiliary disciplines, his great book is still worth reading. Chapters 22–24 deal in particular with the reign of Julian. A. H. M. Jones' book, mentioned above, provides a description and analysis of the changes in society in terms more readily accepted in the late twentieth century. Recent studies which offer an introduction to the questions at issue and to the answers proposed include D. Kagan, *Decline and Fall of the Roman Empire* (Boston, 1962); R. Rémondon, *La crise de l'empire romain de Marc-Aurèle à Anastase* (Paris, 1964); L. White (ed.), *The Transformation of the Roman World: Gibbon's Problem after two centuries* (Berkeley–Los Angeles, 1966); F. W. Walbank, *The Awful Revolution: The Decline and Fall of the Empire in the West* (Liverpool, 1969); P. Brown, *The World of Late Antiquity: From Marcus Aurelius to Muhammad* (London, 1971).

Every aspect of life in Constantinople in the age of Julian is discussed critically and in great detail by G. Dagron, *Naissance d'une capitale: Constantinople et ses institutions de 330 à 451* (Paris, 1974). Antioch in Julian's day is treated in P. Petit, *Libanius et la vie municipale à Antioche* (Paris, 1955) and in J. H. W. G. Liebeschuetz, *Antioch: City and Imperial Administration in the Later Roman Empire* (Oxford, 1972).

JULIAN'S FAMILY

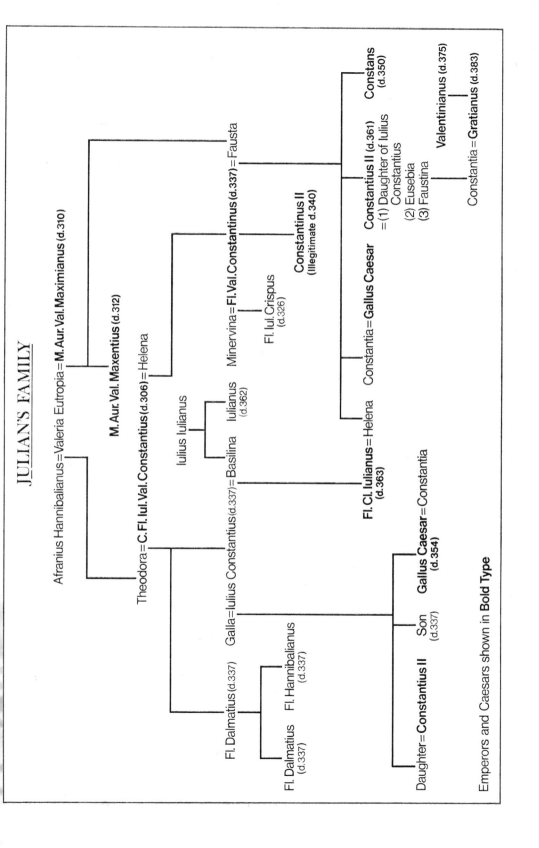

Afranius Hannibalianus = Valeria Eutropia = **M.Aur.Val.Maximianus (d.310)**

M.Aur. Val. Maxentius (d.312)

Theodora = **C.Fl.Iul.Val.Constantius(d.306)** = Helena

Iulius Iulianus

Iulianus (d.362)

Basilina = Iulius Constantius(d.337) = Galla

Minervina = **Fl.Val.Constantinus(d.337)** = Fausta

Fl.Iul.Crispus (d.326)

Constantinus II (Illegitimate d.340)

Fl.Cl.Iulianus = Helena (d.363)

Constantia = **Gallus Caesar**

Constantius II (d.361)
= (1) Daughter of Iulius Constantius
(2) Eusebia
(3) Faustina

Constans (d.350)

Valentinianus (d.375)

Constantia = **Gratianus (d.383)**

Fl. Dalmatius(d.337)

Fl. Dalmatius (d.337)

Fl. Hannibalianus (d.337)

Son (d.337)

Gallus Caesar = Constantia (d.354)

Daughter = **Constantius II**

Emperors and Caesars shown in **Bold Type**

Table of Dates

270–5   Aurelian emperor

284   Diocletian proclaimed emperor by army

286   Diocletian appoints Maximian co-emperor

293   Constantius and Galerius appointed junior emperors

296   Reform of taxation system

301   Edict fixing maximum prices

302–4   Persecution of Christians

305   Abdication of Diocletian and Maximian

306   Death of Constantius; Constantine proclaimed emperor

312   Constantine defeats Maxentius at Milvian Bridge and becomes ruler of the west

313   New policy of favour to Christians proclaimed at Milan

314   Constantine ejects Licinius from Illyricum

318   Beginning of Arian controversy

321   Sunday proclaimed a public holiday

324   Constantine defeats Licinius and becomes sole emperor

325   Church council at Nicaea

330   Inauguration of new capital at Constantinople

332   Julian born at Constantinople

337   Death of Constantine; accession of his three sons; Julian's father and brother murdered by troops

338   King Sapor besieges Nisibis

339   Julian under care of Mardonius

341	Pagan sacrifices prohibited
344–5	Julian sent to Macellum
346–8	King Sapor again besieges Nisibis; indecisive battle at Singara
351	Gallus appointed Caesar; Julian begins study at Nicomedia, Pergamum and Ephesus
	Constantius defeats rebel emperor Magnentius
354	Gallus recalled and put to death by Constantius
November 355	Julian appointed Caesar and married to Constantius' sister Helena
357	Battle of Strasbourg and crossing of Rhine
358	Julian's campaign against Franks
359	Julian again crosses Rhine
February 360	Julian proclaimed Augustus at Paris
361	Julian breaks with Constantius and advances to the Balkans
November 361	Death of Constantius; Julian sole emperor
11 December 361	Julian enters Constantinople
	Edict on restoration of temple property and on return of exiled clergy
Spring 362	Publication of polemics against Cynics and of *On the Mother of the Gods*
	Decree on schools
June 362	Julian leaves Constantinople for Antioch
October 362	Temple of Apollo at Daphne destroyed by fire
Spring 363	Publication of *Misopogon*
5 March 363	Julian leaves Antioch for the front
10/11 March 363	Julian crosses the Euphrates
4 April 363	Julian enters Persian territory
Beginning of June 363	Roman victory near Ctesiphon
	Burning of fleet
16 June 363	Beginning of Roman withdrawal
26 June 363	Death of Julian
June 363	Army proclaims Jovian emperor
July 363	Jovian concludes humiliating treaty with Persia
August 363	Procopius buries Julian at Tarsus

LONDON● ·RICHBOROUGH ●XANTEN
NEUSS
TOXANDRIA COLOGNE
●BOULOGNE BONN
Meuse ANDERNACH● MAINZ
Moselle BINGEN
●REIMS Rhine
Marne SAVERNE
PARIS● STRASBOURG
Seine
SENS● ●TROYES
AUGST●
AUXERRE Saône ●BESANÇON
Loire ●AUTUN

LYON●
●VIENNE

Rhone
●BORDEAUX

NARBONNE● ●MARSEILLE

GAUL IN THE
FOURTH CENTURY A.D.

0   50   100   150   200
|___|___|___|___|___|___|___|___| Miles

0   100   200   300
|___|___|___|___|___|___|___|___| Kilometres

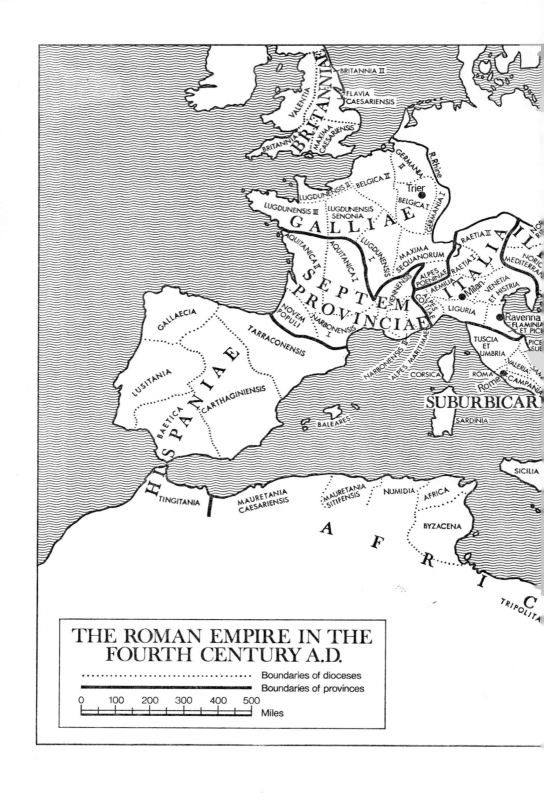

BRITANNIA II
FLAVIA
CAESARIENSIS
VALENTIA
BRITANNIAE
MAXIMA
CAESARIENSIS
BRITANNIA I

GERMANIA II
R. Rhine
LUGDUNENSIS II   BELGICA II
LUGDUNENSIS III   Trier
LUGDUNENSIS   BELGICA I
SENONIA
GERMANIA I

GALLIAE

AQUITANICA II   LUGDUNENSIS I
AQUITANICA I
MAXIMA
SEQUANORUM
RAETIA II

SEPTEM
ALPES
POENINAE   RAETIA I   NOR
PROVINCIAE   VIENNENSIS
ALPES GRAIAE
ET POENINAE   NORI
MEDITERRA

GALLAECIA
TARRACONENSIS
NOVEM
POPULI   NARBONENSIS
I   ITALIA
AEMILIA
COTTIAE   Milan   VENETIA
ET HISTRIA
LIGURIA
Ravenna
FLAMINIA
ET PICE

LUSITANIA
HISPANIAE   TUSCIA
ET   PICE
NARBONENSIS II   UMBRIA   SUE
CARTHAGINIENSIS   ALPES MARITIMAE
VALERIA SAN
BAETICA   CORSICA   ROMA
Rome CAMPANIA
BALEARES
SUBURBICAR
SARDINIA

HISPANIAE

SICILIA
TINGITANIA   MAURETANIA
CAESARIENSIS   MAURETANIA
SITIFENSIS   NUMIDIA   AFRICA
A   F
BYZACENA
R
I   C
TRIPOLITA

THE ROMAN EMPIRE IN THE
FOURTH CENTURY A.D.

.... Boundaries of dioceses
————————————————— Boundaries of provinces

0   100   200   300   400   500
Miles

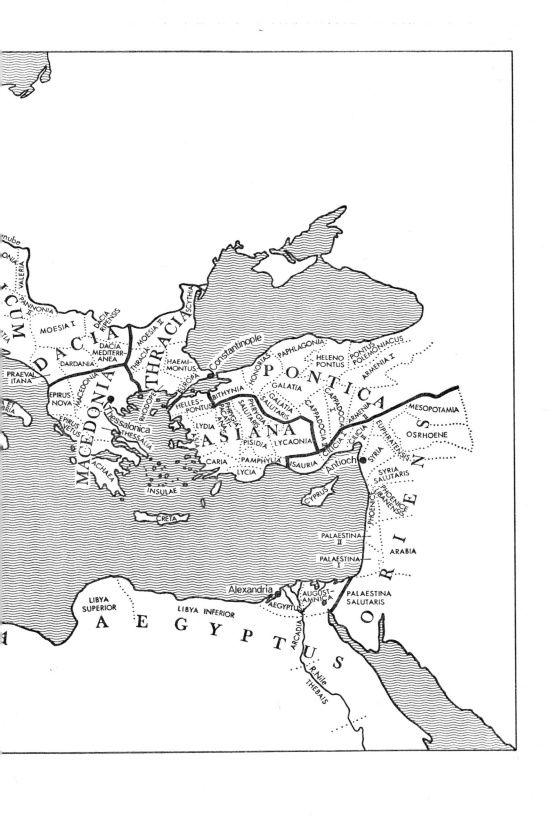

nube

ONIA I

VALERIA

PANNONIA II

TCUM

MOESIA I

DACIA RIPENSIS

DACIA
MEDITERR-
ANEA

DACIA

DARDANIA

MOESIA II

THRACIA

SCYTHIA

PRAEVAL
ITANA

EPIRUS
NOVA

MACEDONIA

RHODOPE

HAEMI-
MONTUS

EUROPA

Constantinople

PAPHLAGONIA

HELENO
PONTUS

PONTUS
POLEMONIACUS

PONTICA

ARMENIA I

MESOPOTAMIA

EPIRUS
VETUS

Thessalonica

THESSALIA

HELLES-
PONTUS

BITHYNIA

HONORIAS

GALATIA

GALATIA
SALUTARIS

CAPPADOCIA
I

OSRHOENE

ACHAEA

LYDIA

PHRYGIA
PACATIANA

PHRYGIA
SALUTARIS

CAPPADOCIA
II

ARMENIA
II

EUPHRATENSIS

ASIANA

PISIDIA

LYCAONIA

CILICIA I

CARIA

PAMPHYLIA

ISAURIA

CILICIA II

Antioch

SYRIA

INSULAE

LYCIA

CYPRUS

SYRIA
SALUTARIS

CRETA

PHOENICE

PHOENICE
LIBANENSIS

O R I E N

PALAESTINA
II

ARABIA

PALAESTINA
I

Alexandria

LIBYA
SUPERIOR

LIBYA INFERIOR

AUGUST-
AMNICA

AEGYPTUS

PALAESTINA
SALUTARIS

A E G Y P T U S

ARCADIA

R. Nile

THEBAIS

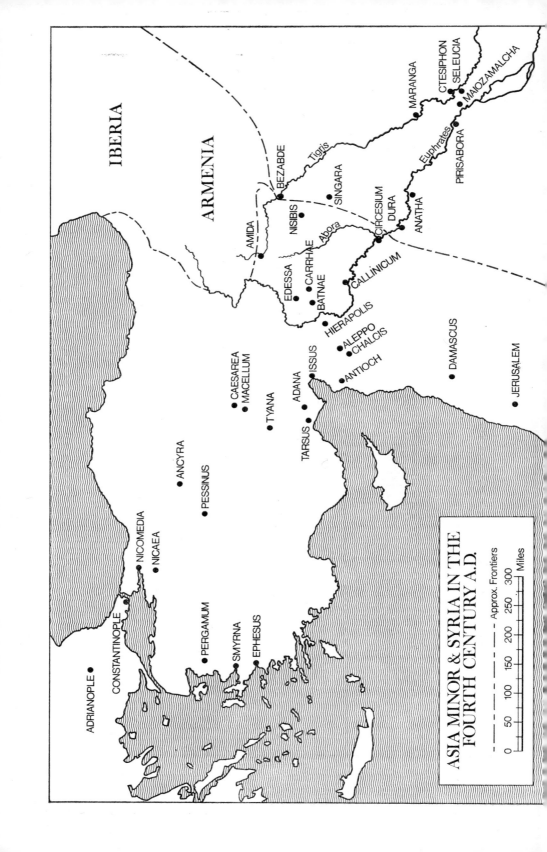

ASIA MINOR & SYRIA IN THE FOURTH CENTURY A.D.

IBERIA

ARMENIA

MARANGA
CTESIPHON
SELEUCIA
MAIOZAMALCHA
PIRISABORA
Euphrates
Tigris
BEZABDE
SINGARA
AMIDA
NISIBIS
CIRCESIUM
DURA
ANATHA
Abora
EDESSA
CARRHAE
BATNAE
CALLINICUM
HIERAPOLIS
ALEPPO
CHALCIS
ANTIOCH
DAMASCUS
JERUSALEM
ISSUS
CAESAREA
MACELLUM
ADANA
TYANA
TARSUS
ANCYRA
PESSINUS
NICOMEDIA
NICAEA
PERGAMUM
SMYRNA
EPHESUS
CONSTANTINOPLE
ADRIANOPLE

Approx. Frontiers
Miles
0 50 100 150 200 250 300

Index

adaeratio, 6

Adana, 144

administration, cities, 119, 132–3, 148, 151, 153–6; provincial, 5; state, 4–5, 18–19, 26–30, 126–31

Adrianopolis, 117

Aegae, 144

Aelius Aristides, 151

Against the Galileans, 174–5

Agilo, 124, 127

Aidesios, 55, 58

Alamanni, 69, 80, 82–8, 91, 94–5, 111

Alexander the Great, 144, 190

Alexandria, 9, 136, 144, 160–1

Alexandria Troas, 63

Aligildus, 120

Alypius, 176

Amida, 100, 108, 166, 189, 194

Ammianus Marcellinus, on Barbatio, 73; editions of, 229; final judgment on Julian, 225; on Gallus, 59; in Gaul, 68, 82, 87; on Julian as emperor, 121; on Julian's appearance, 65–6; on Julian's death, 213, 214, 215, 218; on Julian's edict on teachers, 169; on Julian's inauguration as Caesar, 70–2; on Julian's march against Constantius, 114, 115; and Julian's Persian campaign, 193, 198–9, 202, 204, 206

Amphilochius of Iconium, 226

Anatha, 199

Anatolius, 127

Ancyra, 46, 144, 183

Andreotti, Roberto, 234

Antennacum, 98

Antioch, as centre of power, 26; after Julian's death, 219; Christianity and paganism in, 157, 160, 161, 177–86; Constantius II in, 28, 34, 108; description, 48–9, 144–9; Gallus in, 59; Julian in, 144, 149–58, 183–4, 191; Julian marches from, 195

Antoninus Pius, 130, 134

Apamea, 146

Apodemius, 125

Apollinarios, 173

Apollo, 4, 13, 20, 25, 27, 138, 181

Aquileia, 39, 117

Arbetio, 124, 127

Arethusa, 136

Argentoratum, 85–8, 115

Arians, 23–4, 50

Arintheus, 216

Aristophanes, 37

Aristophanes, governor of Macedonia, 220

Aristotle, 40, 55, 190

Arius, 23

Armenia, 187–9

army, Julian's appointments to, 127; religious practices, 110, 138, 161; under Diocletian, 8–9; under Constantine, 18, 19

Arnold, Gottfried, 230
Arsaces, King of Armenia, 194, 196, 209, 210, 216
Arsacius, 179
Asclepiades, 182
Asklepios, 175
Atarbius, 127, 186
Athanasius, 39, 50, 183, 219
Athens, 64–6, 119
Attis, 142, 171
Attuarii, 108
Augusta Taurinorum, 76
Augustine, 160, 226
Augustodunum, 49, 81
Augustus, 27
Aurelian, 3
Aurelius Victor, Sextus, 120, 130, 214

Babylas, Saint, 155, 181
Babylonia, 188
Bacchus, cult of, 11
Barbatio, 73, 84–5
Barsaphthai, 210
Basil, priest, 144
Basil, Saint, 45, 172, 215, 226–7, 228
Basilina, 32–3, 36
Basilinopolis, 168
Bassiana, 150
Bassianus, 150
Batnae, 195
Belaeus, 137
Beroea, 145, 195
Berytus, 173
Bezabde, 108, 189
Bible, 173, 176
Bidez, Joseph, 233–4
Bonitus, 67
Bonna, 98
Bononia, 98, 106, 116
Bostra, 137
Britain, 93, 94, 98, 106, 166, 176
Brotomagum, 82
Brown, Peter, 234
Bryaxis, 182
Byzantium, 27

Caecilian of Carthage, 23
Caesarea, 41, 183
Caesars, 182
Calama, 160
Callinicum, 197
Cappadocia, 40, 144
Carnuntum, 15
Carrhae, 161, 195–6, 198
Cassianus, 216
Cassius Dio, 29
Castra Herculis, 98
Catullus, 142
Celsus, 127, 151, 175
central government and administration, Constantinople as a centre of, 26–30; mobility of the emperors' centre of government, 26; the Tetrarchy, 7, 14–15, 16; under Constantine, 18–19; under Diocletian, 4–5; under Julian, 126–31
Chalcedon, 26, 124, 144, 191
Chalcis, 154
Chaldaean Oracles, 57
Chamavi, 76, 93
Chnodomar, 85, 86–7, 111
Christianity, early growth and persecutions, 9–14; Julian and, 38, 40–1, 43, 44, 46, 59, 108–11, 134–43, 162–86, 222–7; Porphyry and, 53–4; under Constantine, 19–25, 27, 159, 161–2, 168
Chrysanthios, 55–6
Chrysopolis, 16
Cilicia, 96, 145
Circesium, 197–8
cities, government and administration, 119, 132–3, 148, 151, 153–6
Claudius Gothicus, 16
Clement of Alexandria, 10, 23
coinage, 18–19, 156
Cologne, 68–9, 76, 80, 82
comitatenses, 9
Comum, 64
Constans, 16, 28, 39, 48–50, 77, 83
Constantia, 16, 111
Constantia (place), 183
Constantianus, 198
Constantina, 51

Constantine I, central government under, 18–19; Christianity under, 19–25, 159, 161–2, 168; consulship, 156; death, 34; establishes Constantinople, 26–30; and his half-brothers, 31–2; rise to power, 14–17; upbringing and character, 17–18
Constantine II, 16, 28, 34, 39, 48
Constantinople, Constantius buried in, 121–2; establishment of, 26–30; Julian in, 121, 123–43; and Rome, 27–8, 128
Constantius I, 14, 15, 17, 20, 31
Constantius II, 42, 129, 156; becomes Caesar, 16; Persian Wars, 34, 46, 48–9, 99, 107, 108, 166, 189, 192, 195, 225; becomes Emperor, 28, 34–5; and the murder of Dalmatius and Julius Constantius, 34–5; sends Julian into exile at Nicomedia, 35–6, 39; sends Julian to Macellum, 39–40, 43; visits Julian at Macellum, 46; marches against Magnentius, 50–1, 61, 189; appoints Gallus Caesar, 51, 60, 61; executes Gallus, 62; reconciliation with Julian, 63–4; and the Silvanus plot, 67–9; appoints Julian as Caesar and sends him to Gaul, 69–78; Julian's panegyrics on, 74–5, 97, 130; and Julian's Gallic campaigns, 82–98; tries to withdraw some of Julian's Gallic troops, 99–104; Julian negotiates with, 105–12; prepares attack on Julian, 112–13; death, 120–2; paganism under, 159–60
Corinth, 9, 32
Crassus, 195
Crispus, 16, 32
Ctesiphon, 192, 200, 203, 204–8
Cybele, 142, 171, 197
Cybele, cult of, 45, 58
Cynics, 141–3
Cyril, 174–5
Cyrrhus, 150
Cyzicus, 183

Dagalaifus, 116, 204, 216
Dahn, Felix, 233
Dalmatius, 16, 31, 34–5, 52

Daphne (place), 146, 155, 180, 181–2, 185
Darius, 144, 188
Decentius, 99, 101
Decius, 13, 181
Demeter, cult of, 65
Diderot, Denis, 231
Dio Chrysostom, 151
Diocletian, 31, 103, 126; army under, 8–9; central government, 4–7, 128, 130; economic reforms, 4–7; Persian Wars, 166, 188, 192, 199, 216; rebellion in Antioch, 148; the reign of, 4–8; religion under, 9–14; remoteness from his subjects, 7–8; source of his power, 19; the Tetrarchy, 7, 14–15, 156
Diogenes, 141, 143
Dionysius the Thracian, 171
Dionysos, 138
Divine Sun, see Sol Invictus
Domitianus, 62
Donatists, 23
Dynamius, 67

Ecdicus Olympus, 127
economy, Antiochean, 148–9, 152–6; Constantinople and, 30; inflation, 2, 4, 5, 6, 18–19; under Constantine, 6, 18–19; under Diocletian, 4–7; under Julian, 132; see also taxation
Edessa, 48, 108, 161, 195
Edict of Milan, 20, 23
education, Julian's edict on teachers, 169–74
Eleusis, 65, 119
employment, change of forbidden, 5–6
Ephesus, 36, 56, 63
Ephraim, 192, 213, 214, 215, 217
Epicureans, 143
Epirus, 119
Euhemerus, 73, 99, 110
Eunapius, 56, 57, 99, 220
Eusebia, 64, 69, 74–6, 84, 95, 97
Eusebios, 55–6
Eusebius of Caesarea, 21–2
Eusebius of Nicomedia, 35, 36, 37, 39
Eustathius of Cappadocia, 168

Eutherius, 83–4, 106, 107, 125
Eutropius, 214

farmers, taxation, 5, 6
Fausta, 15, 16, 24, 32
Faustina, 121
Faustus of Buzanda, 215, 226
Felix, 127, 184
Festus, 214
Fielding, Henry, 230
Flavius Ablabius, 194
Flavius Dalmatius, 16
Flavius Eusebius, 76
Florentius, 86, 92–3, 96–7, 100–1, 117, 125
France, Anatole, 233
Franks, 69, 80, 89, 91, 93
funeral processions, edict on, 185

Galerius, 14, 15, 17
Galla, 32
Gallus, relationship to Julian, 33; spared when father killed, 35; exiled in Ephesus, 36; reunited with Julian, 42; becomes Caesar, 51–2; dedicates church in Casearea, 41; as Caesar, 72–3, 79, 80; in Antioch, 59–63; transfer of Babylas to Daphne, 155, 181; downfall and death, 62–3, 73, 101, 125, 150
Gamaliel, 149
Gaudentius, 112
Gaza, 161, 183
Geffcken, J., 233
Gelasius I, Pope, 160
George of Cappadocia, 40, 42, 57
Gibbon, Edward, 2, 230–1
Gnostics, 40, 139, 175
Godefroy, 229
Goths, 2
Greece, Hellenic culture of state government, 128–31
Gregory of Nazianzus, 45, 141; attacks Julian, 78, 219, 224–5; fellow student of Julian, 65; and Julian's ban on Christian soldiers, 186; on Julian's death, 213; on Julian's edict on teaching, 172, 173, 174;

on Julian's intended meeting with Constantius, 124
Gregory of Nyssa, 45
Gronovius, Jacob, 229

Hadrian, 156
Hannibalianus, 51
Hekate, 57–8
Hekebolios, 39, 52
Helena (Constantine's mother), 17, 19, 31–2
Helena (Julian's wife), 74, 79, 84, 111
Heliopolis, 136, 183
Hellenic culture, and state government, 128–31
Herakleios, 141, 142
Herakles, 175
Herbin, Johannes, 229
Hierapolis, 46, 120, 154, 194, 195
Hillel II, 149
Himerius, 64, 78, 177
Homer, 37, 38, 72, 174
Honoratus, 73
Hormizd, Prince, 192, 199, 200, 201, 207
Hortarius, 95
Hrotsvitha of Gandersheim, 227
Huns, 221
Hymn to the Sun God, 138

Iamblichus, 40, 54–5, 57, 167
Iasus, 134
Ibsen, Henrik, 232
Ilium, 26
inflation, 2, 4, 5, 6, 18–19
Iovius, 127
Iran, influence on religion, 4
Isis, cult of, 45, 139, 144

Jacobus of Voragine, 227
Jerusalem, reconstruction of the Temple, 176
Jesus, 175
Jews, 167, 176, 202
jobs, change of forbidden, 5–6
John, Saint, 227–8, 229
John Chrysostom, 150, 160, 161

Jouy, Étienne, 233
Jovian, 213, 216–17, 219, 227
Jovinus, 115, 117, 124
Julian, birth and family background, 29, 31–3; childhood and youth, 30–47; at Nicomedia, 35–9; education, 36–9; and Christianity, 38, 40–1, 43, 44, 46, 59, 108–11, 134–43, 162–86, 222–7; and Neoplatonism, 40–1, 44–5, 53–9, 65, 129–30, 133–43, 159–61, 167, 171–6, 184; chastity, 46–7; at Macellum, 40–7; leaves exile, 52; recommences his philosophy studies, 52–9; studies in Athens, 64–6; reconciliation with Constantius, 63–4; appointed Caesar, 69–73; first panegyric on Constantius, 74–6, 130; prepares to go to Gaul, 73–8; in Gaul as Caesar, 79–104; first battle, 81–2; second oration to Constantius, 97; troops called to Mesopotamia by Constantius, 99–105; troops proclaim him Emperor, 102–4; negotiates with Constantius, 105–12; first edict of toleration, 108–9; marches to attack Constantius, 112–20; takes Sirmium, 116; overwinters at Naissus, 117–20; receives news of Constantius' death, 120, 123; becomes Emperor, 120; in Constantinople, 29, 123–43; sets up military tribunal, 124–5; purges the court, 125–6; appointments to civil and military offices, 126–31; first legal enactments, 132; *Hymn to the Sun God*, 138; and the Cynics, 141–3; *On the Ignorant Cynics*, 143; moves to Antioch, 144; in Antioch, 149–58, 183–4, 191; *Misopogon*, 158; issues edict on teachers, 169–74; *Against the Galileans*, 174–5; reconstruction of the Temple in Jerusalem, 176; lays down duties of priests, 177–80; *Caesars*, 182; edict on funeral processions, 185; leaves Antioch, 195; Persian Wars, 158, 187–212; death, 212–18; persecutions after his death, 220–1; achievements, 221–4; legends build up, 220–1. 226–9; in literature, 228–35; works published, 230

Julian (Emperor Julian's uncle), 36, 127, 157, 183
Julian the Babylonian, 57
Julius Constantius, 31–2, 33, 34–5
Julius Julianus, 32
Justinian, 160
Justinianic Code, 221
Juventinus, Saint, 192, 227

Kallistos, 214–15
Kazantzakis, Nikos, 233
Kennedy, John, 235
Kurdistan, 194, 196

la Bleterie, Philippe René de, 230
Laeti, 84
Lampadius, 67
land-tax, 5, 6, 133, 155
landowners, Antioch, 145–7, 153–5
le Nain de Tillemont, Jean François, 229
Leonas, 107–8
Leontius, 127
Libanius, 150, 151, 161, 172, 194, 195, 227; Antioch as home of, 149; correspondence with Julian, 78; on fixed prices in Antioch, 154; friends given official positions by Julian, 127; on Julian's death, 214, 215, 218, 219, 220; Julian's first contacts with, 52–3; and Julian's relationship with Antioch, 157; knowledge of Syriac, 147; as a landowner, 146; on soldiers in Antioch, 152; welcomes Julian to Antioch, 176; withdrawal from affairs of state, 128, 131; works published affairs of state, 128, 131; works published, 230; on the younger generation, 29
Libino, 111
Licinianus, 16
Licinius, 15, 16, 20, 26, 32, 162
limitanei, 9
Litarbae, 195
local administration, 119, 132–3, 148, 151, 153–6
Lucilianus, commander of Pannonia, 116
Lucillianus, *comes*, 198
Lugdunum, 84

Lupercalia, 160
Lupicinus, 98, 99–101, 106, 166
Lutetia, *see* Paris

Macellum, 40–7
Magnentius, 20, 49–50, 60, 61, 62, 105, 189
Magnus of Carrhae, 214
Maiozamalcha, 203–4
Malalas, John, 214, 220, 226
Mamertinus, Claudius, 119, 123, 124, 127, 131–2
Manichaean dualists, 139, 167
Maranga, 211
Marcellinus, 49
Marcellus, 73, 80–1, 82, 83–4
Marcus Aurelius, 7, 8, 126, 130, 134, 190
Mardonios, 36–8, 39, 43, 44, 78
Maris, Bishop of Chalcedon, 137
Marius Victorinus, 172
Mark, Bishop, 136
martyrs, Christian, 11, 137, 163, 227
Maurus, 103
Maxentius, 15, 16
Maximian, 7, 14–15, 31, 199, 216
Maximinus, Saint, 227
Maximinus, 192
Maximinus Daia, 14, 15, 16, 217
Maximus, Senator, 120
Maximus of Ephesus, 127, 135, 185, 193; after Julian's death, 219; at Julian's deathbed, 213; Julian studies Neoplatonism under, 55, 56–7, 58, 142, 163, 190; leaves for Persian Wars with Julian, 195; in Merezhkovsky's novel, 232
Mazaka, 183
Media, 196
Medici, Lorenzo de, 228
Menander, 75
Mercurius, Saint, 226–7, 228
Merezhkovsky, Dmitri, 232
Mesopotamia, 188–9, 196
Milan, 20, 26, 62, 63, 70
Milvian Bridge, 16, 20
Misopogon, 158

Mithras, cult of, 4, 45, 59, 109, 138–9, 159, 161
Molitor, Wilhelm, 233
monetary systems, 18–19, 156
Montesquieu, Charles de Secondat, 230
Mopsucrenae, 121
Mopsuestia, 144
Morel, Frédéric, 230
Mursa, 61, 67

Nabdates, 204, 207
Naissus, 17, 116, 117, 119, 130, 139
Narses, King of Persia, 166, 188
Nazarius, 15
Neander, August, 231–2
Nebridius, 101, 107, 108, 114
Neoplatonism, 40–1, 44–5, 53–9, 65, 129–30, 133–43, 159–61, 167, 171–6, 184
Nevitta, 117, 120, 124, 127, 131, 216
Nicaea, 144
Nicaea, Council of (325), 50
Nicomedia, 14, 15, 26, 28, 34–6, 39, 52, 144
Nicopolis, 27
Nikokles, 38–9
Nisibis, 183, 196, 213, 216–17
Noricum, 105
Novaesium, 98
Nymphidianus, 127

Oecumenical Council (680), 160
Olympias, 194
On the Gods and the Universe, 139–40
On the Ignorant Cynics, 143
Oreibasios, 73–4, 97, 99, 110, 195, 212, 226
Origen, 10, 23
Ostia, 160
Ozogardana, 200

paganism, *see* Neoplatonism
Palladium, 27
panegyrics, formal, 74–6
Pannonia, 16
Paris, 89, 90, 95, 100–2, 108, 233

Paul 'the Chain', 125
Paul, Saint, 227–8, 229
peasantry, Antioch, 147
Pegasios, 63
Pentadius, 101, 106, 107, 125
Pergamum, 55, 133
Persian Wars, 34, 46, 48–9, 99, 144, 152,
    158, 166–7, 187–218
Pessinus, 144
Petau, Denis, 230
Petraea, 137
Philoppopolis, 117
Phrygia, 212–13
Picts, 98
Piganiol, André, 234
Pirisabora, 207
Piroz, King of Persia, 120–1
Plato, 3, 40, 70, 75, 140, 143, 175, 225;
    see also Neoplatonism
Plotinus, 3, 40, 53, 175
Pola, 62
political power, Diocletian reforms, 4
Porisabora, 200–1, 202
Porphyry, 40, 53–4, 175
price-controls, 4, 154–5
priests, pagan, 177–80
Priscus, 55, 65, 110, 195, 213, 219
Proclus, 220
Procopius, 196, 209, 210, 213, 216, 217
Prohairesios, 64, 172
provincial administration, 5
Prudentius, 113, 225–6
Pseudo-Amphilochius, 215, 227
Pseudo-Cynics, 143

Quadi, 69
Quadriburgium, 98

Raetia, 111
Regensburg Chronicle, 228
Reims, 80–1, 84, 115
religion, state: under Constantine, 19–25;
    under Julian, 133–40, 159–86; see also
    Christianity, Neoplatonism
Renan, Ernest, 233
Rhangavís, Kleon, 232

rhetoric, 75–6
Richborough, 98
Rome, Constantinople and, 27–8, 128;
    decrease as centre of power, 26; Senate,
    25, 26, 160

Sachs, Hans, 229
Sainte-Beuve, Charles-Augustin, 233
Sallustius, Flavius, 156, 192, 198
Salona, 15
Salutius Secundus, appointed Praetorian
    Prefect to the east, 127, 164; background
    and personality, 77–8; Constantius recalls
    from Gaul, 97; Julian discusses religion
    with, 163; Julian's growing intimacy
    with, 79; as Julian's guide to Roman
    affairs, 78, 130; On God and the Universe,
    139–40, 167; refuses to become Emperor,
    216; and the removal of St Babylas' body,
    181–2; and the tribunal after Constan-
    tius' death, 124
Sardica, 15, 26, 83
Sardinia, 132
Sarmatians, 69
Sassanians, 188
Saxons, 69
Schiller, Friedrich, 231
Scots, 98
Sebastianus, 196
Second Sophistic, 131
Seleuceia, 205
Seleucus, 220
Seleukos, 48, 145
Senate, Constantinople, 131–2; Rome, 25,
    26, 160
Senonae, 82–3
Serapio, 233
Serapion, 86
Serapis, 138
Severus, 14, 15, 84, 85, 86, 94–5
Shapur II, King of Persia, Julian's campaign
    against, 158, 194–5, 200–1, 204, 208–
    11, 214, 216; Julian plans to replace
    with Hormizd, 192; reopens hostilities
    against Constantius, 69, 166, 189
Silvanus, 64, 67–9, 81, 86

Singara, 166, 216
Sintula, 100, 101
Sirmium, 26, 51, 99, 115, 116, 117, 120
Socrates, *History of the Church,* 172
Sol Invictus, 3–4, 12–13, 19–20, 22, 45, 109
Sozomen, 215, 226
Spanheim, Ezechiel, 230
Spoleto, 96
state government, *see* central government
state religion, under Constantine, 19–25; under Julian, 133–40, 159–86
Stoics, 171, 178
Strasbourg, 85–8, 115
Succi, 117, 120
Suomarius, 95
Symmachus, 127

Tarsus, 121, 144, 195, 217, 218
taurobolium, 113, 138
Taurus, 117, 125
taxation, 5, 6–7, 18, 23, 24, 92, 133, 155
teachers, Julian's edict on, 169–74
Tertullian, 140
Tertullus, 160
Tetrarchy, 7, 14–15, 16
Thalassius, the Elder, 150, 151
Thalassius, the Younger, 150–1
Themistius, 29, 78, 127, 129–30, 131
Theodora, 17, 31
Theodoret, 172
Theodorus, 181
Theodosian code, 166, 221
Theodosius, 7, 133
Theolaifus, 120
Thessalonica, 9, 26
Thrace, 16, 117
Tiberius, 40
Titus, Bishop of Bostra, 137
Toulouse, 32
Toxandria, 93
Trabert, Adam, 233

trade, Antiochene, 147
Trajan, 8, 89, 156, 188, 190
Tres Tabernae, 88
Tricasini, 81
Tricensima, 98
Trier, 15, 26, 28
Troad, 25
Troy, 63
Tyana, 144

Ursicinus, 68, 73
Ursulus, 125

Vadomar, 111–12, 124
Valens, 196, 219, 221
Valentinian I, 198, 219
Valerian, 13
Valois, Henri de, 229
Varronianus, 216
Vatican, 24
Velez de Guevara, Juan Crisóstomo, 229
Vetranio, 50
Vettius Agorius Praetextatus, 127
Victor, 203, 206, 216
Vidal, Gore, 234–5
Vienne, 76–7, 79, 108, 113, 135
Vigny, Alfred de, 232
Viminacium, 28
Vincent of Beauvais, 227
Vingo, 98
Visigoths, 221
Voltaire, François Marie Arouet de, 231

Xanten, 108
Xerxes, 188

York, 14

Zaitha, 198
Zonaras, John, 220
Zoppio, Melchior, 229
Zosimus, 220